More Praise for This Book

"Microlearning is one of the hottest topics in our industry. This book provides the answers needed to determine if microlearning is right for your organization, and a road map for putting it into practice."

—David Kelly, EVP and Executive Director, The eLearning Guild

"The top challenge for talent development is, quite simply, a lack of time. *Designing Microlearning* goes beyond the hype, showing you how to create a microlearning plan that actually gets performance results."

—Kevin Kruse, CEO, LEADx, *New York Times* Bestselling Author

"*Designing Microlearning* is the quintessential guide to understanding the way employees learn in the modern world. A must read for any instructional designer!"

—Jeff Joanisse, Creative Director, Th3rd Coast Entertainment & Training

"To help people do their best work, L&D pros have to leverage a blend of tools and tactics that fit their workplace culture. Carla and Sue provide an extensive toolkit that can help bring microlearning to life within your organization."

—JD Dillon, Chief Learning Architect, Axonify

"The authors have created a thorough yet approachable book that not only shows how to create useful, engaging microlearning, but also provides a framework for evaluating its value and showing its impact. I would recommend it for any practitioners who are getting started in the microlearning realm."

—Chad Udell, Managing Partner, Strategy and New Product Development, Float

"If you need to design, develop, or deliver microlearning, this is the book. It contains all the tools, concepts, explanations, and instructions you need to create the right piece of microlearning for the right learning outcome. Stop reading this cover and buy the book already!"

—Karl Kapp, Professor of Instructional Technology, Bloomsburg University, Co-Author, *Microlearning: Short and Sweet*

"In this must-have resource, Carla Torgerson and Sue Iannone share clear, practical approaches for using modern microlearning. It provides not just theory and design but also advice on planning, media selection, implementation, and evaluation. *Designing Microlearning* is full of tips from professionals, tools, and job aids you can use right now."

—Megan Torrance, CEO, TorranceLearning

"Carla and Sue have masterfully answered questions about the why, the how, and the what of microlearning. Written by two individuals who are clearly experts in their field, this book offers readers a road map to designing microlearning content that delivers results."

—Jack and Patti Phillips, Co-Founders, ROI Institute

"Immediate and matter of fact, *Designing Microlearning* brims with ideas, examples, and resources learning professionals can leverage to design and develop more meaningful and relevant learning solutions."

—Brandon Carson, Author, *Learning in the Age of Immediacy*

"With *Designing Microlearning*, you'll get two for the price of one: Two knowledge-able authors sharing their industry expertise and practical experience. It's a perfect combination of descriptive theory and tangible tools. This new book belongs on every instructional designer's bookshelf!"

—Cindy Huggett, CPLP, Author, *Virtual Training Tools and Templates*

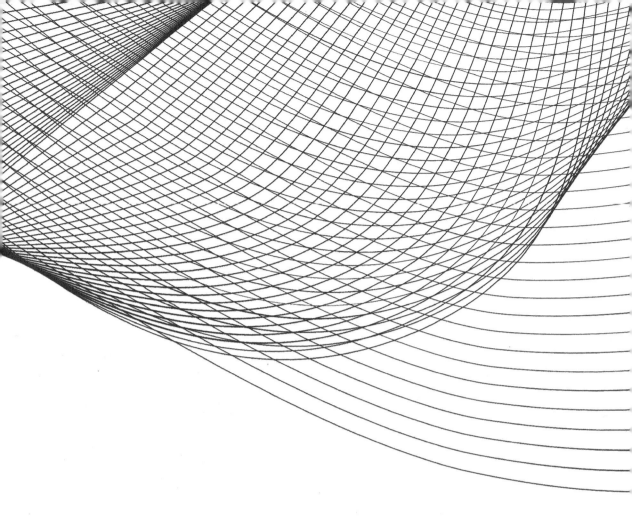

WHAT WORKS IN TALENT DEVELOPMENT

Designing Microlearning

Carla Torgerson and
Sue Iannone

ATD
PRESS

ATD Press is an internationally renowned source of insightful and practical information on talent development, training, and professional development.

ATD Press
1640 King Street
Alexandria, VA 22314 USA

Ordering information: Books published by ATD Press can be purchased by visiting ATD's website at td.org/books or by calling 800.628.2783 or 703.683.8100.

Library of Congress Control Number: 2019956103

ISBN-10: 1-950496-12-0
ISBN-13: 978-1-950496-12-9
e-ISBN: 978-1-950496-13-6

ATD Press Editorial Staff
Director: Sarah Halgas
Manager: Melissa Jones
Community Manager, Learning & Development: Eliza Blanchard
Developmental Editor: Jack Harlow
Text Design: Shirley E.M. Raybuck
Cover Design: Shirley E.M. Raybuck

MILE model graphics, 4 Uses of Microlearning graphics, and 5 Formats of Microlearning graphics designed by Jennifer Hoeke.

Printed by P.A. Hutchinson Company, Mayfield, PA

Contents

About the Series

ATD's What Works in Talent Development series addresses the most critical topics facing today's talent development practitioners. Each book in the series is written for trainers, by trainers, and offers a clear pathway to solving real issues. Interwoven with the latest findings in technology and best practices, this series is designed to enhance your current efforts on core subject matter, while offering a practical guide for you to follow. Authored by seasoned experts, each book is jam-packed with easy-to-apply content—including job aids, checklists, and other reference materials—to make the learning transfer process simple.

The What Works in Talent Development series is a unique core collection designed for talent development practitioners at every career level. To date, the books in the series include:

- *Starting a Talent Development Program*
- *Blended Learning*
- *Effective Onboarding*
- *Designing Microlearning*

Introduction

Are you busy? Crunched for time? Sometimes even overwhelmed? Of course—we all are! In the modern workplace, there is no shortage of things to do. The employees we train are no different. They have a lot to do at work, and it can be hard to find time for training. This is natural; except in rare cases, employees' operational tasks are their number 1 priority. That's what they were hired to do, and that's what keeps the organization going. Training will always be priority number 2 or lower. This is why microlearning is so powerful. It allows learning professionals to provide small amounts of training quickly so employees can get back to their operational duties—or even learn while doing those duties.

Have you been feeling pressure to offer training that is shorter, and you want to get started? Have you already created some microlearning and want to learn more? Maybe you find all the buzz about microlearning confusing, and are just looking for a clear definition with some tools and resources to help?

Whatever your situation, you've come to the right place. This book is a great place to begin or enhance your microlearning journey! We will answer many of your questions, providing case studies, tools, tips, and practical resources to help you along the way. We also share some of the successes and challenges we have encountered on our microlearning journey so you can be fully prepared as you introduce microlearning resources and programs to your learners and your organization.

Why Is Microlearning Important?

Today's learners move fast! They carry multiple devices, process information superficially, and are easily distracted. But most important, they have limited time for learning on the job; in fact, employees spend less than 1 percent of a typical workweek on training and development (Bersin by Deloitte 2014). The evolution of the modern learner means learning professionals need to take these factors into consideration when designing any learning resource.

How does microlearning help the modern learner? Think about a time when you were working on something critical and you got stuck—you realized you didn't know how to complete the task. Chances are you tried to quickly find the answer so you could finish the task and move on with your day. In that moment of need, microlearning can be a great solution! By providing learners with a small, targeted piece of learning, you help them quickly and effectively accomplish a job task so they can get back to work. This rapid desire for learning and answers sets the stage nicely for microlearning.

But microlearning is more than just-in-time training. Consider annual compliance training. Employees find it challenging to complete their compliance training because it's so hard to make time for it. Microlearning can certainly help by offering the training in shorter bursts that can be fit within the employee's busy day.

These are just two examples, and throughout this book we'll offer more. Microlearning can be used in many ways to train employees quickly and efficiently. That is why microlearning is so exciting—as thoughtful learning and development professionals, we want to use our employees' time wisely to meet their needs within the confines of their busy day, and microlearning offers a variety of possibilities to do that well.

Chapter-by-Chapter Overview

Each of the books in the What Works in Talent Development series follows a similar framework. The chapters in this book discuss what microlearning is, how to design it, how to implement it, how to evaluate the outcomes, and what you can do to prepare for the future of learning in your organization. Like other books in this series, each chapter ends with a list of thought-provoking questions, which serve to summarize the chapter's content and guide topics of discussion that you and your organization should consider as you begin your journey with microlearning. You will also find job aids, templates, and checklists to support your efforts. Additional resources are provided throughout the book so you can continue to address your specific needs.

Chapter 1. Getting Started: What Is Microlearning and Where Does It Fit?

Chapter 1 introduces microlearning by discussing what microlearning is, and what it is not. This chapter explores the lively debate around the definition and parameters of microlearning. It also addresses key things to consider before you design microlearning resources or programs, such as understanding the background of your learners and the business need of your organization. In this chapter we also share how to create a vision for microlearning and include how to approach and engage your stakeholders to increase your likelihood of success. Chapter 1 helps you ready yourself before diving in by offering questions to assess the current situation, considerations before getting started, and what to do early and often throughout the journey.

Chapter 2. Shaping the Future: Why Choose Microlearning?

Chapter 2 arms you with the benefits of microlearning so you can get others in your organization bought in to this approach. It's important to understand the research and thinking behind the value of microlearning so you aren't just chasing another fad. Microlearning works, and it's important to understand not only why it works, but also why your learners and your organization are asking for it. Also in this chapter is a look at some of the key barriers that prevent organizations from going micro so you can overcome these barriers yourself.

Chapter 3. Designing Your Microlearning Program: How Do You Start?

Chapter 3 helps you think strategically about microlearning in your organization. Where can it have the biggest impact within your learning ecosystem and how can you make that happen? This chapter discusses four key ways that microlearning can be used in organizations, and helps you consider when each will be most valuable to your learners. This is critical because microlearning used in the wrong way or at the wrong time will not have the value you seek, even if it is well designed.

Chapter 4. Implementing the Plan: How Do You Execute an Effective Microlearning Resource or Program?

You've determined why microlearning makes sense and how to use it in your organization, and now it's time to get down to business. Chapter 4 gets tactical, helping you design and develop each microlearning resource. It introduces MILE, the MIcroLEarning Design Model, which takes you through all the details of creating your microlearning resources. You will consider your performance objective for each resource and how you will design the optimal solution. You will also consider the technology required to distribute your microlearning and how to engage people to use your resources. This is critical because if your learners don't know your resources exist, or they don't remember them at their moment of need, they won't use them.

Chapter 5. Transferring Learning and Evaluating Results: How Do You Demonstrate Success?

In chapter 5, you will learn how to evaluate the effectiveness of both a single microlearning resource and a larger microlearning program. You'll consider what your organization really cares about, and how to speak to that with both quantitative and qualitative data. Equally important is how you collect those data, and how to do it in a way that uses your time wisely. While all learning professionals would love to have a data analyst on their team, few have that luxury, so understanding what data you are collecting and what information you can glean from them is critical. This chapter also looks at topics for evaluating an entire microlearning program, such as Kirkpatrick's four levels of evaluation, Brinkerhoff's Success Case Method, and Phillips' ROI Methodology. Most important, this chapter considers ways you can measure different kinds of microlearning efforts, so the data you obtain have meaning to you and your organization.

Chapter 6. Planning Next Steps: Where Do You Go From Here?

Chapter 6 provides you with a springboard to the next step in your microlearning journey. It helps you reflect on the current state of microlearning in your organization, and how to capitalize on past successes or manage through programs that weren't as successful as originally intended. This chapter gives you practical advice to gain momentum for using microlearning in your organization, and what to do if your microlearning efforts don't seem to be working. It also has a forward focus, considering where microlearning could go in the future.

How to Get the Most Out of This Book

Designing Microlearning gets you started on the journey to designing, developing, and implementing different types of microlearning for your learners. It is meant to be a guide and overview for the topic, with tools and resources to help you implement short-form learning in your organization. However, to be most successful, you'll need to consider the nuances of your own organization—your learners, your operational processes, and your organizational culture—as you decide how to implement microlearning most successfully for your organization.

As you read the book, you may notice the ebb and flow of approach from instructional design practitioner to performance consultant. This is intentional and is essential to the ultimate success of any microlearning content you create. The advice and direction outlined in this book are a reflection of the two authors' expertise and experiences with microlearning (and other learning approaches!) as they have been used with a range of organizations and learners across industries. Pay attention to both the performance need and the tactical implementation. An outstanding piece of microlearning that doesn't meet the performance need is no better than a poorly designed piece of microlearning that tackles the exact need of the learner.

There are a lot of tools and resources in this book. Don't feel obligated to use them all—choose the ones that will help you the most for the areas where you need support. Talk to others who are using microlearning well and learn from their approaches. But most of all, just try it. Start small, try something, and iterate along the way. Your learners and your organization will appreciate your efforts.

Why a Book About Microlearning?

You might be thinking how ironic it seems to write a whole book about microlearning when microlearning itself is short. Learning how to design and implement microlearning requires specific knowledge and skills that, frankly, can't be explained to the point of mastery in a three-minute learning experience. We provide that depth and richness in this book.

Icons Used in This Book

Icon	What It Means
	Tips from professionals will make your job easier and give you ideas to help apply the techniques and approaches discussed.
	Tools identify templates, checklists, worksheets, models, outlines, examples, illustrations, and other prototypes that can be a useful place to start.
	Resources are the books, blogs, articles, or even people that you can access to add to the information you've gained already and take your learning deeper.
	Case Studies provide real-world examples of ideas being applied by practitioners like you.

References

Bersin by Deloitte. 2014. "Meet The Modern Learner." Infographic.

Bull City Learning. 2012. "6 Strategies for Engaging the Modern Learner." Webinar. vimeo.com/140815130.

Torgerson, C. 2016. *The Microlearning Guide to Microlearning.* Torgerson Consulting.

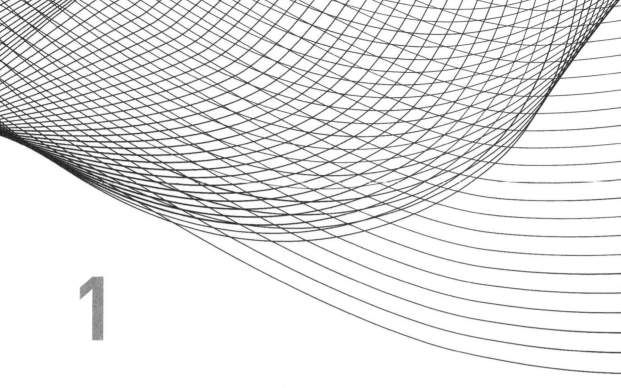

1

Getting Started: What Is Microlearning and Where Does It Fit?

In This Chapter

- Microlearning defined
- Assessing the current situation
- How to engage stakeholders
- How to build a plan for microlearning
- Other considerations when getting started

*M*icrolearning is a huge buzzword in the learning and development field. It seems everyone is doing it—or wants to be doing it. But what is "it," and how do you use it in a way that makes a difference for your learners and for your organization?

To date, microlearning has been poorly defined, creating hype but no follow-through. Without common definitions, learning professionals cannot compare best practices and techniques. And without a clear understanding of what "good" looks like or what works, you can't really evaluate microlearning examples. So let's start with a definition.

Microlearning Defined

What is microlearning? In many ways, microlearning is just a mash-up of many things learning professionals have already been creating and providing: just-in-time learning, performance support, post-training refreshers, and much else. The common thread for these pieces of learning is that they can be *consumed quickly*.

So, microlearning can be any learning content that stands alone or supports other learning activities, such as instructor-led classes, e-learning modules, and simulations. Microlearning can be used in four key ways, and we'll address all of them throughout this book (Figure 1-1):

- preparation before a learning event
- follow-up to support a learning event
- stand-alone training
- performance support.

Figure 1-1. Four Ways to Use Microlearning

That pretty much covers any time someone could be learning. So, if microlearning can be *any* kind of learning and the common thread is its length, then the next natural question is, "How long is a piece of microlearning?" Commonly people say that microlearning is any learning content that can be consumed in about five minutes or less. In our work on countless projects we've found that it's more nuanced; it really depends on how you'll use the microlearning:

- **Preparation before a learning event:** This depends on the length of the long-form learning event and difficulty of the content, but for a full-day class, five to 10 minutes per resource works well.
- **Follow-up to support a learning event:** If you are sending a boost email, then about one minute is best. If you are extending knowledge in a new way, then up to five minutes per resource is ideal.
- **Stand-alone training:** If learners are not required to complete the resource (informal learning), then four or five minutes should be your maximum. But if they are required to complete it (formal learning), then you can go up to eight minutes or so.
- **Performance support:** If learners will use the resource while doing the job, then you should aim for something that can be used extremely quickly, potentially at a glance, and ideally 30 seconds or less. But for more complex tasks where they may be stopping their work for a few minutes to consume some learning, then up to five minutes works well.

Think about how and when your learners will use the microlearning content. What would make most sense for them? With informal learning (learning that is not required), people will tend to gravitate to things they can consume in about four minutes or less, so shorter is definitely better (Bersin 2017). Further, our experience with formal learning is that it may need to be five to eight minutes to really teach a concept effectively.

The real definition is that microlearning is short-form content that is **just long enough** to give learners what they need at that moment and get on with their work. But it's always helpful to be specific, so we'll define microlearning as **any learning content that can be consumed in less than 10 minutes**. This includes:

- three to five pages of structured, well-spaced text
- a five- to eight-minute e-learning module
- a four minute video
- a one-page infographic
- a five-minute podcast.

The Microlearning Definition Debate: To Include, or Not Include, a Seat Time?

Who would have thought the definition of a concept like microlearning would spark such a debate? While in this book we chose to include five to 10 minutes as a guideline, many learning experts disagree with including any seat time when defining microlearning. Why? The need should dictate the length, so "just long enough" allows for a range in length to accommodate the specific need without putting a stake in the ground on a seat time.

While this is true (and we wholeheartedly agree), it makes it difficult to coach and inform others without a concrete definition including an approximate seat time. Imagine a learning professional who commonly creates one-hour e-learning modules. From their perspective, microlearning could reasonably be 20 minutes, because it is shorter compared with what they were previously creating.

Therefore, five to 10 minutes is not a hard and fast rule, and is certainly more of a guideline. We have created all kinds of microlearning in various formats that have been as short as one minute and as long as 10 minutes. The common theme is that these were "just enough" for what the learners needed.

Short Is Not Always Useful

Have you ever watched a five-minute (or less) video on YouTube or LinkedIn and, as you watched it, thought to yourself, "This is a waste of my time," and either stopped watching it or continued only because it was required?

We've posed this question to hundreds of learning professionals across the country, and the answer is always the same: a resounding yes. It's because we've all been there, consuming some short piece of content that we thought would be useful or maybe just funny, and we stopped because it didn't use our time well.

As human beings we are always self-assessing, and as busy people we are always asking ourselves if our time is being used well. There is no shortage of things to do, and we are constantly evaluating and prioritizing how to use one of our most valuable resources: time.

Any piece of learning content that is just five minutes long but not useful to your learners is a **waste of five minutes.** (Thanks to Diane Elkins, owner of Artisan E-Learning, who has been saying this for years!) This may mean trimming a piece of learning content to three minutes to give learners just what they need. Or it may mean expanding the content to eight minutes to provide the depth and clarity that learners need to properly grasp it. So again, any recommendation about length is a *guideline*; microlearning is any content that aids in learning or supporting performance that is short in length that meets the needs of the learner.

Now, let's consider each of the different microlearning content types in detail. There are five common formats for microlearning:

- text-based resources
- e-learning modules
- videos
- infographics
- podcasts.

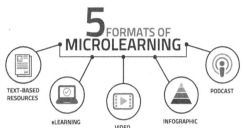

Text-Based Resources

Text-based resources take many forms. They include job aids and performance support, but also things many people think of as simple communications, such as newsletters, blogs, emails, and more. Sometimes when we go micro, we only want to share a paragraph or two of new information or a single page of text with images, so a basic text-based resource could do the trick. It could live on your learning management system (LMS); be less formal, like content on your social collaborative system; or something you send out by email.

TOOLS TALK

Generally, text-based resources will be created using tools like:

» a word processor such as Microsoft Word
» social collaborative system like Jive or Yammer
» your LMS, if it has content creation tools
» desktop publishing software like Adobe InDesign or Microsoft Publisher.

Text-based resources are simple, which gives them power. You should use them when you need to get something out fast. As we work to meet needs at the speed of the business, sometimes that means the training has to get out now, even though you may have only had a few days or a week to wrap your arms around the content. The ease of updating them also serves well if the content is constantly changing. To be clear, it still takes careful instructional thinking to make a good text-based resource, but you can produce and update them much faster than the other formats.

Text-based resources are also important for things where learners need to self-pace—that is, they may need time to linger over any part of the content, and different learners could need different amounts of time to consume the content. This commonly happens when learning a process with multiple steps: Some people will find certain steps easy and others won't. For example, imagine you are fixing your leaky faucet and get stuck midway; you have tools on the counter and maybe even some water spraying into the sink. You will want a good text-based resource with photos. A short video will work too, but the power of the text-based resource is that you can skim the text and find just what you need. And if you are like us, when you find the right bit of content, you'll want to read it several times to make sure you understand it, while other people with more plumbing experience will read it once and move on.

Text-based resources can also be excellent when there are lots of technical details to learn. Again, self-pacing is the primary issue here. If someone has more experience, they'll be able to consume that detail quickly, but others will need more time to think, ponder, and reread.

CASE STUDY: MEET JOHN

John creates training at a high-tech software development firm in Silicon Valley. His training materials teach customers how to use the company's software, which is complex and always being updated with new releases every quarter. The customer training serves as part of the organization's sales and marketing strategy because they know that if people find the software easy to use, they will continue to use the product and recommend it to others.

The software development team works on software changes for the entire quarter, doing final bug fixes just before the scheduled release. John attends developer meetings so he knows what the features will be, but it's not until the last minute that he will know exactly how they function or how the screens will look.

John's team had been building e-learning modules with screen-capture videos to demo the new software features and explain them to clients. But this was always done in the final days before the software release because they couldn't record any screen before it was final, causing undue stress for his team and lots of errors in the content.

His solution? Use a short text-based resource that explains the new features with text and screen-capture images. This can be created quickly and released with the software, using less effort than for an e-learning module. Then his team creates the e-learning modules in the two weeks after the software is released. He has better access to the developers who are his subject matter experts (SMEs), the time to make sure the modules are clear, and time for review by those SMEs who previously didn't have time for him, ensuring the training modules are accurate.

E-Learning

E-learning modules are pervasive in the training field. Unfortunately, much of this e-learning is of the "page turner" variety, with the learner reading a page of content and then clicking a "next" button to reveal another page of content, and continuing in this way until reaching the end of the module. We prefer to create e-learning that is more engaging and interactive, capitalizing on e-learning to ask questions and reveal unique feedback based on the learner's different choices.

For longer-form e-learning, many say that interaction is critical for an effective module. But this is not always true for microlearning—sometimes the best solution will be highly interactive and sometimes it will not.

As seasoned instructional designers who have spent our careers trying to make learning engaging and interactive, this feels odd, as if the instructional design gods should strike us with lightning right now! We are not saying that instructional designers shouldn't try to create interactive learning materials when they go micro. But we are saying to consider the modern learner and what they would find helpful at that moment when they are using the learning resource. The reason to include interactions is to make the learning active—especially because the mind can wander quickly if it's not engaged, and those interactions provide practice, feedback, and the ability to learn from mistakes. However, if the e-learning is only three minutes long and the learner will apply the content quickly, you may not need interactions. You may even frustrate the learner by including interactions that effectively act as a speed bump, slowing the learner down from getting the information they need and moving on to using it in their work. This is especially true when the learner has some familiarity with the content or is likely to grasp it quickly.

Microlearning is often used just-in-time and as you get closer to the moment of performance—the time when the learner is actually going to use that knowledge or skill to influence their workplace behavior—your instruction can often be shorter and less interactive. Why? It's not that people don't need practice to cement new skills; it's that the learner may be highly motivated to seek the answers they need, and the workplace provides that opportunity for practice. For example, let's say you're having trouble creating a pivot table in Excel for a report that is due at the end of the day. You do not need an interactive module to enable you to practice in a simulated environment; instead, you can refer to a text-based resource or a video-based e-learning course to get the information you need and then go to your real project in Excel to apply that knowledge. When learning is contextual to your real work it is most powerful. This is why we simulate these environments in interactive e-learning modules, but it's also why practice in the real environment is so effective too.

So why use less interactive e-learning if a text-based resource could work instead? E-learning enables you to control the order in which the learner is consuming the content, and also allows you to chunk the content into small pieces to express relationships or build content in a hierarchical fashion. These can be especially valuable when designing for learners who are unfamiliar with the content. E-learning also allows you to emphasize emotion (with video or audio), which makes it a more expressive medium than text alone.

Of course, if you can find effective ways to make the content interactive, e-learning will be your best option. Can you use scenarios that require the learner to apply the content, or get the learner to practice the new skill? Or perhaps you can use those scenarios to provide different feedback that addresses common mistakes. If so, the interactive features of an e-learning module will be critical.

Another reason to use an e-learning module is if you need to track whether the learner completed the learning program. Many LMSs allow you to post other formats, such as a PDF, a video, or even an infographic, but the e-learning format is the only one where you can track if the learner accessed every page. Of course, this doesn't necessarily mean they read every page, but most organizations like this format as a way of tracking completion on topics where training is required by regulating authorities.

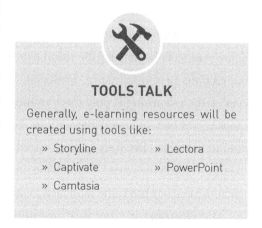

TOOLS TALK

Generally, e-learning resources will be created using tools like:

- » Storyline
- » Captivate
- » Camtasia
- » Lectora
- » PowerPoint

PRO TIP

A lot of people use e-learning because they can quiz the learner at the end of the module and store the learner's score on the LMS. We generally avoid quizzing at the end of a piece of microlearning though. It is so short that the questions are likely to be meaningless and the learner will think you've wasted their time. The learner will only tolerate a quiz at the end of a piece of microlearning if it's obvious to them that the organization must track a score (usually for compliance purposes), or in those far fewer cases in which they see how the quiz helps them learn the material better.

CASE STUDY: MEET TANISHA

Tanisha creates training for sales reps at a pharmaceutical company. Her reps know their product extremely well, and they have mastered their company's sales process.

However, the reps struggle to understand common American health insurance terms such as co-pay, co-insurance, health savings account, flexible spending account, Medicare, Medicaid, and others. Tanisha has a great way of explaining these, using scenarios and stories. Much of the content builds on itself, though; for example, it's hard to explain what a health savings account is unless you've explained what a high deductible health plan is first.

Being in a highly regulated industry, her organization also insists on knowing if the reps have completed the training—not just knowing that the learner opened and looked at the file, but if they actually read each page of the content.

Her solution? Develop a short-form e-learning module (about five minutes) to explain these common terms. She tells the story of Mary, a 70-year-old widow on Medicare, and her three adult children, and how each of them has a different kind of insurance (Medicaid, commercial insurance, and a high deductible health plan from the health exchange). By sharing the story of each of these four people, Tanisha shares the basics of the different insurance options that her sales reps need to know.

She uses an e-learning module because she can combine text and pictures easily. She can also build the module so the learner can choose which insurance product they want to learn about and access them in a nonlinear way. But she also builds it so that when learners experience a story, the content about that character is sequential and builds on previous concepts in that story.

Tanisha is also able to track that learners have accessed the character stories for all four insurance types, and by putting this module on her LMS, she can keep records of which reps have completed which parts of the module so her organization has this information for compliance purposes.

Video

Videos are becoming increasingly popular because the equipment to create instructional videos is getting cheaper and more accessible. And because we all have a video camera on our phones, we've gotten accustomed to seeing videos that are not professionally scripted, directed, and produced. That is not to say that there aren't times when you will want to hire professionals to help with your videos, but you have more options now than ever before to create video without a long timeline or a large budget.

There are four main kinds of video:

- interview (seeing a person talk to the camera or being interviewed by someone)
- live action video (seeing people act out a scene)
- animation (seeing illustrated characters act out a scene)
- computer simulation (seeing how someone interacts with software screens, an app, or a website).

Videos are especially powerful for showing anything that happens over time, like processes or procedures. For example, showing how to safely draw blood from a patient is a great use of video.

In addition, video is excellent for showing emotion. For example, if you want to express the importance of the work done in a pediatric hospital, a video is absolutely the best way to go. (Just have tissues handy!)

Video is also excellent for showing dialogue between people, especially if there is emotion involved. For example, if you have a course for new leaders about having difficult coaching conversations, video is the best way to demonstrate this skill, because learners can hear the dialogue, see the interaction, and observe the nonverbal cues that would be missed in other formats. Similar cases where video would be valuable are showing sales reps in a sales conversation with a prospect, or any staff learning to improve customer service skills.

Video can also be used to simulate a computer screen. Software simulation videos are ubiquitous because they are so helpful—there's nothing like watching someone click through the steps to build a pivot table in Excel to enable you to do it yourself.

Note that your level of effort with video is highly dependent on the kind of video created, with interviews and computer simulations taking less time and skill than live action and animations. Of course, you can also increase the level of complexity by making the video interactive, such as with virtual reality.

TOOLS TALK

Generally, video-based resources will be created using tools like:

Interview and Live Action Video
- » Filming: Anything from a cell phone to high-end video equipment.
- » Editing: There are lots of inexpensive editing tools; you likely have one on your phone and you can find others on the Internet. Or you could use software like Adobe Premiere.
- » For the highest-quality videos, you are likely to hire a supplier with particular skills in this area.

Animation

There are so many tools in this area that everyone seems to have a different favorite. This is definitely not a complete list!
- » Animoto
- » Powtoons
- » Vyond (formerly Go Animate)

Computer Simulation
- » Captivate
- » Camtasia
- » WalkMe
- » Assima

CASE STUDY: MEET MOHAMED

Mohamed creates leadership training for a large retail store chain. He knows that one of the most challenging things for any leader is to deliver performance feedback. Most employees say they want more feedback, but managers often struggle to give such feedback because they fear the reaction of their employees—will they respond defensively or aggressively? As a result, managers tend to play it safe and don't give feedback.

Mohamed has a robust leadership development program that new leaders take in the first 90 days of starting their leadership role. Knowing this is one of the topics they are most interested in, he offers a class on delivering coaching feedback. He knows people come to the class very motivated and they engage well, but they still go back to their offices feeling uneasy about having difficult coaching conversations with their employees.

His solution? Develop a series of videos that can be used after the classroom experience. These short videos are available on demand so leaders can view them just before they have a coaching conversation. Each video shows a manager having a coaching conversation with a direct report, and follows the coaching model learned in the class.

He has several different videos for the most common employee responses: defensive, aggressive, questioning, agreeable, and so on. Managers can pick which response type they want to watch, and can observe an "expert" having the conversation and modeling how to navigate the steps of the coaching model and achieving a successful outcome to the conversation.

Mohamed uses video because it's the perfect medium to show the employee emotion inherent in these situations, and how the manager works through the coaching conversation.

He also puts the videos on a portal that makes it easy for managers to go back and watch them as many times as they want. With the analytics on the portal he can track which videos get the most views, which ones people watch multiple times, and if people generally watch the videos to the end. Mohamed uses this information to determine if the videos are helpful to managers, which topics are of most interest to them, and if there are any videos that don't seem to be useful enough for learners to watch them to the end.

Infographics

An infographic is a visual way of presenting information, often with limited text. You can think about an infographic as telling a visual story. It's a great choice when you have a lot of content or data that you can organize visually to simplify the information. Infographics are presented as a single image, which means they should fit on a single page or screen, rather than having users scroll up and down to view. If presented electronically, the image can be clickable to provide access to additional information or resources.

Infographics are particularly powerful because they are quick for the learner to consume, sometimes at a glance. Much like text-based resources, they are particularly useful if the learner wants to skim or self-pace through the information. If different learners want more or less time to linger over the content, an infographic is ideal. For example, let's say you are creating an infographic for call center employees outlining the five steps for de-escalating an angry caller. An infographic is perfect because the agent can follow the steps in the infographic and pause as long as needed on any given step—even while on the phone with a caller.

Because infographics generally simplify information very well, they are especially useful when the learner is time crunched or needs to access the information quickly. Let's go back to the call center example, where employees need to be able to de-escalate an angry caller. In the heat of this situation employees need to find the information immediately; they can't flip through the pages of an e-learning module or even a multipage PDF. They must be able to see at a quick glance the tips they should use. They don't have time for anything more in-depth.

There are many kinds of infographics; most professional infographic designers say there are eight to 13 different kinds. The ones that are most relevant to microlearning are:

- list (lists information about a subject)
- data or visualized numbers (provides statistics about a topic, where the number itself or an image representing the number is the focal point)
- how-to guide (provides step-by-step instructions)
- flowchart (starts from a single point and branches based on decisions)
- timeline (tells how something changed over time)
- comparison (compares and contrasts two subjects)
- hierarchical (stacks information based on previous levels or steps).

TOOLS TALK

Generally, infographic-based resources will be created using tools like:

- » Microsoft Word's SmartArt
- » PowerPoint
- » Desktop publishing software like Adobe InDesign or Microsoft Publisher
- » Venngage
- » Piktochart
- » Canva
- » Vector art software like Adobe Illustrator.

RESOURCES

For a list of all the infographic styles and examples of each, see "13 Types of Infographics: Which One Works For You?" by Nayomi Chibana.

And here are just a few of our favorite resources about creating compelling infographics:

- » "The Power of Infographics: How Do They Create Impact?" by Elliot Cowan
- » "101 of the Best Infographic Examples on 19 Different Subjects" by Samantha Lile

Also, if you aren't familiar with basic graphic design principles, you should read *The Non-Designer's Design Book,* 4th ed., by Robin Williams.

When creating infographics, you really need to focus on keeping the text brief and use strong visuals to convey key information. Sometimes you'll get pushback from SMEs in the early stages because they want to add more content. But if you can get to a point of showing what that information could look like on a single page, you'll likely garner their support. A quick sketch or mock-up can often do the trick. Focus on the learner and the use case, and the SME will probably agree that the depth of information you are providing is what the learner would need.

CASE STUDY: MEET MOHAMED (AGAIN!)

Remember Mohamed from our last example? He has a robust leadership development program that new leaders take in the first 90 days of starting their leadership role. Knowing it is a very important topic for these learners, Mohamed has designed a class on delivering coaching feedback. He follows that with a series of short microlearning videos that learners can watch after the classroom experience, so they can watch experts model the behavior.

As he designed the class, Mohamed recognized that it would be incredibly helpful to learners if he provided a model for them to follow. This behavior is so stressful and nuanced that it helps learners to have a stepwise path to follow. He chose to use the Situation-Behavior-Impact Model (SBI) from the Center for Creative Leadership.

He teaches the SBI Model in the classroom, and people practice it in role plays. His microlearning videos also show people using the SBI Model in conversations, and he even includes on-screen text highlighting when the leader is discussing the situation, the behavior, or the impact.

But still he finds that employees want more support, something they could glance at just before having the conversation with an employee.

His solution? Mohamed develops an infographic to explain the SBI Model. It's short, having just the name of each step and a brief description. Visually, he uses three background colors to distinguish the steps and a very large S, B, and I.

S
B
I

He has three different ways of offering this infographic job aid:

» a printed card that can fit in a pocket or sit on a desk

» a PDF that can be stored on a computer, and is provided on his department's website

» an image that can be easily accessed on a mobile phone.

Mohamed knows that just having more resources isn't helpful; he needs to get people to use the job aid in practice if they are going to use it in real situations. So he provides it in the class, and tells participants the three ways they can access it. In class he hands out the print version, and helps people find and download the PDF on their laptops and the image on their phones.

Then, during the in-class role plays, participants are encouraged to use the job aid. He reminds them that in this mock setting they are using the job aid so they can get good at using the skill, because they won't be able to pull out the wallet card in a real conversation with an employee!

In addition to the microlearning videos, the department's website also hosts the image of the infographic. Mohamed encourages people to refer to it as they watch the videos to see how the S, B, and I are used. He also reminds people to put the image on their laptops and phones, so they can refer to it before they meet with an employee.

Podcasts

Podcasts are audio recordings that the learner listens to. They are particularly powerful in cases where the learner has a lot of idle time but is able to listen to something during that idle time. While podcasts are not used a lot in corporate training, they make a ton of sense in cases where employees such as sales reps or technicians travel between sites. For these employees, their time in the car (or "windshield time," as it's called) can be extensive. So, those who train people in these kinds of roles have created podcasts and audio files to share information, knowledge, and formal training.

Another situation when podcasting can be useful is when employees have long commute times or do a lot of air travel for work. This may infringe on their "off work" time, but some employees will appreciate having a library of podcasts they can listen to if they wish. The key here is that any listening during personal time is optional, and generally it can only be made available to salaried employees.

TOOLS TALK

Generally, audio files will be recorded and edited using tools like:

 » Audacity » Sound Forge » Garage Band (Apple only).

The files can then be hosted in any of your typical corporate tools (LMS, social system, LXP, and so on). Or for more sophisticated usage, you may use a specific tool designed for hosting podcasts, which enables more features specific to listening to audio files. Some tools include:

 » uStudio » Podbean.

(A special thanks to our friend Josh Williamson, who is a podcasting master and shared some of his favorite tips and tools with us!)

To create an effective podcast, you want an engaging story with a clear message, and it must be brief and to the point. For example, you could do an expert interview. Each question you ask is about something the learner would find interesting, and it's addressed in a short amount of time. This works especially well when your audience has very specific questions; they can skip around and listen to only those ones for which they would like to hear the answer. For example, Sue did a project where a thought-leader physician was interviewed on how they treat a certain type of patient; she asked a number of different questions, which enabled the physician to talk about different challenges and successes in treating the condition.

To create a podcast that people want to listen to, production quality is very important. If it sounds like someone is talking into a tin can or are shouting (even if it's only because there is background noise), the learning will suffer. Find a quiet place to record, think through what people will say in advance, and use a good-quality microphone to record it.

CASE STUDY: MEET SOPHIA

Sophia creates training for staff in the call center of a major retailer. These agents take calls from customers calling the 1-800 number to place an order, or when they have trouble while placing an online order.

Sophia offers classroom training on how to take customer calls and process their orders. She even has job aids that hang in agents' cubes. Their customer service and trouble-shooting skills are very good, but she knows that agents routinely do not offer related products and services (like extended warrantees) to the customers at the end of the call. They think it is "upselling," which makes them uncomfortable, but what they don't realize is that offering these services to people who would want them actually enhances the customer experience.

Her solution? Sophia believes that additional classroom training would not help; this is more about getting the agents comfortable with selling additional products and services. So she develops a series of brief audio recordings, each with a sample call including the optimal agent response and the customer's reaction. These recordings are provided for agents to listen to during times when call volumes are low. Managers also play a sample call at the start of their monthly staff meetings, and then lead a discussion about how that call was handled and the impact on the customer experience.

Instructor-Led Training and Virtual Instructor-Led Training

In most cases, microlearning is asynchronous—that is, content that the learner can access on their own, at any time they want. Microlearning generally isn't consumed by groups of learners at the same time because of the logistics of getting everyone together for a five-minute lesson in a classroom or virtual classroom environment.

However, it's worth making a mention of this format, because creative designers who know their learners well have been using micro content in live settings too. We've seen the following used successfully:

- Take the first five minutes of an all-employees meeting or staff huddle for a short micro-lesson.
- Have 15-minute lunchtime webinars where you offer short, targeted microlessons.

CASE STUDY: MEET KYLE

Kyle does compliance training in a large organization. His team has the challenge of delivering the "boring training" that no one wants, but must be taken for compliance purposes. For example, they deliver an instructor-led class on employment law for leaders. They know leaders don't like the class and only come because it's required.

His solution? Kyle's team talks to these leaders and realizes that despite the groans about taking compliance training on employment law, leaders throughout the organization are very interested in many of the topics. They do want to function in a legal way, doing the best for their employees around topics like sexual harassment, vacation and leave policies, managing foreign workers' immigration status, and a host of other topics. Sometimes the topic of greatest interest at a given moment is based on current events, and other times it's based on what the leader is dealing with on their team.

Armed with this knowledge, Kyle's team starts doing 15-minute webinars at lunchtime. They know that most leaders are so busy that they eat lunch at their desks. So they create "lunch and learn" sessions that can be taken virtually from the leader's desk while they eat. There is a brief presentation based on the questions Kyle's team knows leaders have with time for questions throughout—and they always finish in 15 minutes.

The program (which is not mandatory) is popular enough that they end up offering a regular webinar every two weeks. And if current events cause a particular topic to be top of mind, they quickly change the topic for the next webinar—these are usually the sessions with the best attendance!

PRO TIP

Sometimes when you go micro, the learning material you create may not feel like much more than a communication. The boost learning, stand-alone microlearning, or performance support may simply be communicating when things are new or changing. There is a lot of debate as to whether this is really learning, or whether it is just a "communication," and thus doesn't need an instructional designer involved.

Our answer: Regardless of what you call it, there is value in having the learning professional involved. We need to ensure the material addresses the need of the learners, is clearly expressed, and influences or changes behavior. These are all the primary skills of the instructional designer.

Getting Ready to Start

Now that we have presented our definition of microlearning and run through some ways to use it, you might be asking yourself, "How and where do I start? How do I prepare the organization, the leadership, the learners, and the training team? And, how do I prepare myself to introduce microlearning?"

TOOLS

Consult the "Examples of Microlearning Resource Formats" tool at the end of the chapter for quick definitions of the various formats and ways they can be used.

Getting started on anything new can be overwhelming, but having a plan and tackling it one step at a time is always a good way to begin. Whether you are considering one small microlearning solution or an entire microlearning curriculum, it's important to think about your approach carefully. A great microlearning solution can be awesome in and of itself, but if you haven't considered the impact on the organization, leadership, or learners, it can have little to no impact because of issues with adoption, usage, or even change management. The general steps in getting started are:

- **Assess the situation:** Get an understanding of the current state of the business needs in your organization, identify specific learning or performance needs, and figure out the best opportunities for microlearning.
- **Talk to stakeholders:** Prepare for and approach stakeholders to gauge the receptivity and possible impact of microlearning.
- **Build the plan:** Think about and approach the design and implementation of a plan for microlearning.
- **Consider policies and procedures:** From IT to HR, determine how to ensure alignment and success across departments when considering the implementation of a microlearning resource.

Realistically, you will find that there is overlap with these steps and you will go back and forth as needed. For example, to completely assess the current situation, you will probably need to engage with and talk to stakeholders to complete the full picture of the current state.

Assess the Situation

First things first—as every good learning practitioner knows, start by assessing your situation. If you are well entrenched in your organization and understand the business needs, the current culture of the organization from a learning perspective, and the current range and effectiveness of your learning solutions, you may be able to complete this step rather quickly. If you are new to the organization, a business unit, or a department, this step may take a little longer to complete. In either case, **don't skip it!** Even savvy learning professionals can make mistakes if they make assumptions instead of assessments.

TOOLS

Use the "Assess the Situation for Microlearning Worksheet" tool at the end of the chapter to identify and capture the answers needed to fully understand the current state of your organization's situation and its readiness for microlearning.

To determine whether microlearning is the right fit in your situation, it's also helpful to home in on some specific areas that we have identified in our experience as good opportunities for microlearning. Use the "Microlearning Compatibility Assessment" tool that Carla developed, which provides nine questions you can ask to see if microlearning fits into your learning ecosystem.

Only after you have a handle on where the organization and learning curriculum is currently can you determine the best opportunities to use microlearning. Consider the following questions as you conduct the needs assessment:

- What are the **current business objectives** of the organization, business unit, team, and department you support? Do you know the future business objectives?
- Are **current learning objectives** aligned to the business objectives?
- On which business objectives will **the learners be expected to have a positive impact**? Are there business objectives that the learners are not able to influence, given their job role?
- Are there specific behaviors or tasks that **the learners haven't mastered or achieved**? How critical are they to meeting learner and business objectives?
- What is the status of your **overall curriculum**? Is it aligned with the current and future business needs?
- Do you **already have microlearning solutions in place** that you didn't realize were microlearning until now? (Refer to the definition at the beginning of this chapter if you aren't sure.)
- Are there parts of your **curriculum that need updating**? Could this be an opportunity to implement microlearning?
- Do you have any **short-format learning resources** in your arsenal?

- What kind of **learner feedback** have you received about the training program? Is there difficulty in completing certain job tasks? Are there job tasks that aren't completed frequently enough for employees to remember? Are they too complex to remember?

CASE STUDY: ONE TRAINER'S APPROACH TO ASSESSING THE SITUATION

Carole, a training manager at a large pharmaceutical company, is responsible for the sales-training curriculum for a product that has been on the market for several years. According to company policy, the modules about the disease that the product treats, its impact on the body, and how the product alleviates its symptoms will become dated and expire in the next year. This means they will need to be reviewed and updated. The modules are lengthy—each one is up to 50 pages in a PDF format—with no interactivity. All new hires responsible for promoting this brand are required to read and take assessments on all the modules.

Carole has received feedback from the new hires that it takes too long to read and learn the content. They also struggle with recalling the demographic patient data for this particular disease. This is a challenge, because the product meets a need for a specific patient population.

Carole knows that the company review process will not allow her to scale down the content, but she also knows that there must be a better way to meet the learners' needs. How can Carole support the new hires' efforts to learn and remember the key data points?

Before jumping to a solution, she meets with the marketing team and sales leadership to discuss the feedback she has received from the new hires. She explains the concept of an infographic and conveys the importance of providing this content in a short-form solution that will support the new hires' ability to recall and communicate key demographic data to customers. The remaining content will be redesigned as a 20-minute e-learning module. They agree with her plan and appreciate her consideration to the business' and learners' needs.

Carole uses this opportunity to build a new microlearning solution: an infographic. With the support of a supplier partner, she builds a two-page, interactive PDF that includes clickable graphs and images. The most important demographic data are presented in an easy-to-use format, can be reviewed in five minutes, are self-directed, and can be explored in any order by a learner.

After reviewing the infographic with marketing and sales leadership, she submits it to the company review process to receive legal approval. Then, she includes the infographic in the curriculum for the next training class as a pilot. She tracks the number of downloads and views to ensure that all learners have received and viewed the content. The feedback is overwhelmingly positive from the new hires, and Carole shares the microlearning resource with the rest of the sales team.

Talk to Stakeholders

It's important to gather as much information as you can to get a clear picture of the organization's needs by engaging and interacting with the people who know what's going on. As you find the answers to the questions in the assessment phase, you will start to get a picture of the current state. To focus this picture of your initial

TOOLS

Use the "Microlearning Intake Form" tool at the end of the chapter as a starting point for talking to stakeholders about the performance need and how microlearning can help.

findings, set up time to speak with the business leaders or key stakeholders to validate the current state. While this is considered a best practice when assessing any new learning solution, you should also start to think about microlearning and how its potential introduction will resonate with your stakeholders. If you approach your stakeholders in a meaningful way, it can be a wonderful opportunity to showcase your capabilities as a business partner by asking some really great questions and introducing them to this incredible learning opportunity called microlearning. You will likely be viewed as someone who is well versed in your craft and explores new ideas and techniques for the good of the business.

In preparation to meet with your stakeholders, consider this: Is the culture a learning culture, where microlearning would be an easy entrant to the learning curriculum? Or, would it create pushback from people unwilling to try something new? Reflect on these two questions prior to meeting with your stakeholders. If the organization exhibits a learning culture and will accept a new change such as introducing microlearning, then your job will be relatively easy. Think about how you can market the approach to the organization and the learners, then discuss with your stakeholders.

Or, it may not be the right time for the organization to receive microlearning. There may already be too much organizational change, and even though introducing a microlearning solution might seem simple, it may not feel that way to the organization. In this case, see what microlearning formats are available that are closer to what you're already doing. For example, text-based resources and e-learning may be more palatable than introducing video,

TOOLS

A solid business case for introducing a new microlearning resource or program is important for gaining buy-in from stakeholders and securing any resources you might need. For ideas on how to make an argument for a new microlearning program, see the "Microlearning Sample Business Case" example at the end of the chapter.

and the change would be minimal—or not even really perceived as a change. Incremental change is always easier to implement than large change.

In either case, having a productive and transparent discussion with your stakeholders about your intentions and purpose for introducing a microlearning approach just makes good sense. You further your position in the organization as a learning and performance consultant every time you consider the business needs in an objective way.

PRO TIP

Tell a story about how your microlearning solution will solve a problem and drive a business outcome. You already know that stories are engaging. Stakeholders will listen intently to a story that involves solving a business problem—especially if they are directly affected by that problem. Be sure to include the business' point of view, the employees' perspective, or both.

But what's the best way to plan for a meeting with stakeholders? That depends on how formal or informal your organization and the stakeholders are. If your stakeholders are the executive leadership team at a large company and the opportunity to meet is limited, a formal presentation may be required. If you're meeting with the manager of a small team and have weekly standing meetings, then a less formal approach will probably suffice. In both scenarios, the key information to include is similar to building a business case:

- the identified business need
- the feedback you have received about the current state
- a list of questions for which you desire the leader's insights or wish to validate your understanding
- where there is opportunity to include a new microlearning approach or solution
- pros and cons to introducing the solution, with a focus on positive business and learner impact (if the cons outweigh the pros, you may want to cancel the meeting and rethink your approach)
- budget or resource requirements
- proposed next steps.

If, during a meeting with a stakeholder, it becomes apparent that the cons outweigh the pros, that's OK. Being agile is part of the process! And, anytime you can go to a business partner and say, "I thought this new approach would meet your needs well, but as we talk, I realize it won't," you will strengthen your relationship and become a trusted adviser.

PRO TIP

Do you wonder if you should first ask stakeholders for permission to implement a new learning solution, or go ahead and roll it out and ask for forgiveness later if they don't agree with the approach? While it may be tempting to implement even a "small" new solution before discussing with business leaders, especially if you know it's the right thing to do, resist the urge. Even a small microlearning solution can have a dramatic impact if it is radically different from what is typically expected by the organization. Asking for forgiveness can be a career-limiting move if the solution is not well received.

For example, let's say you learn that customer service representatives have been struggling with handling a specific customer complaint; it's one that doesn't come up very often, and it's complex to address, requiring several steps to execute. You believe that a short video is ideal to help the customer service representatives adopt and reinforce this skill. Thinking the solution is small and simple, you go ahead and roll it out to the customer service team. Within a day of you introducing the video, the customer service manager comes to you and is pretty upset. Why? Unbeknownst to you, the customer service manager had pulled the customer service team together the week prior to review the customer complaint and practice the best way to handle it. And, the approach to handling the complaint that you rolled out was somewhat different from the approach of the customer service manager. Had you taken the time to speak with the customer service manager before you rolled out the microlearning video, you would have learned about the planned training and the difference of approach, and could have partnered to develop the ideal solution. Not only did you upset the customer service manager, but the microlearning solution was misaligned and now requires more work to rectify the situation.

 Learning professionals build strategic partnerships with stakeholders by "asking permission" and working with them rather than having to ask for forgiveness when a solution has gone wrong.

Build the Plan

Now that you have engaged your stakeholders and received the green light to move forward with your proposed microlearning solution, it's time to really dig in and build your plan for design and implementation. The level of detail will of course vary depending on if you are building one new microlearning

TOOLS

Check out the "Sample Microlearning Plan for a Single Solution" tool at the end of the chapter for a rough outline of the components to consider when building a microlearning plan.

resource or if you are considering a whole new microlearning program. It will also be affected by any decisions to use a new format instead of an existing one that is familiar to your organization.

The steps to build your plan are:

1. **Draft:** Build a draft of your plan. This should include the items discussed with stakeholders.

2. **Iterate:** Gather feedback along the way and incorporate it into the plan.

3. **Socialize:** Share and review the plan with your supervisor, your key stake-holders, and anyone else who may need to know. Be sure to communicate the boundaries of what is changeable and what isn't. This helps to secure buy-in prior to implementation and is another chance for stakeholders to chime in if they have any concerns or ideas.

4. **Finalize:** Incorporate any last-minute feedback and put the finishing touches on the plan.

5. **Communicate:** First, stakeholders need to know the plan is done; then, supervisors need to know that their employees are going to receive something, and it would be great to have their support because it will help their staff to do their jobs more effectively; and finally, learners need to know what, when, how, and the "what's in it for me" (or WIIFM) to complete the training.

PRO TIP

Good, solid data lend credibility to your request. They let stakeholders know that "this micro-learning thing" isn't just a flavor of the month. Data communicate that you did your homework and have a rational, reasonable request. Here are some resources that you might consider for your own use:

» **Employee surveys and feedback:** Look for prior surveys or feedback that was collected, which may have identified a performance problem or opportunity for microlearning. If none exist, launch a short survey directed to the learners and even their managers to reveal the opportunity and highlight a need. (Or, the results may show that it is not needed. Both are OK!) Showing a cut of the data can go a long way to build the rationale for microlearning.

» **Employee-level scorecards:** Some organizations create performance scorecards, espe-cially for employees in sales and customer-service-related roles. Scorecards can reveal challenges with remembering or executing complex job tasks, customer dissatisfaction issues, or other performance-related gaps.

» **Industry reports:** You may not need to go to this extent, however, sometimes stakehold-ers want to know how other companies do it, and the learning arena is no different. If these reports exist for your industry, browse them for some data nuggets.

Consider Policies and Procedures

In building your microlearning plan, consider company policies and procedures. Think about how they would come into play when building a microlearning solution for your organization. Anytime you are looking to leverage systems, structures, technology, or equipment to deploy learning—whether it be microlearning or something bigger—you can bet that there are policies in place to provide the boundaries of what can and cannot be done.

HR and Training Policies

It's prudent to get familiar with any HR-related policies that may affect when you can implement microlearning, how you can implement it, and who can receive it. You are, of course, identifying your learner audience up front, so that can be a good place to start. When you think about the learners, what is their work environment like—do they have access to devices and systems to be able to conveniently access your microlearning? For example, an employee working on the shop floor of a manufacturing plant may only be able to access learning materials when not in the middle of work, and may need to go to another location to access them. While this might put a crimp in your informal micro-learning, there may also be an HR or other safety policy in place that prohibits employees from doing anything but their specific operational tasks while on the clock.

Some other considerations in this realm might be the number of hours an employee can or must spend in training. This surfaces in the compliance-training area, because some regulating bodies mandate the minimum number of hours an employee must spend on specific topics. If you are creating microlearning, the length might be ideal for the learner, but may not meet policy requirements.

When Sue was managing a team at one organization, she remembers being assigned manager training on how to address sexual harassment in the workplace. Her first reaction was, well, dread. Her next reaction was wondering how she was going to fit this training into her already packed schedule. She knew that if she didn't finish it in the allotted time (30 days), her name would go on the wrong kind of list and the head of the business unit would come looking for her. The e-learning modules totaled two hours, which likely met some compliance requirement. When she took them, she found that the video-based scenarios were actually done really well, but she had to commit two hours of her day to complete them. Did it include any microlearning? No, but in thinking about how she would have designed the curriculum, she knew it would have been great to have some microlearning videos—one for each of the scenarios—that could be viewed before the course, some support after the course was done, or some in the "moment of need" if she needed to review a scenario at a later time when it was relevant. Instead, all she got was the two-hour course.

The point here is that while policies may be in place, it's not going to kill the opportunity for microlearning. You just need to think critically and isolate the specific performance need, and you can build your microlearning for it. Sometimes you will consider microlearning as more of an adjunct or support to the core learning resources available.

PRO TIP

The thought of making friends with the IT folks might make you cringe. With them being knee-deep in techy stuff, processes, and geek-speak, it can feel overwhelming and adversarial to ask for technology help with your learning strategy. It can also be easy to get frustrated by all the IT restrictions your company places on your work devices: on how we use our computers, what we can download, even the websites we can visit. You may have been told no by IT a few times already.

Put that aside, and consider befriending your IT business partner. Not only can it drive your knowledge of how systems, technology, tools, and equipment all work, you can gain an advocate if you share your learning technology vision with them. Many IT professionals are great at problem solving, and may be able to figure out a way to make your microlearning vision come to life. They can also help to grease the skids when you are trying to make a business case for funding new learning technology to bring into your organization.

Leverage your social and relationship skills to build bridges with the IT team. With the day-to-day IT folks, don't be afraid to say, "I don't understand; can you explain this to me?" and take the opportunity to learn from them. IT leaders may be somewhat easier to communicate with. Be sure to share your vision with them. They can provide feedback on your approach and may be aware of other technology solutions that you didn't even know about! In any case, it's always a good idea to build strong relationships with the IT team—from both a practical and strategic perspective.

Learning Technology Strategy

Because microlearning is generally used individually and on the learner's schedule (on-demand or asynchronous learning), a microlearning solution usually can't be implemented in a vacuum. You'll need some technology to help you distribute your microlearning resources.

Does your organization have a learning technology strategy? Sadly, we've found that many learning professionals do not know what a learning technology strategy is, let alone have one in place. Many learning professionals are handed the tools from the IT department and view them as exactly that—tools. What's also concerning is that a Brandon Hall Group Learning Technology Study revealed that a third of companies do not have any learning technology in place (Wentworth 2016).

A learning technology strategy is more mindful and goes beyond the tools to link the learning technology opportunities and gaps to the business goals and learning objectives. By doing this, existing technology can be effectively leveraged, and budget dollars can be secured and allocated for new technologies needed to see the learning objectives come to fruition. This enables you to also be proactive, rather than reactive, regarding the learning technology you use and how you use it.

What exactly is a learning technology strategy? It governs any technology that can be used to build, implement, store, or curate digital learning and how you will leverage it to enable learning and performance effectively within your organization.

Imagine you learn that one of your learner groups is moving to a completely mobile scenario next year—meaning they will only have smartphones and tablets—yet your LMS is not mobile-friendly. What would you do? Sue found herself in this exact situation at one organization; her business partners in IT had made the decision to equip an outside sales force with smartphones and iPads instead of laptops, without consulting other business partners. That might sound strange, but at the time most of the leadership for this new business unit had not yet been

TOOLS

Use the prompts in the "Learning Technology Strategy Questions" tool at the end of the chapter for thinking through everything you need to consider when getting ready to implement a microlearning program.

hired (including Sue), so they had to make the decision without much input. The LMS in place at the time was being accessed via its desktop version, because most employees were not completely mobile. It worked really well for salespeople in other divisions; however, the division Sue was going to be supporting had a different need. After investigating the situation and learning that the LMS was in the piloting stage of its mobile app, she realized that this was too risky to use for onboarding and training a brand-new sales team—let alone consider any microlearning for them! As a next step, she identified the specific learning needs for this new team and then put together a technology strategy that would not only enable the sales team to access the training courses, but would have a minimally frustrating learning experience as well.

The strategy included investigating and identifying the best mobile-friendly LMS at the time that could deliver content in an easy-to-consume way for the learners that also aligned with her budget. Then, as a learning team they identified internal and external technology that could help them build new content in a more mobile-friendly way. They also made decisions on which technology would be outsourced rather than hosted internally, such as using a cloud-based service to provide boost learning after live training.

CASE STUDY: ONE TRAINER'S APPROACH TO ASSESSING THE SITUATION

Ron was excited about building the curriculum for a new field-based customer service team. This new team would be responsible for servicing high-end medical equipment in hospitals and outpatient clinics in their territory. The medical equipment is complex, with multiple configurations and a host of associated software solutions. Ron was assigned to support the new team from a training perspective and was excited to take on this challenge.

The existing teams at Ron's organization were issued laptops, iPads, and smartphones to use for a variety of purposes, including communicating with customers, participating in any corporate training, and general administrative duties. Ron assumed that the new team would be provided the same equipment as the other teams—he had no reason to believe otherwise—and planned his curriculum accordingly.

He was looking forward to introducing a new microlearning approach to address an anticipated need of the team. Given the large list of machines and the multiple configurations of each, the customer service team would not likely be able to recall the troubleshooting steps for every machine. Ron worked with a supplier to produce mini instructional videos for the more complex configurations and planned to use them during new hire training, as well as make the video series available for the team to access as performance support while in the field on customer visits.

At an internal cross-functional team meeting one month prior to the team's hire date, Ron learned that the new customer service team would be equipped with iPads and smartphones only and would not receive company-issued laptops. While Ron was familiar with the capabilities of their current LMS, he was unaware of its mobile capability. He set up a call with the LMS supplier and learned that a mobile app had only recently been launched and was still in the pilot phase. With a few weeks left Ron started to panic, realizing the unpredictability of how well his microlearning series would function, and if it could easily track each of the learners.

What could Ron have done differently? Had Ron not assumed what equipment the team would receive, he could have had more time to figure out how to make his curriculum work with the equipment situation, or made a case to the business to provide laptops for training purposes.

In the end, Sue's example of developing a learning technology strategy meant identifying all the learning technology systems and tools she needed to implement digital learning—including microlearning—for a unique and new learner population in her organization. She chose a mobile-friendly LMS to enable learners to access digital learning content. And she and her team pulled this concept all the way through, ensuring they captured the metrics the organization needed to track formal learning and provide a solid digital learning experience people could access anywhere, anytime on the device they had in their hand. **A learning technology strategy enables you to review your learning and performance goals and needs, then determine the best path forward with existing or new learning technology to underpin and support your overall learning strategy.**

Consider all the systems and tools available that you can use to create and deploy digital learning for your learners and customers. It can be really overwhelming to think about everything out there! You might be knowledgeable in specific learning technologies, such as tools to develop and author content like e-learning, or maybe you know a virtual classroom platform to interact and engage with learners. But there are so many other systems and tools. Don't allow yourself to be enticed by a great new tool or platform, and then put little thought into the big picture of a learning technology strategy. Even if you inherit all the available digital learning technology, take the time to itemize what you have and determine how it can support your learning and microlearning goals.

Technology provides the infrastructure and backbone for the implementation of learning solutions today, and there's no question it will continue to do so in the future. When working properly and providing the functionality needed, technology can be a tremendous asset in effectively deploying learning solutions. On the other hand, when technology is dated, buggy, or doesn't provide the right platform or features needed, it creates a scenario where frustration abounds—for you and the learners. To save yourself some headaches, answer the following questions about your learning technology prior to building a new microlearning resource or program:

- If you could execute your full vision for microlearning, what learning technology is available to design and develop the microlearning resources? Here you want to think about authoring tools. What does your organization have, and what might you need to be able to build microlearning content?
- Do you or does someone on your team have the technological know-how to build certain types of microlearning resources? If not, do you have the budget

to engage a supplier? Should you insource or outsource the solution? If you wanted your mobile learners to listen to a series of podcasts at their leisure, could you build the resource in such a way that they could access it anywhere? What if they travel internationally, and may have inconsistent WiFi access? Does this change how you build the resource (for example, embedded audio files in a downloadable, interactive PDF versus a live-streaming option). A decent-quality video can be produced using a smartphone; however, a high-quality video requires high-end equipment, a studio, and a videographer. The bottom line: if you don't have the staff or capability in-house, go to a supplier.

- What learning technology is in place to enable implementation? For example, if you wanted to provide pulsed knowledge questions (a question or two sent every few days for several weeks after a learning program) as reinforcement, does your LMS have the capability to do so? If not, is budget available to work with a supplier on a hosted solution?

- Does the current state of your systems and technology support future technology needs? You may have sufficient systems in place now, but will they be sustainable for the near and distant future? Are patches or upgrades needed? How costly would it be to continue with the current systems or consider replacement? These questions are not only relevant for microlearning considerations but also for the bigger picture for any learning organization. This is when it can be great to have a learning technology strategy.

When considering the range of options for microlearning formats, be sure to identify the types of equipment you and your learners have and may need. This seems pretty obvious; however, this mistake can unintentionally be made if it is not thought through carefully. The wrong equipment can derail the best of plans, even when the systems and technology are right.

RESOURCES

Sarah Mercier has created two great resources about learning technology strategy:
- » The video, "Learning Technology Strategy—An Introduction" td.org/videos/learning-technology-strategy-an-introduction.
- » A *TD* magazine article, "Where to Start When Developing a Learning Technology Strategy."

Figure Out Who Else Needs to Know

When considering introducing microlearning to your organization—or anything new for that matter—it's always a good idea to think about who needs to know what your plans are. Who you engage, and to what degree, probably depends on the extent to which you are thinking about adopting and integrating microlearning in your organization. Engaging the right people at the right time in the process can enhance your path to success. Learning professionals who ignore this step may find their efforts hindered, or even halted. So far in this chapter, we've tackled talking to stakeholders and involving or collaborating with the IT team. Let's run through a couple scenarios that will help shape your thinking about who else needs to know.

If you are considering an entire microlearning curriculum, then it's wise to get approval from any senior leadership or key stakeholders before you roll out your plan to ensure their support and avoid anyone feeling blindsided. By taking the time to communicate the value of your microlearning approach, you not only gain approval to proceed—you may even cultivate a sponsor for your efforts. They key is to articulate the value of your microlearning curriculum and how it links to achieving business outcomes.

If your goal is smaller, such as piloting a new microlearning resource, it can be communicated as exactly that—a pilot. Still, it may be important to inform the recipients as well as their supervisors. They need to know your plan to initiate microlearning, especially if it is going to "feel different." A good place to start is by explaining the WIIFM.

As you reflect on who needs to know, you should also **ask yourself if you have a champion.** This person serves as an advocate and proponent for your microlearning. You can have multiple champions if the scope of the project is large, and you may pick up more along the way as your microlearning solution launches with a good learner experience. If your project is small in scale, a champion can make the difference in driving utilization. For example, let's say you created a text-based job aid for a key skill that employees are struggling to execute. You emailed it to the learners, but it is not being used. How can a champion help? By spreading the word of the availability and value of the job aid, and by explaining how it helped them perform more effectively.

If you have a good internal network and already have a champion for your efforts, let them be the mouthpiece to communicate the value of microlearning. And, be sure to thank them often!

PRO TIP

In our excitement and haste to talk with stakeholders, the training team, IT, and others about our plan for microlearning, it can be easy to overlook the manager of the learners. In a small organization, the stakeholder and the manager can be one and the same. In a large organization, there may be many managers that are discrete from the senior stakeholders.

Don't forget the manager! They are critical to the success of your microlearning plans for several reasons. First, they can provide valuable insights about learner performance strengths and opportunities, usually in great detail. They are, after all, the person who usually evaluates the learners' performance. Second, by involving the manager early in the process, you may get an idea of how well (or poorly) your microlearning resources will be received. Third, no one likes to be blindsided! By involving the manager early, you apprise them of what's to come and initiate buy-in, so the manager is more likely to support and pull through the microlearning resource later on, when it is time for their learners to participate in the training. It's a win-win.

We have yet to address the training team on this subject. **Is the training team aware of microlearning, the opportunities, and your plan?** It's possible for the training team to actually be the demise of a new microlearning initiative. We assume that because you are reading this book, you are already interested in, and possibly excited about, introducing microlearning in your organization. But is the rest of your team on board? Do they know what microlearning is, how it can be introduced, and the potential business value? If the answer to any of these questions is no or "I'm not sure," then the team could hesitate.

Think about it: Let's say the training team is a bit old school. Its members are used to building page-turner e-learning modules, creating PowerPoint decks for webinars with a few polling questions, and delivering live workshops. There may be nothing "micro" about the current approach, and from their perspective, it works. But then, you get really excited about creating pulsed knowledge questions to deploy after the training program. It's micro, it's a great idea, and, if done right, it would sustain the learners' knowledge well beyond the time they leave the program. However, your team members are so busy, they may just see the idea as more work to take on, and they just don't have the time. Begrudgingly, they do their part, or they speak negatively outside the department about this new initiative. Not a good scenario.

The solution? **Take the time to educate the team about the value of microlearning, or learn about it together.** Talk openly about the pros (short and targeted resources, modern-learner friendly, enhanced learner performance, increased learner retention of key knowledge from training, and more efficient use of learner time) and cons (time to write questions, LMS or another platform functionality). When everyone is on the same page, encourage the team to explore microlearning ideas and opportunities that would create value for the learners.

What to Do Early and Often

We've covered a lot of ground already in this chapter about preparing to start introducing microlearning in your organization, whether the initiative is big or small. While the previous sections covered a more methodical approach, we now take a look at principles and best practices for setting yourself up for success.

As you think about getting started, begin with a **vision** for introducing microlearning to your organization. It's important to take time to think about what microlearning will look like, the role it will play in the context of how learning is implemented, and the impact it can have on the learners and the business. If you don't have a clear vision, no one else will either.

Identify all stakeholders, including managers. Engaging your stakeholders might initially feel as if it will slow you down; however, starting early here makes your job easier and possibly faster in the end. Doing this can help avoid problems in the long run. Managers can not only be stakeholders; they could also be cultivated into champions.

Speaking of champions, we've noted their importance to the success of your microlearning introduction to the organization—**find and cultivate at least one champion.** Champions contribute credibility to the acceptance of microlearning, especially if they are in an operational role in the organization. Why? They are not senior leaders telling the learners what to do. People closer to those who are experiencing the microlearning can have tremendous impact on adoption and utilization, especially if the champion is well respected in the organization.

Champions can also be helpful in identifying **quick wins** for your microlearning introduction. A quick win in the business world can be defined as a new and visible contribution to the success of the business made quickly. What is a more specific timeframe for a quick win? Theoretically, you could send out a text-based email today and have an impact in a few hours. Realistically and with some planning, a microlearning quick win could be successfully implemented in a week to three months, depending on the amount of time and resources needed based on the format you have chosen.

When applied to microlearning, a quick win could be supported by capturing and communicating the early success of your microlearning resource. This could be tracking early user data, click-through rates, or other utilization metrics. This positive early user experience allows you to communicate and promote early successes to your stakeholders, garnering ongoing support for your initiative. Quick wins may be less relevant if you are considering only one microlearning resource. However, if you are considering a microlearning program, or anything more involved than the introduction of one microlearning resource, then consider identifying a quick win before you begin.

RESOURCES

Do you have a quick win? Maybe not, but think about this: Among high-performing new leaders, most of them managed to secure a "quick win," or a new and visible contribution to the success of the business early in their tenure. To learn more about the quick wins paradox, read Mark Van Buren and Todd Safferstone's *Harvard Business Review* article "The Quick Wins Paradox."

A very important activity to do early, sometimes very early, is to **assess the organization's systems, technology, and tools.** What works? What doesn't? What's missing? Get a handle on this quickly, because you'll need to decide if it is worth the time and money to fix any that are problematic, or bring in new IT solutions instead. Nothing kills your dreams faster than the realization that the technology isn't there to make your microlearning dream come true.

An opportunity for all learning practitioners who wish to introduce microlearning has, ironically, nothing to do with microlearning in and of itself. **The perceived value of training in your organization can help or hinder your efforts** depending on its status. By assessing and monitoring the perceived value of training in your organization, you will be able to predict with some accuracy the level of difficulty you will have with your microlearning introduction. If the perception is good now, keep your finger on the pulse to ensure that it stays this way. If it's not good, then you have an opportunity to address it. In either case, this understanding will give you a sense of how hard you might have to work to get your microlearning initiative off the ground.

Have you spent time around marketers? Learning professionals can gain a few tips from the successful ones. Just as a good marketer develops marketing messages for a product or service, learning professionals can, and should, develop "sound bites" for their microlearning. Why is this important? Sound bites are quick and impactful messages that can grab the attention of the listener. For learning professionals, sound bites succinctly convey key messages that resonate with your stakeholders. We're sorry to say that the term *microlearning* is training jargon, and most likely will not resonate with your stakeholders. Your job is to figure out what will resonate. Sound bites should convey the potential impact of microlearning—for the learner and the business. Refer to the sound bite tool at the end of this chapter for some examples you can tailor to use in presentations or conversations with your stakeholders.

PRO TIP

Avoid using training jargon when communicating with nontraining people, especially leadership. If you can't help yourself, then define your terms so everyone is on the same page. For example, *microlearning* would be considered training jargon. Try using *short-form learning* or *learner support* as alternatives.

What's Next?

Now that we have defined microlearning and walked through the high points of getting started, you may be pondering a number of questions about your organization and how to introduce microlearning. That's great! Take the time to consider the key elements discussed in this chapter and reflect on the performance needs of your organization. As the background and business needs come into focus, you will be able to see the possibilities for where introducing microlearning makes the most sense.

To really understand the needs and motivations of your learners, read chapter 2 to learn more about what makes the modern learner tick. In addition, there will be more specifics about why microlearning makes good sense in many cases, and not in others. We will also talk about four main areas where microlearning can be implemented and the value it can bring to the learners, the business, and you as the learning professional.

Questions to Explore

- How well do you understand the business goals and objectives of the organization? Of the learners you support?
- What do you already know about the performance needs and gaps of the learners? What isn't clear and what don't you know that you need to find out?
- How do you currently approach stakeholders with a new learning idea or opportunity? How can you tailor a microlearning message for them that will be simple and resonate?
- Whom do you know in your organization who could be an advocate or a champion for microlearning?
- Where could introducing a microlearning resource or program provide the most value to the learners, and have the greatest impact on the organization?
- What learning formats do you use most often? Are these formats conducive to microlearning? Do you need to consider some new formats? Which formats do the learners prefer?
- What data and metrics would convey the best case for microlearning in your organization?
- What business processes and policies exist that you should be mindful of when considering microlearning? How can you ensure alignment?
- Do you have the right infrastructure and technology in place to support introducing microlearning?
- Would an external expert or peer be helpful to learn more about how other organizations use microlearning?

Tools for Support

Examples of Microlearning Resource Formats

This table provides quick definitions of the various microlearning formats and the ways they can be used.

Format	Definition	Ways It Can Be Used
Email	An extremely short piece of text that typically offers review, tips, or extension of knowledge regarding a very specific detail of a single topic. It may include graphics, headers, and bullets. It can also include links to other, more in-depth materials.	☐ Preparation before a learning event ☑ Follow-up to support a learning event ☑ Stand-alone training ☐ Performance support
Abstract or Summary	A short text document that typically covers a single topic at a high level. It may be highly visual with graphics, and should be well organized and skimmable with headers and bullets. It can be interactive with links or embedded objects.	☑ Preparation before a learning event ☑ Follow-up to support a learning event ☑ Stand-alone training ☑ Performance support
Backgrounder or Article	A medium-length text document that provides deeper coverage of a given topic. It can be interactive with links or embedded objects.	☑ Preparation before a learning event ☑ Follow-up to support a learning event ☑ Stand-alone training ☐ Performance support
Job Aid	A tool used by the learner to help apply key knowledge and skills—especially those that are complex, difficult to remember, or rarely used. It may take the form of a flowchart, checklist, or step-by-step guide, among others.	☐ Preparation before a learning event ☐ Follow-up to support a learning event ☐ Stand-alone training ☑ Performance support
E-Learning	Generally an interactive multipage piece of learning software. It allows for chunking and sequencing content and provides interactions to enhance learning.	☑ Preparation before a learning event ☑ Follow-up to support a learning event ☑ Stand-alone training ☐ Performance support

Format	Definition	Ways It Can Be Used
Infographic	A highly visual resource that conveys a key concept using graphic imagery and some text. It can be stand-alone or embedded in another resource.	☑ Preparation before a learning event ☑ Follow-up to support a learning event ☑ Stand-alone training ☑ Performance support
Audio File or Podcast	Brief audio recordings to supplement learning (such as subject matter expert interviews). It can be used on its own or embedded in another resource.	☐ Preparation before a learning event ☑ Follow-up to support a learning event ☑ Stand-alone training ☐ Performance support
Video	Videos can cover a wide range of topics. Generally, the shorter, the better. It can be used on its own or embedded in another resource.	☑ Preparation before a learning event ☑ Follow-up to support a learning event ☑ Stand-alone training ☑ Performance support
Question Bank	A set of questions used for self-checks, quiz assessments, and self-study. Also an important form of follow-up to reinforce or "boost" learning.	☑ Preparation before a learning event ☑ Follow-up to support a learning event ☐ Stand-alone training ☐ Performance support

*Note that many of these formats can be used on their own or embedded in another resource.

Assess the Situation for Microlearning Worksheet

Use this worksheet to identify and capture the answers needed to fully understand the current state of your organization's situation and its readiness for microlearning. Use the space provided to answer each of the questions as you learn more about the needs of your organization.

1. Business Needs and Drivers

What are the current business objectives of the organization/business unit/team/department you support?

Are there specific business needs that are not fully being met? Are there business objectives that could be accelerated? Can training play a role and have a positive impact in ensuring the organization's success in meeting or accelerating the objective?

On which business or performance objectives can the learners have a direct or indirect positive impact? Which ones can they not influence? (Do not build learning resources for objectives that the learners cannot influence.)

Are there business objectives that, if not addressed by training, would put the organization at more risk, such as an objective to meet an industry-related compliance expectation?

Whom can you speak with to fully answer these questions? Are there any data or reports (such as organization goals and objectives, market research reports, and sales and marketing data) you can review?

2. The Learners

Are there behaviors or tasks that most learners have not mastered or achieved? If so, why?

How critical are these behaviors or tasks to meeting or achieving the business objectives? (If they're not very critical, do not proceed.)

How complex are these behaviors or tasks? Could they be easily isolated and taught in an asynchronous way, or do they need to be taught in a live classroom or virtual classroom setting?

What learner feedback exists about the existing curriculum, courses, or learning resources? What do they repeatedly ask the training team for help with?

How receptive to new learning courses, curriculum, or formats are the different learner groups in your organization? Would introducing a new format be viewed as an unwanted annoyance or a welcome change? Try to think about the learning culture in your organization, and to what degree change management would be needed.

3. The Curriculum

Is your current curriculum aligned with the current needs of your organization? Is it deployed in a manner that optimizes learning?

If business needs change in the near future, will the current curriculum continue to support future needs?

Are critical behaviors addressed in the current curriculum? Are there any gaps?

How much updating is needed? (Quantify by resources, courses, or a rough overall percentage.)

4. Microlearning Opportunities

Did you already have microlearning in place, but didn't realize it was microlearning? (Consider any learning content that can be consumed in five to 10 minutes or less.)

Do you have any short-format learning resources in your curriculum?

Review any gaps or opportunities in section 3. Would any of these be potential opportunities to introduce microlearning?

In reviewing the curriculum, are there opportunities to use microlearning in any of these ways:
• Preparation before a learning event:
• Follow-up to support a learning event:
• Stand-alone training:
• Performance support:

5. Resources

Is there budget to address any curriculum changes or new technology to deploy it? If not, how can you secure the budget? What data and information may be needed to build a case for more resources? (You may not have specific answers without building a plan first, but here you can start to think about a ballpark idea of what you might need to ask for.)

Can you build and deploy microlearning without additional budget? What other support would you need, such as staff or someone with a specific capability, like video editing or other software knowledge?

Microlearning Compatibility Assessment

Use these nine questions to identify whether microlearning fits into your learning eco-system, and if it doesn't, how you can modify your approach to make it fit best.

		Yes	No
1.	Is your content compliance related?		
2.	Is the seat time mandated by law?		
3.	Is your content related to other formal training (such as instructor led or e-learning)?		
4.	Is your content complicated, or does it need to be covered in depth?		
5.	Will your content provide support at the moment of need?		
6.	Is it hard to break your content into discrete chunks?		
7.	Will you provide content learners are intrinsically interested in, even if it may not be related to a formal training event or specific job task?		
8.	Is the content new to the learner?		
9.	Is it important to keep your content top of mind?		

Scoring

- **Odd-numbered questions:** If you answered yes to any of these questions, microlearning is likely a good fit for you.
- **Even-numbered questions:** If you answered yes to any of these questions, microlearning likely isn't the best fit. In these cases, you'll want to use other learning approaches, use microlearning in support of longer-form learning, or modify your approach to the content.

Note: a lot of people find that regardless of their score, there are one or two questions that are particularly important for their content or organization and create the justification to go micro or not.

Here's a little more about why each of these questions is important:
1. Is your content compliance related?
   - Generally, compliance training is where you should start any microlearning effort. Many employees see such training as a waste of time, so shortening it will earn you a lot of credibility. And any savings in seat time is generally experienced across the entire employee population, giving the organization a significant payoff too.
2. Is the seat time mandated by law?
   - If the seat time is mandated by law, this will be a barrier to going micro. However, see if you can break that into segments—for example, can you satisfy a requirement of 60 minutes a year with just five minutes every month?
3. Is your content related to other formal training (such as instructor led or e-learning)?
   - You can use microlearning to ensure all learners have the same level of knowledge before coming to a formal learning environment, or to continue extending their learning after the event.
   - You can also use microlearning as reinforcement after a formal learning activity. This is a great way to encourage long-term retention.

4. Is your content complicated, or does it need to be covered in depth?
   - Material that is complicated or needs to be covered in depth is not a good fit for microlearning. Remember that with microlearning you want to be able to provide the content in short bursts. If the content can't be broken down this way, use formal learning to teach the content and use microlearning to support it (see question 3).

5. Will your content provide support at the moment of need?
   - You can use microlearning to give just-in-time learning or support when an employee is stuck or needs help. This is generally your most effective use of microlearning, because it directly affects the learner's immediate productivity.
   - To be most effective, this content needs to be found easily at the employee's moment of need. Usually, this requires that the resources be housed somewhere with good search capability and be supported by strong tagging.
   - To be most effective, the content also needs to be targeted to the learner's specific need, which may require you to have a stronger understanding of the user and the use case.

6. Is it hard to break your content into discrete chunks?
   - Material that cannot be broken into discrete chunks is not a good fit for microlearning. To go micro, find ways to break your content apart. Focusing on your enabling objectives can help with this.

7. Will you provide content that learners are intrinsically interested in, even if it may not be related to a formal training event or specific job task?
   - You can use microlearning to address informal learning topics that have wide appeal to your employees, such as time management, having difficult conversations, or leadership skills. Employees will appreciate the efforts made to foster their personal development, and will be motivated to use these learning resources because of their intrinsic interest.

8. Is the content new to the learner?
   - Because microlearning resources are so short, the format is not as good for material that is very new to the learner. Microlearning is likely to be more effective if you can scaffold on top of something the learner already knows.

9. Is it important to keep your content top of mind?
   - You can use microlearning to reinforce new content or things people should already know. This is an excellent way to keep concepts top of mind, even if the employee uses them infrequently. Many compliance and leadership topics fit extremely well here.

Used with permission from Torgerson Consulting.

Microlearning Intake Form

A solid business case for introducing a new microlearning resource or program is important to gain buy-in from stakeholders and secure any resources you might need. Using an intake form can help you home in on the best path forward for creating the optimal microlearning solution to meet the business need.

1. What is the performance gap or need? How do you know?

2. Who is the audience or potential learner group? Is there learner feedback regarding learning or performance needs?

3. How much time would those learners realistically have to complete the training; for example, five minutes a day, an hour a week, or a portion of the monthly staff meeting?

4. Is this training ☐ required? ☐ not required?

5. How will this training material be used?
   ☐ preparation before long-form training
   ☐ follow-up to support long-form training
   ☐ stand-alone training
   ☐ performance support.

6. What are the preferred delivery methods?
   ☐ text-based ☐ e-learning ☐ video ☐ infographic ☐ podcast

7. Where will this training be hosted?
   ☐ LMS ☐ Learning Experience Platform (LXP) ☐ website or portal
   ☐ social collaborative system ☐ other

Sample Microlearning Business Case

A solid business case for introducing a new microlearning resource or program is important to gain buy-in from stakeholders and secure any resources you might need. Here is an example of a business case for a microlearning program.

Background

FastFood is a restaurant chain with 250 locations in the southeast United States. FastFood provides customers with a range of steak and chicken options in a clean and pleasant environment at affordable prices. Customers can order off the menu or choose from an array of buffet options.

FastFood hires for a range of roles, including short-order cooks, servers, and hostesses. Typical training for new hires includes three days of computer-based training (e-learning) and shadowing other experienced employees on the job.

Business Need

Fifty percent of new hires quit after only two days on the job. In reviewing exit surveys and interviews, employees stated the e-learning experience was a primary factor in their decision to quit.

First, the training was often conducted in a very small room with no windows where the employees had to sit at a computer for hours to complete the online training so they had a negative initial impression of working for the organization. Second, employees complained that the training was boring and they thought that if the training was boring, then the job may not be so great. Finally, and most importantly, they also felt overwhelmed by the amount of content in the e-learning and feared they would not be able to successfully do the job.

Because so many new hires quit, the on-site managers spend an inordinate amount of time interviewing and hiring employees; while that's important, it is taking too much time away from running the day-to-day operations of the restaurant.

FastFood wants to reduce its new hire turnover, ensure new employees have a positive and engaging onboarding experience, get new employees into the restaurant faster, and reduce managers' time spent on hiring.

The Opportunity

In conducting an audit of the e-learning modules, there is an opportunity to improve the new hire training experience by redesigning much of the content into short-format microlearning, enabling access on any device to get the new hires out of the less desirable training room. There's also an opportunity to explore making some of the training program available on the job in the moment of need.

The Proposed Solution

To address the new hire's needs, we will create a series of short-format e-learning modules to replace most of the existing training materials. Each module will be no more than five minutes long and will contain interactivity relative to the task at hand. For example, a short-order cook can watch a short video on how to cook a steak, then practice cooking a steak via a short simulation. Specific topics for microlearning include proper dress code, proper personal hygiene, and how to communicate with customers according to the FastFood way.

New hires do not have to sit through all the training at once. In fact, the training program will be designed so that over the course of a day, new hires can spend some time going through the training program, then go into the restaurant to immediately apply what they learned with mentor or manager oversight.

The training could be accessed through a FastFood computer or iPad or even the employee's own smartphone or tablet if desired.

The Outcomes

If implemented as outlined, the following outcomes could be expected:
- a reduction in new hire turnover within the first week of employment
- a reduction in the amount of hours managers spend hiring new employees to fill vacancies
- an increase in the amount of time managers spend on the day-to-day operations of the restaurant.

These outcomes may be measured by tracking the number of training completions of the total new hire program, conducting surveys with restaurant managers three months post-launch of the new microlearning program, and tracking the number of new hires who quit in the first week on the job.

Resources

To implement this microlearning program as outlined will take approximately 10 to 12 weeks, and can partially be funded using the existing training department budget. If agreeable, the training department will ask for the balance of funding from other department heads.

Sample Microlearning Value "Sound Bites"

When you think about engaging stakeholders to discuss the business case for a micro-learning resource or program, sound bites can be very useful in conveying the need for introducing microlearning. Here are several examples of sound bites for making the case for microlearning.

"Studies demonstrate learners forget 90 percent of what they learned after they leave a training program if no additional coaching or support is in place. By providing microlearning to the participants after they leave the program, their retention rate can be maintained." *(For more detail on this, see the information on the forgetting curve in chapter 2.)*

"Sales representatives struggle to remember the complex process of how products are reimbursed. By providing microlearning in the form of a job aid, sales representatives can refer to it prior to going into a sales call, increasing their confidence level in communicating a difficult process, and enhancing their ability to support their customers."

"Next quarter, a new software update will be pushed out to customers. An investment in a short video tutorial can minimize the number of calls received to the customer service desk, saving time for our agents."

"Our employees are busy—we don't have time to take them away from their role to complete a full day of training. By developing small, shorter-form learning, we can provide more value to the employees without disrupting the business . . . fitting into the day in a practical way."

"Compliance training needs to be more than a 'check the box' activity. By repeating the key compliance tasks, it increases the likelihood of employees living up to the expectations. If it's really important, repetition can help. (A sign posted in all common areas that employees see every day about the number of days without a safety incident can keep safety top of mind and motivate employees to keep the positive streak going.)"

Plan for Creating a Single, Stand-Alone Microlearning Resource

Before creating your microlearning, consider the different elements to be included in your plan. Here is an example of a plan for creating a single, stand-alone microlearning resource.

Identified Business Need	Customer questions about IT security with installed diagnostic equipment have increased in the past six months. Sales representatives are not confident in addressing customer concerns and are unsure of the best way to handle complaints. Customer service call volume is also increasing due to increased security announcements.
Impact if Successful	Increased sales representative confidence and ability to handle customer complaints in an effective manner; decreased call volume to customer service.
Solution Type *(microlearning as preparation before long-form training, follow-up to support long-form training, stand-alone training, or performance support)*	Stand-alone training
Solution Description	This short e-learning module will review the most common IT security breaches, provide key talking points, and demonstrate how to effectively respond to customers
Audience	Sales representatives, district managers
Format	E-learning module, HTML5
Length	5-7 minutes
IT Requirements	Hosted on the LMS and viewable on the learner's iPhone, tablet, or laptop; completion is tracked on the LMS
Resource Requirements *(budget, time, or people)*	Budget dollars
Timing	Q2 of next year

Learning Technology Strategy Questions

Use these questions to think through your learning technology strategy and how it might influence microlearning implementation in your organization.

What technology is available to build or author content?

What technology systems are available to deploy content?

What technology systems or platforms are available to store and curate content?

What is the learner experience at the point of consuming the content?

How old is the technology? Will updates be available in the near future?

Which technology supports microlearning? What else do I need? (Think about video, podcasts, mini e-learning modules, and so on.)

What technology is missing to support the creation and implementation of microlearning resources?

References and Additional Resources

Allamano, C.B. 2018. "How to Make the Business Case for Learning." Udemy for Business, September 3. business.udemy.com/blog/how-to-make-the-business-case-for-learning.

AllenComm. 2019. "What Technology Can Do for Your Learning Strategy." Insights, June 26. td.org/professional-partner-content/what-technology-can-do-for-your -learning-strategy.

ATD Staff. 2016. "The ATD Talent Development Framework: Learning Technologies." Insights, September 16. td.org/insights/the-atd-talent-development-framework -learning-technologies.

Center for Creative Leadership. 2019. "6 Strategies to Make Digital Learning Work." Center for Creative Leadership, January 17. ccl.org/articles/leading-effectively -articles/6-strategies-to-make-digital-learning-work.

Chibana, N. 2015. "13 Types of Infographics: Which One Works For You?" Visme, November 21. visme.co/blog/types-of-infographics.

Cowan, E. 2016. "The Power of Infographics: How Do They Create Impact?" SEMrush blog, February 16. semrush.com/blog/the-power-of-infographics-how-do-they -create-impact.

Hill, B. 2012. "How to Write a Good Marketing Message." *Houston Chronicle* small business blog, July 19. smallbusiness.chron.com/write-good-marketing-message-51621.html.

Lile, S. 2017. "101 of the Best Infographic Examples on 19 Different Subjects." Visme, May 6. visme.co/blog/best-infographic-examples.

Love, S. 2016. "How to Conduct a Lightning-Fast Needs Assessment Clients Will Love." Insights, June 15. td.org/insights/how-to-conduct-a-lightning-fast-needs-assessment -clients-will-love.

Mercier, S. 2016. "Where to Start When Developing a Learning Technology Strategy." *TD* magazine, August. td.org/magazines/where-to-start-when-developing-a -learning-technology-strategy.

Mercier, S. 2017. "Learning Technology Strategy—An Introduction." ATD, August 31. td.org/videos/learning-technology-strategy-an-introduction.

UNC Executive Development. 2015. "Making the Case for Learning and Development: 5 Steps for Success." Executive Development blog, April 23. execdev.kenan-flagler .unc.edu/blog/making-the-case-for-learning-and-development-5-steps-for-success.

Van Buren, M., and T. Safferstone. 2009. "The Quick Wins Paradox." Harvard Business Review, January. hbr.org/2009/01/the-quick-wins-paradox.

Wentworth, D. 2016. "Mission Critical: A Fully Developed Learning Technology Strategy." *Training* magazine, May 26. trainingmag.com/mission-critical-fully-developed-learning-technology-strategy.

Williams, R. 2015. *The Non-Designer's Design Book*, 4th ed. San Francisco: Peachpit Press.

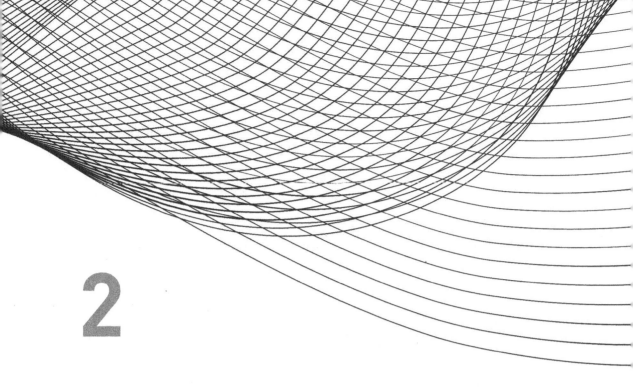

2

Shaping the Future:
Why Choose Microlearning?

In This Chapter

- Why learners are asking you to go micro
- Why organizations are asking you to go micro
- The learning benefits of going micro
- The value of microlearning to instructional design processes
- Barriers that may prevent you from going micro

Microlearning is a hot topic. It seems everyone wants to be doing it without really knowing what "it" is or how it can make a difference for their learners or their organization. In chapter 1, we defined microlearning as any learning that is short—five to 10 minutes (or less)—and just as long as needed to give the learner what they really need. But why should you go micro?

We've been using long-form learning for decades and it seems to work just fine, right? Of course, we all know that the field of learning and development is evolving as our understanding of optimal learning environments improves. So, for example, the university lectures Carla's dad sat through in the early 1970s really were as bad as we all imagine. Nearly every story he used to tell her of his university experience was about "listening to a lecture" followed by talking about how hard he and his friends "studied" afterward—what they were really doing was making sense of the concepts, asking one another questions, and helping one another learn the material. Listening to someone talk for hours without interacting with them was no less effective then than it is today, but now we're realizing that we can (and should!) do things differently: Engage the learner with demonstrations, add activities, and ask them questions.

We know that long-form teaching and learning can be done well, and it can be very effective. But as our understanding of how to teach optimally has evolved, we've also realized the importance of supporting the learner after a longer learning event with things like job aids and follow-up materials, and we've also realized that we can teach important concepts in short bursts. Of course this has also evolved because the technology has evolved too. In 1970, the most powerful learning technology Carla's dad had was a pocket calculator!

Let's take a look at some of the reasons you should consider microlearning as part of your design and development toolkit.

The Modern Learner Is Asking You to Go Micro

Three major societal factors are coming together right now, and this confluence of factors is creating a situation where the power of microlearning is recognized more than ever before. These influences are mobile devices, social connectedness, and time scarcity (Figure 2-1). These societal influences have made modern learners consider how they are learning in their personal lives—how they consume content to get better at their hobbies, understand their physical ailments, fix their homes, and even raise their children. Now they are asking how those same approaches could be used in their workplace learning too. As a result, modern learners and modern organizations are asking for sho content.

Figure 2-1. Flywheel of Factors Driving Microlearning

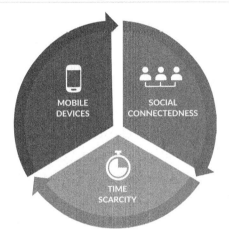

Source: Torgerson (2016).

Mobile Devices

That phone in your pocket is more powerful than the computer NASA used to put the first man on the moon in 1969 (Grossman 2017). Some say millions of times more powerful (Puiu 2015). With that powerful device, we are able to get nearly any information we need anytime we need it.

For example, consider how often we use Google Maps, and how positively it affects us. Most people use it to get turn-by-turn directions to new places and to help them when they're lost. But people also use it for routes they know well; as they walk out the office door each day, they map the directions to their house. It's not that they don't know the way; it's that there are multiple equally good routes, and they are checking to see if one is faster than the other due to an accident or traffic congestion. And as they get into their car with the preferred route selected, it provides the expected arrival time. Before they drive away, they can even call or text their family to tell when they expect to be home, knowing that the Google Maps estimate is going to be accurate within minutes.

This is a perfect example of performance support. If there's a route you don't know well, you have turn-by-turn directions to guide you while you drive. And given two good options, you have a tool that will tell you how to perform optimally every time, despite changing conditions each day.

That's a very specific example, but of course your phone serves as performance support in countless other ways too. One of the most important is that whenever you need some piece of information that you don't know, you can look it up on the Internet from your phone. We don't think it can be overstated how powerful it is that we all have access to every website on the Internet at any time and location.

This access to information anywhere, anytime has made people realize the value of looking up information when they need it. They don't have to remember phone numbers, addresses, or other facts they once had to memorize to function in society. And now they're asking if that power could help at work too. Are there things that employees could look up rather than having to remember? Are there ways to make their jobs easier by giving them the information they need just when they need it?

The idea of performance support has been around for decades, but the power of personal computers and mobile devices has enabled learning professionals to think very differently about how employees can be supported at work.

Social Connectedness

Human beings are highly social and have always learned from one another. For example, Carla's grandparents were farmers in a rural community, and she remembers what it was like when someone came over for coffee. So much learning was happening! It really was the equivalent of the modern-day office watercooler. They were sharing all kinds of information that was important to them—things about their livestock, tips about their machinery, better ways to can their food. What they were learning isn't important; the point here is that they were constantly learning from their friends and neighbors.

Carla's grandparents didn't have a telephone. Let that sink in for a minute . . . imagine your life if you didn't have a cell phone, you didn't have a landline, and you had no other way of communicating with the community around you except for physically driving a mile or more to your neighbor's house. Someone coming over for coffee was a regular occurrence, and it's not because Carla's grandparents were neighborhood socialites. Everyone worked this way because this was how they connected with one another. Sure, it was enjoyable to see their friends, but they always got something valuable out of it. This is how they did much of their informal learning.

Fast-forward to today. Not only does everyone have a telephone, but they are mobile and connected to other people via the Internet. And that connection to the Internet is key. If you regularly go to a physical office, you have the value of talking to, and learning from, the people around you. And regardless of whether you go into a brick-and-mortar building surrounded by other people or not, you are connected virtually to many networks and thousands of people. Everyone is connected in lots of ways: work networks by email, Microsoft Teams, Yammer, or something else; professional networks on LinkedIn and Twitter; personal networks on Facebook, Pinterest, and Instagram. The list goes on.

All that social connectedness has enabled people to supercharge the informal learning they do with one another. They are constantly interacting with people via these virtual networks and interacting with countless others every day—even if they are just reading what other people are posting on an email group, LinkedIn, or Facebook. Even if they aren't interacting with that content in a formal way by using it at that moment, they are still learning from it.

People have gotten so accustomed to all this informal learning through their online networks that they're now asking how they can maximize that at work. In many ways, they're asking how they can harness the power of informal learning at work—maybe we make it a little more formal, or maybe we keep it informal and offer more content or encourage people to participate more. Regardless of the form it takes, it's clear that informal learning and learning from each other is driving everyone's interest in microlearning.

Time Scarcity

In our teaching and speaking across the nation, we often ask, "Do you have too much time?" No one raises a hand. Sometimes people will laugh or someone may call out "Yeah right!" but not one hand goes up. This reaction is because everyone knows the same truth about society: There is no shortage of things to do to fill the time, no shortage of commitments and priorities, and the idea of actually finishing all of them is laughable. This is true both in people's personal lives and at work.

As a result, when people need help with a task in their personal lives, they expect to find the knowledge they need right away, so they can get on with their day—for example, finding directions to a new place, finding out if a business is open, watching a product review video before deciding to make a purchase. We have gotten used to being surrounded by instructional and informational content in our everyday lives, and having it available to help us right at the moment we want it.

Of course, people now bring that expectation to work, expecting to be surrounded by learning and support materials that enable them to make better use of their time. It really is all about getting the learning and support they need as quickly as possible, integrating that learning into the flow of their work, and using that to get on with their day as efficiently as possible. Of the three factors, this is the one that most causes learners (and organizational leaders) to demand microlearning at work.

* * *

Because of these three factors, people are seeing the power of short-form learning in their personal lives, so it's natural to want to use short-form learning in the workplace too. The modern learner and the modern organization are demanding this. Often, they are the ones asking the training people to think differently about how we teach them. They see the ability to add learning into the flow of their busy day, and ways to support them as they do their job.

In countless organizations, the employees are asking for shorter-form learning, and they are telling the learning people that this is a better way to go. It's because, as the users of that learning, they instinctively know what would help them most. Just like many universities have evolved the classroom from Carla's dad's lecture experience in the early 1970s to a more student-centered and learning-focused experience, workplace learning needs to evolve to better support employees with content when, where, and how they need it. The modern learner is demanding we go micro, and we need to listen to them about how to meet their needs.

The Organization Wants to Meet Targeted Learning and Business Needs

One of the greatest powers of short-form learning is meeting targeted learning and business needs, and doing that without disrupting the flow of the business. Instead of pulling people off the job for a day of training, you can give them little bits of content that they can consume as they have time over several weeks or even longer.

This is important because your learners were hired to do an operational duty—that's their job—and that job will always be their top priority. Learning and getting better at that job will always come in second (or lower!). This makes sense: If someone doesn't do their operational duty, then they are not furthering the core work of the business and the business will not survive. In for-profit and not-for-profit organizations, the business won't make enough money to sustain itself. In government and charitable organizations, the organization won't provide the services that it exists to provide, which results in reduced funding or donations.

CASE STUDY: ADDRESSING BUSINESS NEEDS WITH MICROLEARNING

Susan works for a large financial services firm with physical banks across the nation. The firm also has online and mobile banking, and phone banking services.

In personal banking services, the company is rolling out a new product: a new type of savings account with several features that the bank has not offered before. It's particularly well-suited to high-school students and helping them save for college. It is marketed to parents, but used exclusively by teens.

Susan works on a team that creates product training for the personal banking staff. The training she creates is used by branch tellers across the country and call center staff in their headquarters in a large city.

The Current Way

For a new product rollout like this, Susan normally designs a 50-minute class (to ensure that employees are back on the phones within one hour) that can be offered live and virtually. She offers a live class at headquarters for the call center staff. It works well because they are physically in the same location. Classes are offered at a few different times; staff sign up for one of the offerings and are scheduled off the phone lines to attend. Because, the staff at physical banks are dispersed, she offers them a few virtual instructor-led training (VILT) sessions using their web-based conferencing system.

For both the live and VILT classes, Susan creates a PowerPoint deck that explains the product, its features, the target market, and ideal times to talk about it with target customers (in this case, parents) who are unaware of the new offering. It's a mix of product-specific training and sales training, but because she can only get the employees off the phones for one class, she makes sure to cover everything well in the one opportunity she has. She works hard to make sure the training and examples are relevant and the class is interactive, but she also knows that they cover a lot of information in an hour, and people likely forget a lot.

Susan has been under pressure to consider alternative ways of teaching this content. She has to inform the call center a month prior to the class offerings to get the classes "on the schedule" so people are covered when they're off the phones and balance the phone line staffing. This prevents her from getting training out quickly.

In addition, while the staff at physical banks appreciate the efforts to provide webinars, it's challenging for staff to attend them. Sure, sessions are offered during "slow times," but many of the smaller banks only have a few tellers working then, so invariably there's a 15 to 20 percent no-show rate at any given webinar, because staff have customers to attend to and need to reschedule for a different session.

A New Way

Susan decides to try a new approach for her next product training. She creates a five-minute PowerPoint presentation about the new product. It's just a couple slides with the key information about the product and the new features. Managers are expected to share it at a team meeting within a given two-week period.

Then she follows this with a month-long email campaign. Each week she sends one email reminding people of the new product and linking to a short e-learning module on the LMS. Each module takes less than 10 minutes to complete and has just one focused topic:

- Week 1: who the product is for and the importance of those customers to the bank
- Week 2: features and benefits of the product
- Week 3: key questions customers ask and addressing concerns
- Week 4: when and how to tell customers about it.

The Result

Susan finds that the branch staff really appreciate the opportunity to learn at different times of the day, and that each piece is short enough that they can fit it into their day. Sure, this is partly the advantage of an asynchronous approach, but keeping the pieces to 10 minutes or less also makes it easier for the branch staff to consume within their busy day.

Susan's greatest challenge with this approach is making sure employees complete all the learning pieces, but she asks managers to help her ensure that their staff complete the one module per week. She also purposely gives learners just one week to complete each training, because this helps them manage their time and keeps completion rates strong. And because the material is on the LMS, she is able to track usage and completion, and even tell managers when someone is not completing the training.

The call center staff still need to have their learning time scheduled, so Susan has a new challenge, but she works with scheduling to have a 15-minute block for learning time assigned to every employee once a week for a month. Because she has a program that has one piece every week for four weeks, she's able to submit this as a single request to scheduling.

The unexpected surprise is that staff now know the product better and bring it up more often with customers. Because people forget so much of what they learn in a single learning event, Susan's approach of spreading the content out over five short learning bursts actually helps them better remember the new product.

Ultimately, Susan was able to create more effective training while being less disruptive to the business. She needed strong relationships with her operational leaders to get their support of the program, but with those in place, she was able to make a positive change in her approach to this training. The managers appreciated the efficiency and effectiveness of the program and will be willing partners the next time there is a product rollout.

Certainly, you want to use training to enable the organization to continually improve, but at the heart of it, the learner must do their operational duties for the organization to survive. So it only makes sense that operational leaders want to get employees trained and proficient as efficiently as possible. Time not spent in training is time people have for their operational duties or other priorities (like committee work, organizing their workspace, or even just leaving a little early on a Friday afternoon).

As a result, organizations are asking for learning professionals to consider ways to make their training more efficient. It's not that they don't want training—it's that they recognize all the things their employees need to do, all the priorities they have, and training is just one of them. So, if you can provide content that is shorter, or helps just when the learner needs it, you are likely to enable those employees to get back to their other priorities, particularly their operational duties, more efficiently—and with the training to make them more effective at those duties.

As you can see from the case study, microlearning absolutely helps you to be more judicious with your learners' time. When you are targeted with what you teach and provide focused content, you are able to train employees and get them back to doing the thing they were hired to do.

In the end, it may be approximately the same amount of learning time (in Susan's case, she had a five-minute lesson followed by four 10-minute lessons for a total of 45 minutes, instead of a 50-minute class), but it feels like less time to the learner, it's less disruptive to the business, and it has better retention and transfer to the job, which makes the training more effective. And it enables the learner to better focus on priority number one: their operational duties.

PRO TIP

If you are focused on improving a specific performance need, building the case for microlearning will be much easier. It will be easier to communicate your vision, and easier to get buy-in from the organization.

But be careful about creating a vision that is unattainable—you don't want people to dismiss you because they know that training alone (or a single microlearning program) won't solve the problem. Don't try to boil the ocean. Start small, focusing on single behaviors that you can affect.

Learning and Performance Can Improve When You Go Micro

As learning professionals, your ultimate goal is to improve performance—to help people get better at their jobs. Microlearning can absolutely help you as you try to move the needle in your organization. This includes reducing the forgetting curve and improving transfer of learning to the job.

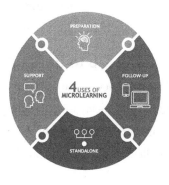

As we said in chapter 1, microlearning can be used in four main ways:

- preparation before a learning event
- follow-up to support a learning event
- stand-alone training
- performance support

There are advantages to using microlearning in all of these situations.

Preparation Before a Learning Event

When microlearning is used to help level-set participants' base-line knowledge before a training event, you make the learning event more valuable for everyone. You can use prework to help get participants ready to learn—or when pushed to an extreme, the learning event can become a flipped classroom, where you give people material before the class to read and consume and then use the classroom time to focus only on the  application and practice of that learning. Of course, the more classroom time you spend on application, the better the learning and transfer to the workplace will be.

Many learning professionals say the biggest challenge with these sorts of techniques is that it's hard to get people to do the prework. Properly completing the prework would make a big difference to the learning environment, but how do you get people to do it? There are lots of strategies, but one is to go micro. Make the prework feel easy to consume by creating bite-sized pieces with just a few that have to be done before the program.

Sometimes it helps to tell your learners that the prework will take just 10 minutes, or that there are only three seven-minute pieces to complete. Of course, that can produce its own challenge, because people will say, "It's just 10 minutes," and put it off until later. Sometimes that means people will hastily do the prework just before the class, and sometimes they still won't complete it. However, using microlearning is a valid way to help get more people to complete more of the prework.

Follow-Up to Support a Learning Event

When someone participates in a longer-form learning event, they will quickly forget what they learned if they aren't practicing and applying their new skills immediately. It can be challenging to sustain learning over time.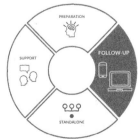

CASE STUDY: PREPARATION BEFORE A LEARNING EVENT

Jim has a leadership development program for new leaders in his organization. Within 30 days of being promoted into a leadership role, new leaders are expected to take his series of classes. Jim has prework for the classes, but new leaders are very, very busy as they try to find the new balance between tactical duties and leadership duties.

Jim used to ask participants to read a chapter from a leadership book prior to coming to each of his classes. Now he summarizes the chapter into a two-page "backgrounder." He tells the learners that it will only take them 10 minutes to read, and that he has summarized the most important points for them so they don't have to read the entire chapter.

The result? More people complete the reading before class, and everyone (even those who don't read it) see Jim more favorably because of his efforts to use their time well. They feel like Jim really understands what they are going through during this career transition.

The Forgetting Curve

The learner in a typical class will forget most of what they learned in that class within days. This is called the forgetting curve (Figure 2-2).

The learning curve and forgetting curve show us that most new information learned in a class is forgotten within days. As you can see in the graph, during a class people acquire a lot of new skills and knowledge. But studies show that the retention of this knowledge rapidly declines if there is no intervention—they simply forget it. The only way to disrupt this is to have the learner immediately apply what they are learning on the job, or to provide ongoing reinforcement or coaching over time.

Figure 2-2. The Forgetting Curve

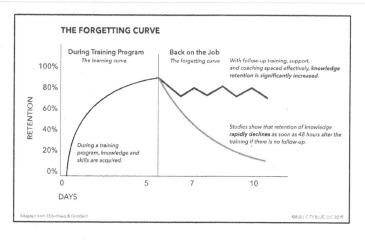

Let's consider an example to make this concrete. Think about your last formal learning experience—it could have been a training class, a webinar, or even a conference presentation. Pause for a minute until you can think of one. Now ask yourself these questions:

- What was the class or presentation about?
- Of all the things that were covered, how much do you really remember (a lot, a moderate amount, or not very much)?
- What were the top things you learned?
- Are you using any of those in your work now?

If you can rattle off the answers to these questions with ease, congratulations! Sadly, for most people, the reality is that they'll forget almost everything they learned in that learning event, unless they have an opportunity to apply it immediately. And unless they applied it immediately, it likely didn't affect their work in a substantial way. This is sad for several reasons—not only was the information forgotten, it was a huge waste of time, and a lot of money spent by the business went down the drain.

That's not to say that such learning is not useful—there's always a small amount that we do remember. We will remember those parts that are most important to us. And we are often surprised by the things that we remember much later—that moment when you think, "Yes, I've heard about that before. . . ." and then you look back in your notes (or on the Internet!) for more information.

However, the big takeaway here is that as instructional designers, if you want learners to really remember something from your instruction, you need to provide repetition and reinforcement. There are a few different ways to do this, but one is to provide small bits of content to reinforce key ideas after the learning program. Many call this boost learning.

Reinforcement or Boost Learning

Using microlearning to reinforce prior learning is one way that makes a great difference. Many people call this boost learning because you really are "boosting" the learning after the learning event.

How does that work? Ideally, you identify the top concepts from the class. Then, you create a short piece of content to reinforce each concept. It may be a few paragraphs of text, an infographic, or a few minutes of e-learning or video. Regardless of the format, your goal is to provide a brief reminder of the concept and why it is important or how it is used, so you can keep the learning alive.

The real power here is that you are improving the retention of the longer-form learning and thus improving the impact of the other learning events, particularly live classes. We know that in general people really like in-person classes, but retention from them is weak. Focusing on good activities and discussions in class is one strategy to increase retention, and follow-up and reinforcement after the session is another.

CASE STUDY: FOLLOW-UP TO SUPPORT A LEARNING EVENT

Sam creates new product training for his sales reps. He does a one-hour webinar each September to present the new products that are coming out for the year.

He knows the sellers are most familiar with the existing product line, so it's always challenging to get them to take time to understand the newest products and include them in their offerings to customers. The webinar is good for familiarizing them with the new products, but they often forget a lot of the details. As a result, they don't include the new products as often when presenting to clients.

So Sam creates a boost program to follow the webinar. He sends a series of brief emails twice a week over the month following the webinar to reinforce the new product information. The reps become more familiar with the products and are more likely to mention them to customers.

Stand-Alone Training

Some concepts are short enough that they can be taught independent of a longer-form learning event such as a longer e-learning module, virtual instructor-led training, or instructor-led training. In these cases you are able to use the learners' time more efficiently by giving them just what they need and no more. All learners notice when there is content in a course they do not need. So instead, focus on what is most important to the learner and then give just those pieces.

To be clear, this form of microlearning will have the same issues with retention as other long-form training—one-time learning is always forgotten quickly. But because it is shorter, it can be consumed multiple times or also used as performance support. Or it can be provided just before the learner applies that skill on the job. This sort of short, just-in-time learning will have greater retention because the new knowledge and skills are applied immediately.

CASE STUDY: STAND-ALONE TRAINING

Jeannette provides training for leaders about employment law. This is an annual training program about how to deal with all kinds of issues, such as employees who chronically miss work, who come to work intoxicated, who harass others at work, and many other topics.

The class lasts an hour, and most leaders are relieved when it is over. They know the content is important, and they know why they have to take the class, but they don't see the content as relevant at that exact moment and they have pressing operational duties to take care of.

So Jeannette changes her approach. She identifies the top 12 employment law issues that people need to be aware of. She creates a short piece of e-learning that takes five minutes or less to consume, and then distributes one piece of stand-alone training every month, with a reminder to call their HR business partner for help with this and any other issues.

She sets an expectation that people will receive one short piece every month and that this will replace their longer class. Leaders still have trouble finding time to consume this shorter-form learning, but she puts it on the LMS so it can be tracked and reminders sent until it is complete.

The result? Leaders are more aware of employment law issues, as evidenced by them calling their HR business partner for support more often. This is seen as a success; calling more often for support means that the leaders are considering employment law more carefully in their day-to-day work.

Performance Support

When people are at work and trying to do their job, they sometimes use checklists and other job aids to help them perform optimally. These aids are called performance support—the things that support them at the moment they are trying to do some aspect of their job.

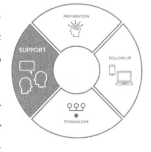

A great example of performance support is the one discussed earlier: Google Maps. If you get lost, it helps at your exact moment of need to find where you are and how to get back on track. There are lots of examples in the workplace too. Have you ever gone into a restaurant restroom and noticed the sign that reminds employees to wash their hands before returning to work? That's a great example of performance support—something that helps ensure people do a task of their job properly every time. There are even laws requiring such signage in restaurants in the United States; those laws are in place because even lawmakers know they will help make a difference in employee performance.

Performance support can also be far more sophisticated than a small poster or sign. When you get stuck while using a piece of software and click the "help" button, you are getting performance support. And when you talk to a call center agent who asks if they can put you on hold for a moment to find the answer to your question, they are almost surely looking the answer up in a performance support database. A good agent can even do this while making small talk with you; you may not even realize that they are looking up answers while having a brief conversation with you about the weather.

When learning is augmented with performance support, employees will generally perform better. The images in Figure 2-3 come from research by Conrad Gottfredson and Bob Mosher.

Figure 2-3. The Value of Performance Support

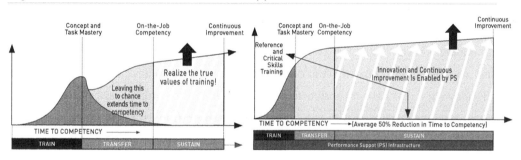

RESOURCES

To gain a deeper understanding of how performance support can be used in your organization, and practical ideas for how to implement it, see *Innovative Performance Support: Strategies and Practices for Learning in the Workflow* by Conrad Gottfredson and Bob Mosher. You can also find their latest work on their 5 Moments of Need website.

The first image shows the traditional training cycle for live classes. As discussed before, there is a lot of learning followed by a lot of forgetting. The phase of transferring learning from the classroom to the workplace is critical to improving performance, and for the organization to capitalize on the value of the training. But as Gottfredson and Mosher say, leaving the transfer phase to chance "extends time to competency." We add that it can also cause many concepts learned in the classroom to never be utilized on the job. This is what has been coined "scrap learning," because all that time spent learning is essentially scrap or waste.

The second image shows a better way to sustain and continuously improve performance. If you train someone and immediately provide them with performance support that helps them transfer that learning to their job, then the time spent learning will result in improved performance, and clearly there will be a payoff to the learner and the organization. You should not be surprised by Gottfredson and Mosher's results—they found they could cut the classroom time in half, and if they provided good performance support, employees reached competency twice as fast!

For example, imagine having a two-day class on the latest features in a customer-relationship management (CRM) program like Salesforce or HubSpot and then sending people back to their work with nothing more than encouragement to use these new features—no additional support, no follow-up from the facilitator or classmates, no manager involvement. Of course, the sales reps who take the class will use some of the new ideas they learned—the ones that really caught their attention. But even by Monday they will have forgotten some of those ideas, and many others may be used once or twice and then never again. **The forgetting curve is serious, and change is hard.** As a result, when learners are expected to incorporate new ideas into their workflow without any support, they likely won't get maximum value from the learning experience.

But imagine trimming that classroom time back to a one-day class that simply teaches the most important features and how learners can get support when they forget how to use that feature. In the class, you provide job aids, and show how to use them. Then, after the class, you follow up with regular emails to remind them of the best tips and features in the program, and their manager routinely checks in on their progress with the new features, particularly those the manager finds most relevant to the work of the team. You can see how the learner would become more proficient so much more quickly!

CASE STUDY: PERFORMANCE SUPPORT

Tom works for a company that leases and sells office technology, like printers and pho-tocopiers, to large businesses. He creates training for the on-site service-repair people. These technicians learn about all the equipment and models that clients may have, but when they are on-site they'll likely need very specific details about error codes and how to resolve them.

Rather than training the technicians on all the nuances of every problem a customer could have, Tom creates one-page guides that walk them through the steps of addressing each error code in each of the products they may service. Then the technician can look up the specific details for the product they are servicing, and work from that one-page guide. The company provides all these one-pagers in a searchable mobile app so the technicians can easily find what they need at any client site.

Tom offers formal training only at a high level to teach about the equipment and the main models they may service. But in the training class, he also shows technicians the one-page guides and gives them a number of scenarios to resolve by using the guides on their iPads. The learners practice using the performance support materials in the classroom, and under the guidance of a trained facilitator, so they become comfortable using the per-formance support and will be able to use it in the field.

Microlearning Improves Your Design and Development Processes

As a learning and development professional, when you consider microlearning, you are taking a more holistic view. You are considering how your training fits into the workflow and the big picture of the employee trying to work most efficiently. You are also consid-ering how you support learning long term.

Going micro may also allow you to become more agile. Folks like Michael Allen and Megan Torrance have been talking about agile development, particularly for e-learning, for a long time. But we believe that with microlearning you may be able to be more agile than ever before. When you go micro, the pieces are smaller, so iterating and taking some out and adding new ones in feels easier and more natural. It's also easier to make tweaks and revisions over time, either because something changed or you found a better way to teach it.

We recently worked on a microlearning program where we delivered about 2.5 hours of content entirely through short-form resources. There were 22 resources, some videos, some interactive e-learning modules, and some noninteractive PDFs. What we found through this experience of creating a program with so many microlearning resources was that we learned more with each piece we created. In fact, it took a long time to develop the first few pieces because we were ensuring the user experience was clear and easy to follow and our instructional approaches were working well. We found things we wanted to tweak and change as we built more and more pieces. At times it was challenging to manage changes to the already completed modules, especially as we got further into the project, but the end product was far superior because we'd been incrementally improving each piece as the entire program was built.

RESOURCES

For more on Agile methodology and how it relates to instructional design and e-learning, check out Michael Allen and Richard Sites' *Leaving ADDIE for SAM: An Agile Model for Developing the Best Learning Experiences* and Megan Torrance's *Agile for Instructional Designers: Iterative Project Management to Achieve Results*.

PRO TIP

Often the most innovative microlearning solutions come from really understanding the learners and their use case (see the discussion about use case in chapter 3). Be careful of listening to colleagues who say "It won't work" when you want to try something different, such as using microlearning or being more agile. If you focus on the learners' performance, and are grounded in an understanding of the use case and the learners' needs, you are likely to create learning materials that they will use and appreciate.

The whole idea of microlearning is "different" to many of our SMEs, and they may question the approach. If this happens, focus on the learners' performance on the job and the use case. How will this help those learners? If you do that, you'll likely win over those naysayers. And if that doesn't work, consider your naysayers as a challenge! Do your research and gather data to support your approach. And be willing to explain it to them—you likely know more about the approach than they do.

Then, call your first rollout a "pilot," and maybe even do it with a smaller subset of your audience. That way the naysayers will be less likely to see the approach as risky, and will be more amenable to trying something new.

The Barriers Preventing Organizations From Using Microlearning

Now that we've discussed some of the reasons why microlearning can work and ways to use it well, let's highlight common barriers in the organization that prevent microlearning from being implemented or adopted—and tips to overcome them. The Association for Talent Development (ATD) published a whitepaper in which it looked at the barriers that prevent learning and development professionals from

RESOURCES

For more data about what instructional designers are doing with microlearning in their organizations, check out ATD's 2017 research report *Microlearning: Delivering Bite-Sized Knowledge.*

using microlearning. It asked nearly 600 learning and development professionals about their use of microlearning in their organizations.

One question ATD asked was about barriers, or the reasons that learning and development professionals might not be using microlearning. Figure 2-4 shows the results.

Figure 2-4. Primary Barriers to Effective Microlearning

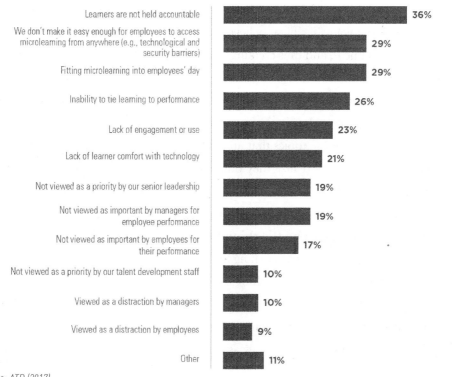

Source: ATD (2017).

PRO TIP

Try to anticipate and identify potential barriers to microlearning in your organization. Then, come up with ideas for how to address those barriers before you start socializing your program. Even if you don't have all the specific answers, knowing how you'll address such questions will be critical to getting organizational support for your program.

Let's look at the top four issues—those barriers that at least 25 percent of respondents thought were problematic in their own journey into microlearning:

Barrier 1: Learners Are Not Held Accountable

Time is the most limited commodity we have, so we are always prioritizing what tasks to do with that limited time. Even when we don't realize it, we are subconsciously making decisions about how best to use our time. As a result, it's absolutely true that we are all more likely to do things if there's a level of accountability. When something is optional at work, it's often not done.

As a result, a lot of organizations are not willing to try microlearning because they believe microlearning is only used as informal learning—that is, it is used only if and when the employee wants it. They believe that because microlearning is not required, people won't consume it, and thus creating those materials is not a good use of the training team's time.

While this logic makes sense, there are a few things to remember. If you are training on topics learners care deeply about, you are more likely to get them to consume it. So start by looking for those topics that are closest to the moment of performance, that moment when the learners realize they don't have the skills or knowledge they need to do a particular job task or duty. **Generally, learners don't care a lot about your training, but they do care about getting their operational duties done, and you want your training to be the thing that helps them with that.**

Also, we can have short-form learning that is hosted on an LMS, and have the learners' completion tracked. There is nothing saying that LMS content can't be short. Also, remember that holding people accountable for their learning is not always about the LMS. This could be as simple as having the employee's manager provide that accountability. The leader can be a tremendous asset in helping identify where this content will make the biggest difference for the learner and continuing to make it a priority among their other work duties.

Barrier 2: Technology and Security Constraints

Any time you create training that is delivered electronically, you'll have to deal with security issues. We've both had experiences with this—one of us spent more than 20 years in training for pharmaceutical and biotechnology companies, and the other spent years in instructional design roles in both financial services and healthcare delivery settings. Your setting probably has its own security concerns too. Few organizations are immune to this.

Technology and security can be a barrier for sure, but you can always start with the technology you've already figured out. How are you delivering e-learning now? Even if that content can only be accessed on company property and from an LMS, you can still go micro. Use your LMS and start by making your content shorter. Then, as your efforts and sophistication grow, you can look into ways to offer that content to people off-site, and possibly with other technologies like a social collaborative system or on mobile devices.

Barrier 3: Fitting Microlearning Into Employees' Days

This is an interesting challenge. Even as we make training shorter, people still say they don't have time for it. It really is about priorities, and the fact that our learners have a lot of operational duties that will almost always be prioritized above training.

Interestingly, you may find that as you go shorter, you have more trouble garnering completion. When the e-learning course is 30 minutes long, people will plan for the time in their day, but when it's five minutes, they are likely to put it off, thinking that it's "just five minutes" and that there will be a better time to do it later. This is the classic time management concept that things that are urgent take precedence over things that are important.

This issue is similar to our first barrier about holding employees accountable. When learning and development professionals hold people accountable to doing their training, they elevate training's importance and then people find time to do it. The question really is about priorities and what are the most important things to be done with limited time.

We are not saying that all training has to be mandatory, but maybe some of it should, to give it the right level of importance and priority within the workday. When you use microlearning, you are more likely to be hyper-focused on the most important things your employees need to know or be able to do. So then maybe some of that content is so important that it can or should be required. There will be times when making training mandatory doesn't make sense or simply isn't possible (such as customer training), but if you have the ability to make any of your learning mandatory, *and* the training covers an important performance or organizational need, then go for it! Alternatively, get managers bought in to holding their learners accountable for completing the microlearning.

Barrier 4: Inability to Tie Learning to Performance

This is a common barrier for all training efforts; this is not specific to microlearning. In fact, many people say that microlearning gets you focused on the content that has the greatest value to improving performance and is often used closer to the moment of performance. These factors likely make it easier to assess their impact on performance improvement.

Certainly, you can consider measuring return on investment with the four levels of the Kirkpatrick Model or the five levels of the Phillips ROI Methodology (which we address in chapter 5). But it can be hard and time-consuming to evaluate the business impact, and even the Phillips model assumes you don't measure to the final ROI level with all programs all the time.

In all cases, we want to use training where it is likely to have the greatest impact on employees and the business, and certainly we'd like to evaluate the business impact where we can. But not pursuing microlearning because it can't be evaluated is akin to not pursuing any other form of learning—e-learning, instructor-led classes, or virtual instructor-led classes—because you can't evaluate it. In chapter 5, we explore a variety of ways to tackle the measurement of microlearning.

TOOLS

Use the "Top Barriers to Going Micro and How to Address Them" tool at the end of this chapter for ideas to overcome the four main barriers to implementing microlearning in organizations.

Microlearning Is Not a Silver Bullet

With a whole chapter devoted to why microlearning is a good idea, and providing research on why it is instructionally sound, we think it is important to close this chapter with a reminder that microlearning isn't a magic elixir that will work in all cases all the time. We certainly wouldn't want to go to a surgeon who studied at the Microlearning School of Medicine, and we're sure you wouldn't either.

With that in mind, here are some common misconceptions about microlearning and why they are problematic.

Myth 1: Employees Will Consume Microlearning on Their Own Time

You'll notice in our case study earlier in this chapter about Susan's training program for bank employees that she did not create a microlearning program with an expectation that bank employees would consume the content on their personal time on their phones. This is a common fallacy we hear: If we give people something short and mobile-friendly, surely they'll consume it off-hours on the train or bus as they commute to and from work, or do it in the evenings and weekends when they have some downtime.

Even the most engaged and dedicated employees are not likely to consume workplace training during nonwork times. Yes, they may consume content from LinkedIn and other professional sources while sitting on their couch on a quiet Saturday afternoon. However, that content is generally of very strong interest to them personally, and they see it as a nonwork task. They are unlikely to engage in content that is for work in nonwork times.

There are usually only two times that training content from the employer will be consumed in nonwork times. The first is if the microlearning is just-in-time learning or performance support and the learner is working after hours when they need help. So, for example, a sales rep is entering his call notes in Salesforce on Saturday, after a busy week of sales calls. If he gets stuck on some feature of Salesforce, he may go to the just-in-time learning or job aids you've provided. He's consuming your microlearning—and he'll probably be very glad you provided it—but his focus is not on learning. It's about getting his job done quickly so he can enjoy the rest of his weekend.

The second time that employees will complete training during off-hours is if the training is a job requirement and they are completing the training after hours to meet a training completion deadline—that is, disciplinary action will be taken if they have not completed their training by a certain time, and that time is almost up.

In all other cases, it's foolish to think that by just providing content that is more easily consumable, our employees will stop having hobbies and outside interests, or that they will give up their precious spare time to consume our training. And even if they would, you should really question such a strategy—your employees will just burn out and you'll be left with retention problems.

Myth 2: Microlearning Content Is Produced Faster Because We Have Less (or No) Analysis

We can absolutely create a seven-minute piece of e-learning faster than a 30-minute one. This is simple project management—the time needed to write the script, create the graphics, and build the e-learning will be less. Sure, it's harder to write content that is concise, but the actual development of a seven-minute piece will take a lot less time than a 30-minute piece.

However, the needs analysis and understanding of the performance objectives is still needed, and this will likely take just as long as for longer-form learning. You still need a good understanding of the problem you are trying to solve and identify one or more learning objectives that you believe will address the problem. We are not advocating for "analysis paralysis," but you need a clear understanding of the learning objective or performance objective that you are trying to achieve with the training. If you don't have a clear understanding of the objective, you will never achieve it!

So, yes, you can produce microlearning resources more quickly, but you still need to take some time up front to make sure you understand the audience and the learning or performance objective well. If you don't do this, you're not likely to achieve your objectives, and you will be wasting your time and your learners' time.

Myth 3: Microlearning Is Just for Millennials

Some people think microlearning is just for Millennials—that younger learners appreciate learning in short form more than anyone else. Or they'll point to research that says Millennials are engaged by work environments that allow them to learn and grow.

We don't think those ideas need a generational qualifier. Most people want to do their best at work, want to believe they are being used to their fullest capability, and want to know that they are learning the skills needed for their next role in the company or their career. We are both far from being Millennials and we feel fortunate to spend our time in a work environment that enables us to learn and grow. We are also just as impatient as any Millennial; we Google everything to find quick resources and videos to solve our problems.

Also, from an organizational learning perspective, older employees tend to have higher-ranking positions and thus more significant job duties and salaries. We should feel compelled for the good of the organization to use their time as effectively as possible, and microlearning is one way to do that.

Microlearning Can Be Powerful

Of course, microlearning can be powerful. That's why people are so interested in it. It may not be faster or cheaper to create six five-minute mini-modules than a 30-minute e-learning module. However, with a good understanding of the performance you are trying to improve, you may be able to identify concepts you don't need to include in training, those things that really aren't important. Or you can develop and release those mini-modules in a stream that appears faster because each piece is released as it is completed. Getting content out faster makes you also appear more responsive to the business.

Moreover, **in going micro, you're using the learner's time more judiciously.** Simply put, going micro is more learner-centered, and will be more effective because learners will engage more and feel better about your training. And if going micro means learners are spending less time in training, it can also be a significant cost savings to the organization. The cost of the training team's time is often insignificant compared with the cost of the employees' "lost work time" while they are in training. So rather than focusing on the time it takes the training team to create such a program, focus on the cost savings of the employees whose training takes less time to help them become proficient.

As we mentioned earlier, when learners are supported with reinforcement and performance support, **their retention will be higher.** They will notice their capabilities are stronger and they will feel more confident and engaged at work. This will produce higher job satisfaction and employee productivity.

What's Next?

Microlearning really has a lot of potential. Considering all the benefits to the learner, to the organization, to performance improvement, and even to your instructional design processes, it's easy to see why people are so excited about microlearning. But it's not enough to just be excited. In the next chapter we offer guidance for recognizing where microlearning fits in your curriculums and how to use microlearning to address real learning and performance needs in your organization.

Questions to Explore

- From where is the desire (or pressure) coming for you to go micro? Is it you or your learning team? The business stakeholders? Your learners?
- How can you garner interest in a microlearning approach from your learners? Your business stakeholders? Your learning and development team?
- How would learners in your organization benefit from microlearning?

- Are there opportunities to create microlearning that is hyper-focused to support business needs?
- Are there opportunities to create microlearning that is targeted to a specific performance issue?
- Are there opportunities to create microlearning to improve preparation before live training?
- Are there opportunities to create microlearning to blunt the forgetting curve after live training?
- Are there opportunities to implement microlearning as performance support, either in support of a class or without other associated training?
- If you have already implemented microlearning, where haven't you considered that would be effective?
- What barriers must you address before implementing microlearning?
- What myths about microlearning must you address within your organization?

Tools for Support

Top Barriers to Going Micro and How to Address Them

Use this tool for some ideas on how to address the common barriers to going micro in organizations.

Barrier	How to Address It
Learners are not held accountable	Find ways to hold learners accountable or make the microlearning a priority for learners: • Make the learning mandatory. • Get leader buy-in to encourage learners to complete the training. • Promote the WIIFM of the training such that learners prioritize taking it.
Technology and security constraints	Start by using systems you already have in place, such as: • your LMS • your social collaborative system • your LXP • a website, intranet site, or SharePoint site.
Fitting microlearning into employees' days	Find ways to hold learners accountable or make the microlearning a priority for learners: • Make the learning mandatory. • Get leader buy-in to encourage learners to complete the training. • Promote the WIIFM of the training such that learners prioritize taking it.
Inability to tie learning to performance	Find ways to connect learning to performance: • Focus on content that has the greatest value to the organization. • Focus on content that can be used closer to the moment of performance (and thus is more likely to improve performance).

References and Additional Resources

Allen, M.W., and R. Sites. 2012. *Leaving ADDIE for SAM: An Agile Model for Developing the Best Learning Experiences.* Alexandria, VA: ASTD Press.

Association for Talent Development (ATD). 2017. *Microlearning: Delivering Bite-Sized Knowledge.* Alexandria, VA: ATD Press.

Quinn, C. 2013. "Extending Learning." Learnlets, May 23. blog.learnlets.com/2013/05/extending-learning-3.

Gottfredson, C., and B. Mosher. "The Five Moments of Need." 5momentsofneed.com.

Gottfredson, C., and B. Mosher. 2010. *Innovative Performance Support: Strategies and Practices for Learning in the Workflow.* New York: McGraw-Hill.

Grossman, D. 2017. "How Do NASA's Apollo Computers Stack Up to an iPhone?" *Popular Mechanics,* March 13. popularmechanics.com/space/moon-mars/a25655/nasa-computer-iphone-comparison.

Puiu, T. 2015. "Your Smartphone Is Millions of Times More Powerful Than All of NASA's Combined Computing In 1969." *ZME Science,* October 13. zmescience.com/research/technology/smartphone-power-compared-to-apollo-432.

Torgerson, C. 2016. *The Microlearning Guide to Microlearning.* Torgerson Consulting.

Torrance, M. 2019. *Agile for Instructional Designers: Iterative Project Management to Achieve Results.* Alexandria, VA: ATD Press.

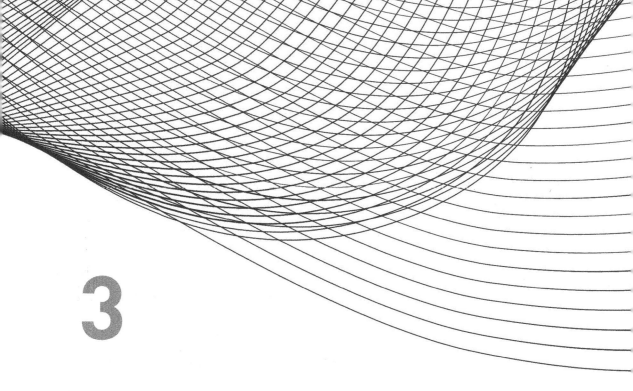

3

Designing Your Microlearning Program: How Do You Start?

In This Chapter

- Thinking strategically
- Focusing on the performance need and the learner
- If and where microlearning fits
- How to determine what should be micro

G oing micro can feel really daunting. You have multiple performance needs and tons of content. So how do you start when it comes to designing microlearning?

Learning leaders typically break all their organizational needs into workstreams or projects. These are generally around different topics and can be incredibly diverse—like designing and delivering annual compliance training, courses on crucial conversations, and best practices for interviewing, hiring, and onboarding new staff. This is the highest level at which "training needs" come to us, and their diverse topics are a reflection of the requests from different business units, each of whom has its own needs.

At this level, the goal for most learning leaders is to work with business partners to understand their organizational need, and then prioritize each of these disparate needs to determine which projects will be taken and which will not. Many teams have an intake process to help manage the flow of requests and their ability to choose which projects to take.

PRO TIP

Sometimes the flow of requests from the business for us to create training is daunting. Of course you want to be strategic to the needs of the business, but most organizations are structured so that each business unit is focused only on its needs and thus wants its request to be your highest priority. As a result, you may find yourself saying yes to everything that comes your way. You might be thinking, "I know this project is important to them, so I'll just find a way to get it done," or maybe you fear the political ramifications of saying no to a particular person or business unit.

While the requester feels good that you accepted their request now, it will likely be worse later on. If you say yes to everything, you'll likely find yourself or your team overwhelmed by the amount of work you've agreed to take on. Ultimately, you may not be able to deliver to the level of quality you promised, or projects may not be completed according to the agreed-upon timelines, and ultimately you are left feeling miserable because you haven't excelled at anything. No one is happy: not you, not your team, and not that business partner who was originally happy that you agreed to take on the project.

While saying no is an important skill, you don't have to say no to everything. In fact, by having a conversation with the stakeholder to learn more about their microlearning request, and asking some pointed questions about needs and priorities, you will start to transform from an order-taker to a valued business partner.

While entire books could be written on this topic (and probably have!), we recommend starting by just getting out of the mindset of taking on every project that comes to you. Prioritizing resources is an important part of business, but it can be very difficult for training people to do.

Any time a new project comes to your department, ask yourself:
- How important is this topic or project to the overall needs of the organization, when compared against all other projects or potential projects you have?
- How important is it to work with this team or leader? Work gets done through relationships, and organizational politics must come into consideration.
- Do you have the resources (staff, time, budget) needed to take on this project? If not, is it feasible to extend your team with contractors or suppliers, extend the timeline, or find additional funding from other sources?

Once you have the answers to these questions, it will be clearer and easier to determine which projects you should take on, which ones you should say "maybe later this year" to, and which ones you'll say no to.

Once you've determined a project to take on, this is the point at which you're now thinking more specifically about what you want to achieve with the program. This is when you also start talking with your stakeholder about the delivery modality and if it makes sense to include microlearning.

Focus on the Performance Need

When starting to design a new program, the first thing you want to ask is what is the performance need? What is the actual behavior you're trying to influence or change?

We cannot stress enough the importance of knowing the performance need. If you don't understand the goal for the program, you will surely fail. As the great Yogi Berra said, "You've got to be very careful if you don't know where you are going, because you might not get there."

TOOLS

See the "Questions to Help You Focus on the Performance Need" tool at the end of this chapter for specific questions you can ask stakeholders and learners to help you determine the behavior you're trying to affect.

Equally important is having a shared understanding of this goal between you and your stakeholder. If you think the goal is one thing, but they have a different understanding of that goal, you will also fail. You will guide your team to a vision of success that won't be perceived as successful by the business leader or stakeholder, who is the ultimate judge of that success.

Knowing your goal will also help you create your evaluation plan, which we'll discuss more in chapter 5.

Focus on the Learner

Now that you know what you want the program to achieve, the next step is to focus on the learner. We believe this is the critical foundation to going micro. **Microlearning is inherently learner-centered, but to be learner-centric, you must understand the learners and their needs.**

To better understand the learner population, ask questions like these:

Who Will Consume This Learning?

Admittedly, this is an extremely broad question, but we've found it's a good one to ask to get your stakeholders talking about the audience and their goals for those learners. Once the stakeholders start telling you about the audience, you'll likely find areas that you can explore further. And it gets at two fundamental areas:

- **workplace factors** such as job role, amount of experience, or tenure with the organization
- **personal factors** such as age, level of education, geographic location, or language proficiency.

What Is Their Typical Workday Like?

A lot of people stop when they know the basic factors about the learner population that we just described, and that's probably enough if you're going to develop a full-day class or even a 30-minute e-learning module. In both of these cases, you've taken the learners away from their work duties in a substantial way to consume the training, so understanding their workday and workflow doesn't matter as much.

But when we go micro, whether it is in follow-up to a training event, stand-alone microlearning, or performance support, it can be important to understand the nuances of that day a little better. Are they desk workers or are they in the field, and what is that experience like? Are they in front of a computer, or do they work primarily on a tablet, a mobile phone, or without technology at all? Are they customer-facing or client-facing, and if so, is that interaction face-to-face or technology-enabled? **Ultimately, you're trying to understand the conditions under which the learners are most likely to consume your content in the midst of their operational duties.**

PRO TIP

We cannot overstate the importance of understanding the conditions under which the learners are most likely to consume your content. Oftentimes, learning professionals overlook this step, whether they think it's not important or they assume it's obvious. But there is significant power that comes from being able to state the use case. This is easy to skip when you are offering a full-day classroom experience, but if you want to use mobile learning or microlearning, you need to consider how the learning will be used while the employees are in the midst of performing their operational duties.

For example, the technicians who fix wind turbines have a very interesting use case. Turbines are monitored from a central office, but if repairs are needed, a technician has to go out to inspect the actual components. As a result, wind turbine technicians climb very tall ladders (sometimes more than 260 feet—that's 26 stories!) while wearing safety harnesses and carrying tools to get to the very thing they are working on. Climbing up and down from the turbine is one of the most dangerous parts of their job.

In the past, these techs would climb the ladder to investigate an issue. Then, if they needed to refer to a schematic or technical specs to better understand something, they would climb back down the ladder to access these materials on computers in an office. Then, with more information and a solution in mind, they would climb the ladder again to fix the turbine.

Of course, considering this use case, the safety challenges, and the desire for the technician not to climb up and down the ladder more than is absolutely necessary, a solution accessible on a mobile device becomes obvious. How can we provide reference materials and short-form content that techs can use while at the top of the turbine, so they don't have to climb down the ladder to access those resources? And how do we make it so usable that the learners can easily find what they need while at the top of the turbine?

Knowing the use case will also help you to come up with unique solutions. For example, do you have learners with a lot of downtime? Or maybe the downtime is limited, but there are regular, short pockets of time when they are not serving customers and thus are idle. Or perhaps they work third shift (all night), and there are ways you can give them training in an e-learning or microlearning format so they don't have to take face-to-face classes with the daytime employees. Or maybe they have a handheld device that they use to perform their operational duties that you can capitalize on to provide brief bursts of training.

Ideally you should take some time to shadow those employees doing their operational duties. Follow one person around for an hour or two. Observe how they work, but also ask lots of questions about what their typical day is like. Also sit in common areas like a break room and just watch and listen. Are there patterns in the behavior you see?

TOOLS

See the "Questions You Can Ask About Your Learner to Help You Understand the Use Case" tool at the end of this chapter for questions you can ask to help you determine the micro-learning use case.

Is Microlearning the Right Solution for These Learners?

Of course, in a book about microlearning, the natural next step is to assume microlearning assets are the right solution for your need. But, as discussed in chapter 1, a good needs assessment will begin to inform your solutions, and you should consider all the options for learning and determine which fits best.

There are lots of ways to train people. Here are just a few:

- Synchronous learning
  - » live face-to-face classes
  - » virtual instructor-led classes.
- Asynchronous learning
  - » e-learning modules
  - » videos
  - » infographics
  - » whitepapers or articles
  - » blogs
  - » podcasts.

Note that in this list, the first two are *synchronous learning*—that is, a bunch of people come together at the same time (whether in person or virtual) to learn together. All the others are forms of *asynchronous learning*—when learners are learning independently and thus can learn at their own time and pace.

Microlearning simply happens when we take any of these forms and get so hyper focused on a single learning need that the duration of the training is short. Because this is easier to do in an asynchronous fashion, microlearning is generally used with asynchronous learning (such as e-learning, videos, and infographics), but you could easily have a five-minute lesson at the start of a team meeting, or a 10-minute live webinar at the start of shift if you wanted. Again, understanding the use case will tell you if those ideas make sense in your situation.

Figuring Out If and Where Microlearning Fits

As mentioned in chapters 1 and 2, microlearning can be used in a variety of ways:

- preparation before a learning event
- follow-up to reinforce a learning event
- stand-alone training
- performance support.

Once you consider the performance need and layer on an understanding of the learners and their use case, it should become clearer where learning needs to be more in depth, and where something shorter could work. Then the places where microlearning can be used will become more obvious.

TOOLS

Use the "Situations Where Microlearning Can Be Useful" tool at the end of this chapter to determine the areas where you can go micro.

Let's consider each of these situations and how you would know if microlearning would be a good fit.

Preparation Before a Learning Event

You'll know you need a longer learning event like a half- or full-day class, a one-hour webinar, or even a 30-minute e-learning module when the content needs to be covered in depth, interconnections between pieces of the content are important, or live social interactions are needed to make the learning meaningful.

You'll also know that microlearning to prepare people for the learning event will be helpful if any of these situations are true:

- **Learners don't have a good understanding of why they are coming to the class.** Telling them the WIIFM at the start of the learning event is fine, but for some topics, it's better to provide a short video or series of videos in advance to express why this area is a problem and why they should see coming to this class as a good use of their time. Facilitators sometimes talk about how learners, especially in live classes, fall into three groups: explorers (those who are very eager and interested), vacationers (those who came because being in class is better than being at work), and prisoners (those who would rather be anywhere else than in your class). If you think you'll have a lot of vacationers and prisoners coming to a class, you can use microlearning in advance of the learning event to help turn them into explorers before they even arrive.

- **There is a lot of didactic content that needs to be understood before the learners can have a thoughtful discussion or activity with it.** If people can't come into the live or virtual classroom and immediately have a fruitful conversation about a topic, then providing a short article, video, or e-learning module would be helpful to prevent you from taking the first portion of the class to "tell them stuff." This sort of microlearning is more useful for fact-based topics or hard skills, where it's likely that participants don't actually know the content prior to the class (like a drug's mechanism of action), and is less useful for soft skills, where it's likely that participants have lived experience that gives them a wealth of knowledge and opinions prior to the class (like leadership topics).

- **There are a wide variety of knowledge levels among those people attending the class.** Again, this is more commonly seen with hard skills than soft skills, but if you have a topic where there's a clear variety of participant knowledge levels, and that lack of knowledge will hold some people back from being able to learn from and participate in the class, then it will be helpful to give participants some materials to bring them up to speed. To make this work, though, you really want to customize the content given to each learner—the experts shouldn't have to take all the same materials that the less experienced people do. Remember that the intention here is to lift up those with less knowledge, not force everyone to consume basic content—and no one likes to be forced to review material they already know well.

PRO TIP

If you looked at the previous list and thought those last two bullets were just describing pre-work, you're right. And if you thought, "I've been doing that for years," you're not alone. This form of microlearning is something that learning professionals have been doing for decades. Prework for a training course is nothing new.

But as we mentioned in chapter 2, it can be really hard to get people to do prework. Some organizations will say a participant can't come to a training class if they haven't completed the prework. But that can be difficult, because operational duties are often seen as a higher priority. For example, Carla previously worked on a training team in a healthcare-delivery system, and many of the participants came from clinical roles, such as nurses, doctors, and other care providers. The training team had pre-reads for many of their leadership classes, which they strongly encouraged people to complete before class. But what happened if a nurse manager came to class and said, "I'm really sorry I didn't get my prework done. We had a code on the floor yesterday and I had to focus on our patients." Or equally common would be something like, "We had two nurses out sick yesterday, and I had to help with patient care."

Frankly, it would have been very difficult for Carla's team to make the case that the prework was so important that those clinicians should have prioritized differently. This is a stunning example because when patients are not cared for, they could get sick or die, but we all face something similar in our organizations—it's very difficult to suggest that prework for a class is more important than operational duties. If Carla's team had not considered the importance of the operational duties of their participants, they would have appeared tone deaf and created terrible relationships with their learners and organizational leaders.

We must always remember that our learners were hired to do their operational duties. That will always be their first priority. Except in rare situations, learning will always come second.

Of course, we know that properly completing prework makes a big difference for all participants in the class, so there are lots of things we can do to get people to do it. As mentioned in chapter 2, one of those strategies is to go micro. Make the prework feel easy to consume by creating it in bite-sized pieces, and just give them a few pieces to do before the program. The less daunting it seems, the more likely people will be to complete it—even if it's just in the 15 minutes before class starts.

Follow-Up to Reinforce a Learning Event

Again, you'll know you need a longer learning event like a half-day or full-day class, a one-hour webinar, or even a 30-minute e-learning module when the content needs to be covered in depth, interconnections between pieces of the content are important, or live social interactions are needed to make the learning meaningful.

You'll also know that microlearning is needed to follow up on that learning event if any of these situations are true:

- **Learners will be able to complete their work even if they do not incorporate their new skills or change their behavior.** This is often the case with soft skills like leadership: Learners come to the class and learn new ideas for how to motivate their staff. But then they go back to their work, and it's up to them if they use those new ideas or not. Contrast this to an organization rolling out a new electronic medical records system. Learners come to class to learn how to use the new software, and they will have to use their new skills to get their work done when the new system is in place. Often, when your learners do not use their new skills it is not malicious or even intentional—as mentioned in chapter 2, the forgetting curve simply takes hold quickly and a lot of ideas learned in class are very quickly forgotten. And of course, integrating new skills into the work behaviors and practices they've been doing for years is challenging to say the least. However, this is more pronounced in situations where the behavior change is not held accountable by the workflow, such as by a tool, a co-worker, or their manager.

- **Learners will need to be convinced and reminded to use their new skills.** Really this is a change management issue, but much like using microlearning to set the WIIFM before a longer class, you can also use microlearning to continue to reinforce the need to apply these new skills and the value they bring.

- **Learners are likely to forget the important nuances of the content.** Reminders about best practices, like a "tip of the week," can help people to remember to use the new ideas and skills long after a class is over. This is particularly helpful if content is very specific and remembering the details is important. Consider a financial services firm that provides an infographic to remind employees of the five kinds of bank accounts the firm offers and their features and benefits as a follow-up to an hourlong training webinar. The infographic can help reinforce each of the bank account types so the employees don't forget them.

- **You want to continue to extend the learning beyond the classroom, especially in a personalized way.** For example, if you do a one-hour webinar on how employment law affects managers in the organization, you may follow that with a series of resources that provide more depth on important national laws, or specific nuances for the different states in which your managers are located. In this situation, you can have general resources that extend the learning for those who want more, or specific details that are relevant only to some participants.

Stand-Alone Training

One of our favorite areas is using microlearning for stand-alone training. This enables you to use people's time more wisely and bring learning closer to the moment when they will actually need it. This makes the learning more contextual and realistic, and more likely to be transferred into workplace behaviors.

You'll know that microlearning can be used for stand-alone training if any of these situations are true:

- **The concept that needs to be addressed is small and discrete.** For example, you have a product that has been recalled. You want reps to know what that product is, why it was recalled, and what the organization will do for customers who purchased it. You can probably cover this in an e-learning piece that is five minutes or less, or maybe even a short PDF document. Or if the recall is for a serious defect, you could use a short video from the CEO to share that content so you can also reinforce the message that the company cares deeply about the issue and its customers. Of course, if the CEO can't express this caring emotion well, then this will come off as hokey or even insincere. But if the CEO is able to express passion for the content, then it can garner buy-in and support from the employees.

- **The content is a larger concept, but it can be broken into a number of small, discrete pieces.** For example, a sales methodology that capitalizes on five different tactics could have a short microlearning module about the methodology and a short module for each tactic. Again, the key here is that the content pieces are discrete. If the learner needs to consume part 1, part 2, and part 3 in order and all at once, then this is really just chunked content and you should instead consider creating a longer piece of e-learning with sections to enable the learner to access the different chunks. But if the content can realistically be broken into stand-alone pieces that the learner can consume individually, then you can take that large body of content micro.

- **The content needs to be able to serve as "refresher material" after the training is over.** For example, understanding managed markets in the U.S. healthcare marketplace is critical for reps who sell pharmaceuticals, medical devices, or any other supplies that could be used in delivering patient care. The nuances of commercial insurance, Medicare, and Medicaid (along with a host of other, even more complex topics) are important for the reps to understand. Detailed training will probably be needed, but it's also likely the reps will want to go back to the key concepts more than once to refer to those things they learned. A five-minute e-learning module serves far better as refresher material than a 30-minute one!

- **The learners already have a basic understanding of the concept.** The key here is that the learners have enough understanding of the topic or concept that you could give them just one small piece of content and they would understand how this content fits into the bigger picture of their behavior. For example, if you already use Excel a lot, then a microlearning library of small tutorials showing you how to do a variety of tasks (conditional formulas, pivot tables, or charts) could be helpful. But if you're completely new to using AutoCAD, then the same type of microlearning library would not be helpful. You would need an overarching big picture of the software and how it's used before such discrete content will be helpful.

- **The learners are highly motivated to consume the content.** This is where self-study content libraries come into play—for example, a portal filled with a variety of resources for improving your time management, your selling skills, your leadership skills, your Excel skills, and so on. Generally, this sort of learning is not required, and the learners self-select to consume what they want when they want.

Performance Support

For us, another favorite area is using microlearning as performance support. This is where the learners may or may not have completed any formal learning, but they find themselves on the job and need some additional support to be able to do a task. We're talking about materials that help the learners to do the job itself, such as job aids, checklists, flow diagrams, and just-in-time training.

You'll know that microlearning can be used for performance support if any of these situations are true (Malamed 2017):

- **A task is performed infrequently or content is easy to forget.** The classic example is the label on every fire extinguisher that tells you to use PASS: pull (the pin), aim, squeeze, sweep. It doesn't matter if you've had fire extinguisher training before; in the midst of a fire, that label is clear and concise, and guides your behavior at that moment of need. Of course, if you were fortunate enough to have a class where you practiced using a fire extinguisher in an empty parking lot, you'd be more confident and capable in that moment of need. But even those who didn't have that opportunity will be able to use PASS at a basic level when faced with a fire.

  Another example is the step-by-step guide that reminds employees how to complete their expense reports. Employees who submit a lot of expenses don't need assistance, but for the employees who only submit expense reimbursements a few times a year, some simple stepwise instructions will enable them to complete their expense reports more quickly and correctly than if they didn't have those instructions.

- **Accuracy is crucial or errors are risky.** For example, pharmaceutical reps need to be able to talk with healthcare providers about potential adverse reactions of their product. Having an infographic that the rep can use when talking to the provider about the most common adverse reactions and their prevalence could be very useful. This is information that the rep and the provider don't want to make mistakes with.

  Another example is providing job aids for first responders. For example, firefighters are often trained in how to start small engine equipment like generators, but in the heat of the emergency, they may flood the engine and be unsure how to clear the excess fuel. A short checklist with the steps for how to start a generator is ideal, and is recommended for use by firefighters in the United States (U.S. Fire Administration 2019). You could even have it in the cab of the fire truck for the (nondriving) firefighters to look at while driving to the fire.

- **A process or procedure is error-prone.** We know of a manufacturing company that has a very complex piece of machinery. In fact, there are 23 steps to using it, and even the most experienced staff find it hard to use. Putting a poster on the wall reminding employees of the steps will help them use the machine more easily. In fact, in this real case, the organization is using an augmented reality (AR) solution so workers can wear special AR goggles while using the machine and be walked through the steps, customized to where they are standing at the machine. This is an ideal solution for this equipment because it is so complicated; in fact, the organization estimated the cost of creating the AR solution was cheaper than the cost of training the employees to mastery.

- **There are multiple steps or decision points.** In the U.S. healthcare sector, it can be challenging for patients to gain access to much needed specialty drugs. There are a whole host of reasons for this, but one of the biggest challenges is the number of steps required of the healthcare provider to receive approval from the payer (typically a health insurance provider) for the patient to have access to and reimbursement for the drug. These processes are in place to ensure the patient only receives expensive specialty drugs when it's the best option, but it is challenging for patients, pharmaceutical sales reps, and medical office staff to figure out the steps. For one organization, Sue developed a two-page step-by-step "if, then" decision guide outlining the steps, common pitfalls, and when to refer to a patient assistance program if no patient health insurance coverage was available. This helped pharma reps and medical office staff, at a high level, to figure out how to help a patient get access to a new drug once the healthcare provider had written a prescription for it.

- **There are topics that learners would commonly want to search for help on.** Learners will want to search for help to solve problems during many of the previous situations. But any situation where the learners would want to look it up or ask for help are cases when performance support is warranted.

See the tools for support at the end of the chapter for a checklist that helps you consider all the times when microlearning can be used with your content.

Understanding Performance Support

Conrad Gottfredson and Bob Mosher have done outstanding work in this area, helping L&D professionals understand where training and performance support fit into their work.

They talk about the five moments of need, or the times when someone at work could need learning materials (Figure 3-1).

Figure 3-1. The 5 Moments of Need

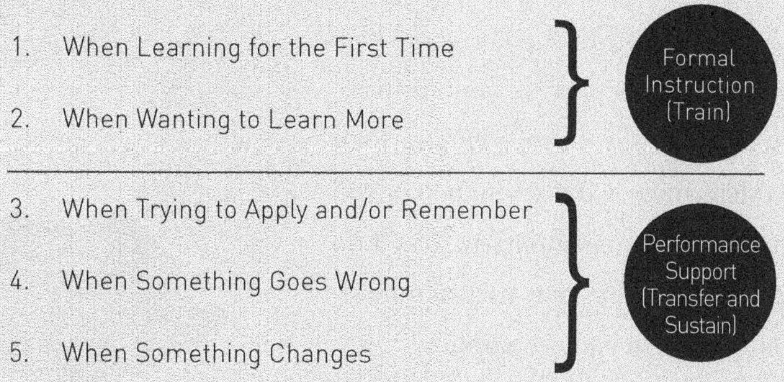

1. When Learning for the First Time
2. When Wanting to Learn More

} Formal Instruction (Train)

3. When Trying to Apply and/or Remember
4. When Something Goes Wrong
5. When Something Changes

} Performance Support (Transfer and Sustain)

Gottfredson and Mosher say that training is needed for moments one and two, while support materials are more appropriate for moments three, four, and five. All of this centers on understanding the moment of need for your employees.

The most important thing in all of this is realizing that so many instructional designers focus only on creating training—which is really only a solution for moments one and two. When you start looking more closely at the workflow and the use case, you start seeing opportunities for just-in-time instruction and performance support.

Figure 3-2. Designing for the 5 Moments of Need

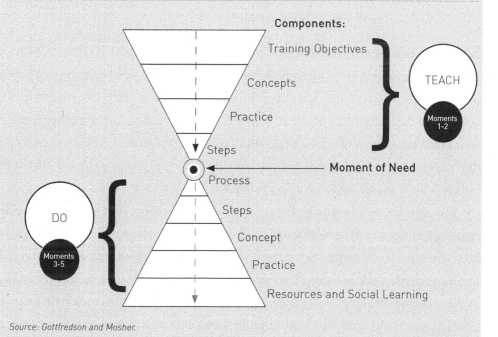

Source: Gottfredson and Mosher.

Determining What to Offer As Micro Content

After you've determined that it's a good idea to use microlearning as part of your instructional solution, or for the entire solution, then you need to determine what content you will offer in that microlearning situation. You'll do this differently for the different uses of microlearning, so let's look at each separately.

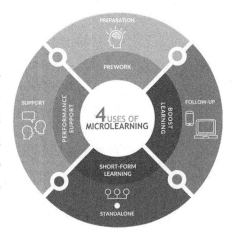

Preparation Before a Learning Event

When you use microlearning prior to a longer-form learning event, the first question you should ask is, what's the purpose of this prework microlearning? Recall from the previous section that this kind of microlearning can be used to:

- Set learner motivation prior to the class.
- Provide didactic knowledge-level content.
- Level-set participants' prior knowledge.

Setting Learner Motivation

If your goal is to set learner motivation prior to the class, you need to really think about your analysis—why was this topic important enough for you to devote resources to it, and why should the learner care about it? Why should they see this class as a valuable use of their time? Learning professionals talk about the WIIFM (what's in it for me) and stress the "me" in that. We do believe that you can also focus on an organizational goal, if the learner is likely to buy in to that as important too.

For example, before a compliance and safety class you could send a short video showing some of the dangers of working in the factory, and how this class is designed to keep you safe, so you can go home from work every day with all your fingers and toes. But let's say you work in financial services and are creating training on a new product; in this case the meaning to the learner is less clear. Before a class on a new financial product, you could send an email to participants reminding them that the company prides itself in providing the best products to ensure a comfortable financial future and retirement for their customers, and that the new product they'll be learning about is designed to help customers reduce debt so they can have a more stable long-term financial outlook. An employee who has bought into the mission of their organization will also be motivated by this kind of message, even though the WIIFM is not directly focused on themselves.

So again, you can focus on the what's in it for me, or what's in it for the organization—but the real point here is that you're focusing on the *why*. Why are we asking you, as a busy employee, to make time for this learning activity, and why are we confident that it will be a good use of your time?

PRO TIP

We sometimes hear people say that they don't need to express a WIIFM—the motivational element that gets (or keeps) people bought in to taking the course—if learning that information is required. The thinking is that if they are required to take the course, you don't need to garner buy-in to get them to consume the material. We suspect that thinking will only become stronger with short-form content because designers will say, "It's only five minutes. And it's required anyway."

While it is true that you often need to have to have a stronger WIIFM if the content is optional, you should not assume that all learners will want to consume your content just because they are required to take it. Thus, if you want learners to take a program seriously, give it their fullest focus, and actually learn from it, you should still have a motivational element within the course and/or use microlearning to set that motivation in advance where possible.

As Michael Allen (2016) says, "You can't learn someone." You can teach someone, but you cannot learn them. It's not a grammatical issue; it's a physical one. You cannot learn for someone else, no matter how much you want them to learn something. Learners must be actively involved in their learning, and for them to put forth the effort needed to learn, they must be motivated. The crux here for adult learners in the workplace is for them to see this learning material as a valuable use of their time when weighed against all their other priorities. As designers, it is our job to position each piece of learning, even if it is required learning, in such a way that learners do want to focus on it and thereby learn from it.

Providing Didactic Knowledge-Level Content

If you are using microlearning to provide knowledge prior to the classroom experience so you don't have to lecture about it in class, then you are doing what some call a "flipped classroom." You start by determining what activities you'll do in the class, which are generally focused on recall or application of knowledge. Then you determine what knowledge people need to participate in those activities and what resources are available to provide that knowledge. Is there an article they can read, or do you need to design something yourself?

For example, new pharmaceutical sales reps have to acquire a lot of knowledge before they can even begin to have conversations with healthcare providers. Even if the reps are focused on only one drug, there are numerous topics to learn: the disease state (what is the disease, what's going on physiologically or biochemically in the body, and how that affects the patient), the drug's mechanism of action (the physiological or biochemical processes that happen or change due to the action of the drug), treatment options, treatment guidelines, how the drug gets reimbursed, the kind of clinicians who prescribe the drug and their clinical specialty, and much, much more.

A rep can't possibly walk into a pulmonologist's office and talk with clinical staff about prescribing a product if they don't know how the product works, which patients it's better for compared with the competitor's product, and the science behind why that is so. This is particularly significant, from a training perspective, in pharmaceutical sales because there is so much scientific knowledge reps must possess to even have a credible conversation. And if reps aren't credible, no clinician will make time for them or prescribe their product.

So a new rep will have lots to learn—but there's a large component that starts by reading and memorizing scientific content so they can apply that knowledge to a variety of situations. To maximize the classroom time, many organizations have moved to delivering this content during home-study. To introduce the science of the disease state, you may have them read articles from medical journals or written by the company's staff clinicians. Also, a great way to introduce the disease state and patient is to create an infographic. It typically includes key data points, such as the number of people afflicted with the disease in a particular region, incidence in men versus women, and other relevant statistics. Another option is an "e-zine": a digital, magazine-style format that covers key topic areas on a given subject. For example, an e-zine topic such as "meet the customer" can introduce information about physicians who practice a certain specialty, how much school they have completed, common reasons for going into the field, the kinds of patients they see, and so on.

Having the participants read this material in advance allows the classroom time to be used for asking questions, understanding nuances in the content, and applying it to their work. There's no need for the facilitator to lecture about this content for hours; just give the learners some materials to read ahead of time, and then they can come to class prepared and ready to participate.

This approach of using prework is going to be most valuable in situations where there is a lot of very detailed content that the learners are not likely to know from lived experience; you must "tell" them things for them to be able to do their work. Conversely, you generally won't find this kind of prework as helpful in areas where the learners probably have a lot of knowledge or opinions about the topic from lived experience. This is why, for example, the pre-reading for leadership development classes is generally much lighter, and why it's so much harder to hold people accountable to completing it.

Level-Setting Participants' Prior Knowledge

If you know that you'll have a varied audience in terms of background knowledge and you want to use microlearning to level-set participants before coming to the classroom, the process is similar to the previous section. Start by designing the classroom experience so you can determine the level you'll target in the class. Then, determine the prior knowledge that people will need to have to be able to participate.

The big difference from the previous section, though, is that then you identify which content is needed for which groups of learners. When preparing for a class on explaining the changes to health benefits offered by the organization, maybe the payroll team needs to get certain content, while the benefits team needs something different and more in depth. Or perhaps when giving a class for marketers about improving your market segmentation skills, there will be detailed content for people at the associate level, but less (or no) content for those who are midcareer.

This notion of providing different content for different learner groups is very hard to do in practice. If it's not clear how to segment the audience, you could provide some sort of quiz prior to the prework learning experience, and give them certain prework to do based on their scores. Of course that requires a very thoughtfully designed quiz. It can also take a lot of time for the learning professional to customize the prework for each learner or learner group.

Another approach that works very well is to give learners scenarios to solve and then provide teaching content when they get questions in the scenario wrong. (This is often called teaching through feedback.) The result is that a person who knows the content can go through it quickly while the less experienced person can stop and learn from detailed materials about the areas where they made mistakes. The key is to make realistic scenarios with challenging common errors and good instructional feedback that is targeted to the error.

Follow-Up to Reinforce a Learning Event

When you use microlearning after a longer-form learning event, the first question you should ask is what's the purpose of this post-event microlearning? Recall from the previous section that this kind of microlearning can be used to:

- Convince learners to implement their new skills in situations where the workflow does not hold them accountable to using the new skills.
- Remind learners of the details of the content that will enable them to implement their new skills on the job.
- Extend the learning beyond the classroom, especially in a personalized way.

Convincing Learners to Implement Their New Skills

This is similar to the pre-learning microlearning that is designed to get learners bought in to the value of a class (or the WIIFM). But this time your focus is on how using these new skills will make a difference to the learner and the organization in the short or long term. Again, start by thinking about the reasons you are devoting resources to this organizational need, and why addressing it is important to the learner. But then take it a step further—how will actually using these skills make that person more efficient or effective at their job? Putting new skills into practice is hard, so why should the learner bother to make that effort?

For example, after a class for managers on developing stronger team cohesion, you could send a follow-up email each week reminding leaders of the value of having strong team cohesion and how it will enable them to have a more effective team. Or, better yet, you could send best practices stories or videos from respected employees telling how they used these skills and how they made a difference. This sort of microlearning is generally not mandatory, so your usage will be a bell curve; some people will watch all the videos, more will watch a few, and others will watch one or none of them. This is OK. Remember, you're trying to create buy-in, and if you require people to consume all the content, you are likely to create resistance instead.

Reminding Learners to Implement Their New Skills

Assuming learners are sufficiently bought in to using their new skills, you can reinforce key parts of the content after the class with microcontent. Look at your course materials to determine the most important pieces and then provide short reminders or even job aids about it. For example, you could reinforce the activities learned in a leadership class that could be used to develop stronger team cohesion. This is often called *boost learning*.

For boosting, we recommend that you have a regular cadence of email messages, text messages, or other push notifications that remind people of the core concepts they learned in the class. Plan to send your first boost message within 24 hours of the class, and then every second day for a total of three boosts in the first week following the class. Then do two boosts in the second week and one or two final boosts in the third week. Then stop pestering your learners. You want to be persistent and timed quickly after the class ends because that will tame the forgetting curve, but you also don't want to "spam" your learners, because then they will ignore you.

You may also want to put a note at the bottom of each boosting message that says why you are sending the reminder. Tell them this will help them remember the content, and you will only be sending these messages for a few weeks. This will be new for your learners, so you may want them to know what you're doing and why.

Extending Learning Beyond the Classroom

In this case, you start by designing the classroom learning material and then decide what would be helpful additional content for learners after the class is over. With this kind of microlearning, you can get into the weeds of concepts that perhaps only 20 percent of people would find useful, because those will be the only people to consume it. Or you could provide content that's relevant to 100 percent of a subgroup within your group (such as specific applications of the content by state, when you have learners from multiple states). The real need here is to focus on what people will find useful when applying this content back on the job; it's less about what learners would find interesting, and more about what they would find useful. We all have great intentions of reading that interesting article after a class, but very few of us actually do it, because all those good intentions are lost in the shuffle of getting our operational duties done, especially after we've been away from the office at a class.

Boost Learning

Many people are doing research in the boost learning area. Some that we know of are Art Kohn, a professor at Portland State University School of Business; B. Price Kerfoot, a practicing urologist and an associate professor of surgery at Harvard Medical School; and Alice Kim, a postdoctoral researcher at York University in Canada.

Kohn's research shows that content that takes five seconds to consume is just as effective as content that takes 30 seconds or five minutes to consume, so he suggests emailing a very short piece of reinforcing content to learners that recalls what was learned. He recommends boosting over a two-month period after the course is over, with three different phases of boosting and different kinds of boosting in each. For more, consider these articles he's written:

- » "Brain Science: Overcoming the Forgetting Curve" (April 2014)
- » "Brain Science: Enable Your Brain to Remember Almost Everything" (May 2014).

Dr. Kerfoot's research with medical students shows that appropriate spacing can increase short-term knowledge recall by up to 50 percent, and strengthen retention for up to two years. His approach is the foundation for Qstream, a spaced repetition program. It is more gamified than Kohn's, with scores and leaderboards. He sends a question to participants every three days, and they immediately get feedback with the correct answer and a brief explanation. Adaptive testing is used, so if a learner gets a question wrong, they get it again very soon, but it's spaced out much later if they get it right. A question is retired after multiple correct responses. He does his boosting program over a year! Here are some resources about his approach:

- » "Learning by Degrees" (Lambert 2009)
- » "Online Game Helps Doctors Improve Patients' Blood Pressure Faster" (American Heart Association 2014)
- » "An Online Spaced-Education Game Among Clinicians Improves Their Patients' Time to Blood Pressure Control" (Kerfoot et al. 2014)
- » "Q&A With B. Price Kerfoot, MD EdM: How Long Do the Benefits of Qstream Last?" (Kerfoot 2018).

Finally, Kim works with Axonify on its adaptive testing algorithm. Axonify is much like Qstream, a gamified approach to spaced adaptive testing where learners have to answer a question every few days. Axonify's approach is based on sending learners two to three questions in a session, but after each question the learner also has to identify how confident they are that they were right. Then learners are given the correct answer and corrective feedback if they were incorrect. Questions are provided a few times a week; an adaptive engine repeats questions that were answered incorrectly or for which the learner had low confidence, and increases the spacing of correctly answered questions over time. Here are some resources describing this approach:

- » "Axonify: Powered by Brain Science" (Axonify 2019)
- » "The Spacing Effect Stands Up to Big Data" (Kim et al. 2019).

Stand-Alone Training

When you use microlearning in a stand-alone fashion, you want to determine if the microlearning resource will be used as a single piece of learning, or if there will be a set of resources offered together. Recall from the previous section that this kind of microlearning is used to present a piece of content that is small and discrete, whether you have just one resource (like explaining the basics of a new law and how it will affect employees), or if you have a set of resources (like a library of resources that help you use Excel better).

In all cases, you want to take the content and break it into the smallest pieces that make sense on their own as discrete chunks. For example, we recently created a series of mini-modules about a lawn care chemical that were designed for distributors of those products and the lawn care professionals who buy them. As is common, this sort of distributor and customer training is completely optional, so it had to be engaging yet informational. We could have created a 20- to 30-minute module about the benefits of the product, but of course that wasn't likely to be consumed. Instead, we created a story about Joe, the owner of a lawn care business. The story had five discrete pieces, each telling you a few features and benefits about the product. You could look at Joe's Facebook page, see an animation of him talking to his distributor, and even watch him talking with one of his customers. Each module was short (no more than three minutes) and could stand alone; you didn't need to experience them in order, nor did you need to consume all of them for the story to make sense. Again, the key was to create a small piece of content that had enough information to stand on its own, but was short enough that consuming it was not overwhelming.

Performance Support

When you use microlearning as performance support, the first question you should ask is, what's the purpose of this performance support resource? Recall from the previous section that this kind of microlearning can be used when:

- Accuracy is crucial or errors are risky.
- A process or procedure is error-prone.
- There are multiple steps or decision points.
- A task is performed infrequently or content is easy to forget.
- There are topics that the learners would commonly want to search for help on.

PRO TIP

A lot of people are starting to talk about how microlearning is workflow learning. An important distinction needs to be made here: Workflow learning is learning that's done while in the act of doing the job. This means very quick reference materials or performance support can be workflow learning; these materials are used to help the learner get their work done at their moment of need.

However, as you can see from our four categories (preparation before a learning event, follow-up to reinforce a learning event, stand-alone training, and performance support), workflow learning is only happening in the final category. Microlearning that supports other learning content, or even microlearning that stands alone, is not workflow learning. When the learner has to stop working on their job tasks, even if for only five minutes, you've removed them from the workflow to pause and learn something.

It's not bad to remove the learner from the workflow to learn new things. That focus enables them to learn new things that make them better at their job, even if it's in short bits of time. But if you're truly attempting to create workflow learning, you should be focusing on performance support, because that's the only form of microlearning that is actually used in the flow of work.

Our approach to all of these is similar, so we'll consider them together. In all cases, start by thinking about the actual tasks that the person does on the job. Where do they seem to have the most trouble or make the most errors? Which ones are just plain scary for the employee? When someone lacks confidence in their ability to perform, that means the task is hard for them. With these in mind, you've probably hit on something that fits one of the previously listed descriptions.

Remember that at this step you're creating something extremely specific. Rather than a five-minute microlesson, you're designing the one-page job aid that enables the learner to solve their problem and get on with their work. If you really think about the moment of need, you'll know the level of detail needed. For example, if the materials are for a person who is back on the job and runs into a problem, they need the answer quickly and will actually be frustrated if you give them more information, examples, practice activities, and so on.

It's All About Improving Performance

In this chapter we've focused on our four categories of microlearning (preparation before a learning event, follow-up to reinforce a learning event, stand-alone training, and performance support). It's easy to slice everything up and talk about how to create effective microlearning assets in each of these categories, but by focusing on the best techniques for different situations we run the risk of losing the forest for the trees. **Regardless which kind of microlearning you're trying to create, always ask, "How will I improve performance?" because that's what your primary focus should always be.**

Carla has a friend who once told her a great story that will put this all into perspective. We'll call him Jim (it's not his real name). Jim was a director of training, and his team created training in one of the most challenging learner environments: for sellers in a multilevel-marketing organization. This is a company where everyday people can sign up to be sales reps and sell to the people they know in their network, like Tupperware, Avon, Mary Kay, or Pampered Chef.

Jim's team created sales training for these sales consultants. Because of the nature of their business, none of the sales training could be made mandatory. The only reason people would take the training course is if they actually saw it as valuable to getting their job done: generally, selling more effectively.

Jim's team consisted of a number of instructional designers; about half of them were academically trained as instructional designers with advanced degrees in education, and the other half were former sales reps of the company who were just naturally good at teaching others. (Cammy Bean calls this the "accidental instructional designer.")

RESOURCES

Have you found yourself in a training or instructional design role despite having no formal background in the field? You might be an accidental instructional designer. Many training professionals find themselves in this position, having come to training from operational roles.

If this describes you, we recommend *The Accidental Instructional Designer: Learning Design for the Digital Age* by Cammy Bean. It will tell you about instructional design concepts and best practices from the field of education, particularly as they apply to e-learning.

Another great resource for new and experienced instructional designers is *Design for How People Learn* by Julie Dirksen. This book addresses the fundamental concepts of instructional design, including principles of learning, memory, and attention that enable your audience to learn and retain the knowledge and skills you're sharing.

Jim told Carla that as he tried to go micro with his team, those with advanced degrees in the field wanted to ask which category the microlearning would fit in; would it be formal learning, performance support, just-in-time training, or something else? But those who were former sales reps didn't get tangled up by this; they just asked if it would have helped them do that task better.

Carla has seen this happen at a few crucial times in her career too. Considering the specific details and nuances of designing different kinds of instruction is helpful—and if you're someone with an advanced degree in education, you'll likely think there's value in that level of understanding. However, instructional designers have a tendency to get in their own way. Don't get tangled up by all these details. Just start by asking the question Jim had to ask every day: Will this training help improve performance, and have we presented that value proposition so well that the learner will want to engage in the training, even if it's not required?

A lot of training people will say that you shouldn't bend to what the learner "wants"—that sometimes learning is hard, and sometimes you know what they need to learn. While this probably holds true at times, instructional designers need to be very careful with this sort of thinking. Your learners are trying to get something done at work, and if what you provide helps them do that thing better, they will use it. But if it doesn't help them, they will see it as a waste of their time and they either won't use it or won't fully engage with it.

And, of course, the accidental instructional designer isn't always right either. Sometimes those folks who know the business so well can miss details that are critical for new learners, and that formally trained instructional designers will catch. It really is a balancing act, and we should capitalize on the skills that both groups bring to the table.

Expressing Your Vision

An important challenge some people experience when going micro is the situation where everyone agrees on the same single objective, but each person is imagining a different depth of coverage in achieving the objective—that is, a vastly different seat time. Everyone is sitting around the table nodding their heads in agreement, but in their heads they are all thinking of something different, which means they really aren't in agreement at all! This can happen when the learning team is trying to push the envelope to provide resources that are shorter and more performance focused, but the SMEs or leaders are thinking of all the things learners need to know.

For example, the learning professional and the operational SME could both agree to the same enabling objective: "Front-line staff will be able to handle calls from difficult customers who want a refund." But the learning professional is thinking of a five-minute mini e-learning course on the most common requests for a refund, and how to de-escalate callers in these situations. Meanwhile, the operational SME who "owns" the business problem is thinking of a 30-minute e-learning module, getting much more deeply into how to address these refunds, when and where exceptions can be made, how to request an exception, and how quickly a refund can be processed in a variety of situations. And if logistics would allow, they'd actually like a two-hour class where they could introduce a de-escalation model, and participants would role play some calls and practice their de-escalation skills.

Our advice: **Be very detailed in expressing your vision for the learning materials or program.** Provide the seat time you're imagining for the e-learning module, the number of pages for the job aids or text-based resources, the number of resources that will be created, or the span of time this program will last (for example, is it a single micro resource, or a series of 10 resources that will be consumed over a month). A lot of times we don't want to get pinned too quickly to a given scope, especially if we don't know exactly what content we'll be covering. But there is significant power in telling someone you're imagining a five-minute mini-module or 30 minutes of e-learning or four hours in a classroom. At this point, we're painting a vision; we're not signing a contract for a particular scope.

Once you have agreement on the vision, you can dig into the content and determine the best depth to address each concept within that approximate scope boundary. No one will quibble if the vision of five-minute learning resources produces materials that are three minutes or eight minutes. You are still working within the same vision as everyone else.

What's Next?

Now that we've considered where microlearning can fit in our learning ecosystem, and we've created a vision for how this form of learning will be used, we need to actually design and create those learning materials. That's the focus of our next chapter! In that chapter we will address how to design microlearning to fit all the different needs: preparation before a learning event, follow-up to reinforce a learning event, stand-alone training, and performance support.

Questions to Explore

- Which projects are most strategically important for your organization? Are there any projects you're taking on that you should say no to?
- For any given project:
  - » What is the performance—the actual behavior—you're trying to affect?
  - » How will the learner use these materials within the flow of their day?
  - » Is microlearning the right fit for that learner and that performance need?
- Can you find ways to use microlearning to:
  - » Support preparation before a learning event?
  - » Reinforce a learning event?
  - » Provide stand-alone training?
  - » Provide performance support?
- How will you improve performance with this microlearning content?

Tools for Support

Questions to Help You Focus on the Performance Need

When starting to design a new program, the first thing you want to determine is the performance need. What is the actual behavior you're trying to affect? Use this guide to get started.

A good way to determine this behavior can be to ask questions like these of your stakeholder (generally an operational leader or a subject matter expert from the business):
- Why is this program important? What is the pain point you're trying to address?
- What's the actual behavior you're trying to change?
  - » What are some examples of people doing this incorrectly that you commonly see now?
  - » How would they do it differently if they were performing optimally?
- What's the risk of not doing this program?
- Why now? Why hasn't this been pursued already, or why not wait?
- If this program was wildly successful, what would we see?
- Who is going to determine whether this program is successful?
- What could prevent success from happening?

Then follow up by asking questions like these of a learner (generally an experienced employee from that operational leader's team):
- Do you agree that this is a pain point? How would it make a difference for you if this was solved?
- Why do you think we're not already doing things this way?
- If this program was wildly successful, what would we see?
- What could prevent success from happening?

You'll notice that these questions are very similar for both the leader and the typical learner. This is intentional. You want to be sure that what you and the stakeholders identify are the real issues for the learners. It's easy for leaders and SMEs to get away from the day-to-day duties and not recognize important nuances that are obvious to the learner.

By talking to learners you're likely to learn about day-to-day challenges that prevent them from performing optimally. Understanding these barriers can help you to understand where training can have impact and where other organizational factors may be more relevant.

Questions You Can Ask About Your Learner to Help You Understand the Use Case

Question
Are they desk workers or are they in the field, and what is that experience like?

Why It's Helpful
Instructional designers generally have **desk jobs**, so it's easy to imagine what that day is like. But even for desk workers, is there anything that makes that role unique? Perhaps there's a lot of evening work, a lot of travel, or something else.

If they are **in the field**, it's useful to know what a day in that job is like. This is where it can be helpful to have someone on your team who previously did that job. For example, that's where Sue's past experience in pharmaceutical sales serves her so well—she actually did the job that she was later training others to do.

If that's not possible, see if you can shadow someone in that role for a few hours. For example, in past roles, Carla has had opportunities to shadow call center employees in both financial services and health insurance, and nurses in hospitals. It's also common for instructional designers of sales staff to do a ride along, where they come on the seller's calls for an afternoon.

There is nothing more valuable than actually sitting on the phones with a call center person, or following a nurse or a salesperson for a few hours, to really understand the pace and pressure of these client- or patient-facing roles.

Another great example of knowing the use case is when Carla worked on a training team in a healthcare environment. They offered live classes from 8 a.m. to 5 p.m. It wasn't feasible to offer classes at other times of day, so it was very helpful to recognize that sometimes we would have a clinician who had worked from 7 p.m. to 7 a.m. (a common 12-hour shift) and then come to our class from 8 a.m. to noon. Anyone who works nights a lot knows that you don't usually finish work and go right home to bed, but still, knowing which participants had been up all night before coming to our class was important.

Notes About My Learner _____

_____

_____

_____

_____

_____

_____

_____

Question

Are they in front of a computer, or do they do their work primarily on a tablet, on a mobile device, or without technology at all?

Why It's Helpful

The employee will always look for their just-in-time learning and performance support on the device they are using at that moment when they need help. So if they are typically working on a mobile or handheld device when they are likely to want that piece of support, you'll want to find ways to provide it on that device. This is a big key to determining when mobile learning will be most valuable.

Of course this is most specific to training that's provided for just-in-time support, but it will also help you to understand how people will take their required training too. For example, many restaurants have a training computer in a back room where employees will do some training at the start of their shift, prior to going on the floor.

How technology is used is also something you'll see if you shadow someone for a few hours. One consulting firm we know of does this a lot. In one case the firm discovered that the workers used a small handheld device, and that midshift they had to bring it to a charging station, where they would wait for five to 10 minutes for it to charge. The firm put instructional posters in the charging area to provide very short bits of training content while people waited for their devices to charge. In another example, that same firm realized every employee had to change clothes at the start of shift, so they started putting instructional posters on the lockers, so people would read them while changing their clothes.

They figured this out simply by observing workers in the field. Take some time to shadow your employees or sit in break areas and just observe what goes on. Then, look for patterns in what you see different people doing. Understanding the environment in which your learners work (especially for those who are not desk-workers) is critically important to providing training they will consume.

Notes About My Learner _____

_____

_____

_____

_____

_____

_____

_____

_____

_____

_____

_____

Question

Are they customer- or client-facing, and if so, is that interaction face-to-face or technology-enabled?

Why It's Helpful

There are lots of things we look up when we are on the job. But how we do that is very different if we are in front of a customer or client, or if we are communicating with them by phone or email. For example, when you are talking to someone in a call center and the agent asks "May I put you on a brief hold?" they are looking up the answer to your question. For simpler issues, they will look up those answers while talking to you, and you may never even know they used support to help them answer your questions!

It's very different for a person who is providing customer assistance face-to-face. Then there are certain things the agent can look up without losing credibility, but other things that they cannot. As designers we must recognize how our materials can be used: Can they be used exactly at the moment of need in front of the customer or not?

We know of another firm that was designing content that the employee was likely to need at key moments, but couldn't look it up in front of the client. This drove them to shorter-form learning so it could be used just before walking into the room with the client. In fact, they called it "broom closet training" in light of the imagined use case: The employee would be about to meet their client when they could duck into a broom closet to quickly brush up on a couple things before the meeting! (Of course we all knew the training could also be done in a hallway, a cafeteria, in the car, or maybe even a bathroom stall—the point was that they were thinking about the use case so well that it helped to guide them in how they offered their content.)

Notes About My Learner
_____

_____
_____
_____
_____
_____
_____
_____
_____
_____
_____
_____
_____

Situations Where Microlearning Can Be Useful

Microlearning can be used in lots of ways and in a variety of common situations. Consider the situations where you offer training. Which of you experience? Check off all that pertain to you. These are the areas where you can go micro.

Preparation Before a Learning Event	Follow-Up to Reinforce a Learning Event
☐ Learners don't have a good understanding of why they are coming to the class. ☐ There is a lot of didactic content that needs to be understood before the learner can have a thoughtful discussion about it or complete an activity with it. ☐ There are a wide variety of knowledge levels of those attending the class.	☐ Learners will be able to complete their work, even if they do not incorporate their new skills or change their behavior. ☐ Learners will need to be convinced and reminded to use their new skills. ☐ Learners are likely to forget important nuances of the content. ☐ You want to continue to extend the learning beyond the classroom, especially in a personalized way.
Stand-Alone Training	**Performance Support**
☐ The concept that needs to be addressed is small and discrete. ☐ The content is a larger concept, but it can be broken into a number of small, discrete pieces. ☐ The content needs to be able to serve as "refresher material" after the training is over. ☐ The learner already has a basic understanding of the concept. ☐ The learner is highly motivated to consume the content.	☐ A task is performed infrequently or content is easy to forget. ☐ Accuracy is crucial or errors are risky. ☐ A process or procedure is error-prone. ☐ There are multiple steps or decision points. ☐ There are topics that learners would commonly want to search for help on.

References and Additional Resources

Allen, M. 2016. *Michael Allen's Guide to e-Learning.* Hoboken, NJ: Wiley.

American Heart Association. 2014. "Online Game Helps Doctors Improve Patients' Blood Pressure Faster." *Science Daily,* May 20. sciencedaily.com/releases/2014/05/140520133210.htm.

Axonify. 2019. "Axonify: Powered by Brain Science." July 9. resources.axonify.com/brain-science/axonify-brain-science-datasheet.

Bean, C. 2014. *The Accidental Instructional Designer.* Alexandria, VA: ATD Press.

Dirksen, J. 2015. *Design for How People Learn,* 2nd edition. San Francisco: New Riders.

Gottfredson, C., and B. Mosher. 2011. *Innovative Performance Support: Strategies and Practices for Learning in the Workflow.* New York: McGraw-Hill.

Gottfredson, C., and B. Mosher. "The Five Moments of Need." 5momentsofneed.com.

Kerfoot, B.P. 2018. "Q&A With B. Price Kerfoot, MD EdM: How Long Do the Benefits of Qstream Last?" Qstream blog, October. blog.qstream.com/blog/2018/10/qa-b-price-kerfoot-md-edm-long-benefits-qstream-last.

Kerfoot, B.P., A. Turchin, E. Breydo, D. Gagnon, and P.R. Conlin. 2014. "An Online Spaced-Education Game Among Clinicians Improves Their Patients' Time to Blood Pressure Control." *Circulation: Cardiovascular Quality and Outcomes,* May 1. ahajournals.org/doi/10.1161/CIRCOUTCOMES.113.000814.

Kim, A.S.N., A.M.B. Wong-Kee-You, M. Wiseheart, and R.S. Rosenbaum. 2019. "The Spacing Effect Stands Up to Big Data." *Behavior Research Methods* August.

Kohn, A. 2014a. "Brain Science: Enable Your Brain to Remember Almost Everything." *Learning Solutions,* May. learningsolutionsmag.com/articles/1423/brain-science-enable-your-brain-to-remember-almost-everything.

Kohn, A. 2014b. "Brain Science: Overcoming the Forgetting Curve." *Learning Solutions,* April. learningsolutionsmag.com/articles/1400/brain-science-overcoming-the-forgetting-curve.

Lambert, C. 2009. "Learning by Degrees." *Harvard Magazine,* November/December. harvardmagazine.com/2009/11/spaced-education-boosts-learning.

Malamed, C. 2017. "How to Get Started With Performance Support." The eLearning Coach, November 20. theelearningcoach.com/elearning2-0/get-started-with-performance-support.

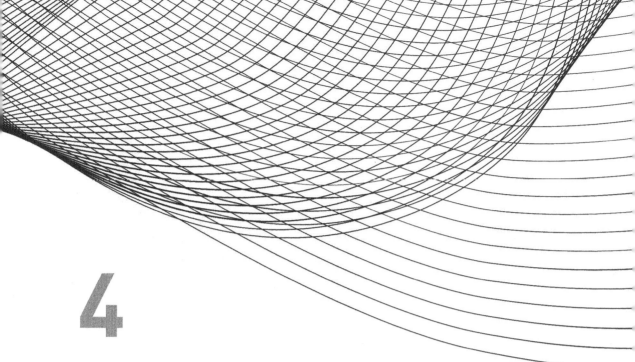

4

Implementing the Plan: How Do You Execute an Effective Microlearning Resource or Program?

In This Chapter:

- The MILE model: A model for designing effective microlearning
- How to identify performance objectives, and the importance of enabling objectives
- Ways you can deliver your microlearning resources
- Obtaining content with the 3 Cs: curate, create, and crowdsource
- Ensuring people use your resources

In the last chapter you identified how you would use microlearning:

- preparation before a learning event
- follow-up to support a learning event
- stand-alone training
- performance support.

You also identified, at a high level, what you would teach in that piece of microlearning. Now that you have a vision for how to use microlearning in your organization, you need to bring it to life! That means having a plan to actually design, develop, and deliver the microlearning resources.

MILE: The MIcroLEarning Design Model

Once you've got a pretty clear idea of what you want to teach or support using microlearning, the MILE model will help you to think through the steps to create that resource or series of resources and get it into the hands of your learners (Figure 4-1).

Figure 4-1. The MILE Model

The MILE model is designed around the concept of a car speedometer. How long does it take to drive a mile (or 1.6 kilometers)? It depends on a lot of factors, like traffic, weather conditions, if you're in a school zone, and even the car you drive.

But generally, you can drive a mile in one to five minutes . . . if you're on the highway, you're traveling about one minute per mile; if you're in a school zone you're closer to about five minutes per mile.

This analogy is meant to help you remember that each microlearning resource you create should be about one to five minutes long. What does that depend on? Lots of factors, like the topic, the learner, their workflow, even their level of experience with the concept. And as we discussed in chapter 1, it's also highly dependent on how you are using microlearning—will it be used as preparation before a learning event, follow-up to support a learning event, stand-alone training, or performance support?

As we said in chapter 1, we don't want to get hung up on the exact seat time, but we do want to keep in mind that this is supposed to be of a short duration.

Now let's look at the steps of the MILE model. These are the things you will do as you bring a microlearning resource or program to life:

- **Identify performance objectives.** This is where you determine what you will teach.
- **Determine program technology and structure.** This is where you determine the technology you will use to distribute the resources and any trade-offs associated with your approach.
- **Create or select resources.** This is where you actually curate, create, or crowdsource the learning resources.
- **Promote.** This is where you tell people about the program and garner their engagement.
- **Monitor, modify, and evaluate.** This is where you determine if the resources or program are working or not.

TOOLS

"The MILE Model Job Aid" tool at the end of this chapter helps you work through all five steps of the MILE model. It includes questions relevant to each step that will help you apply this model to your own work.

The MILE Model Is an Agile Model—A Note From Carla

You'll notice that at the base of the speedometer of the MILE model, it says, "Return to Prior Steps as Needed." This is the most important part of the model! It's the part that reminds you to be agile.

In my current role as a director of instructional design, I lead the crafting of the instructional vision for training projects and managing scope as we create that design. Inevitably, as we near the end of projects, whether they are micro or not, clients ask for changes and have new ideas. When these come up I always start by asking my team, "Will that change make the piece better, or just different?" If it will make the product better, I always consider the change carefully to see if there's a way we can include it, even if the request is technically out of scope. Good ideas are good ideas, and (within reason) we shouldn't disregard them simply because nobody thought of them sooner.

In my experience, **going micro enables you to be more agile than ever before.** Here are two main ways in which I've seen my team become more agile when I've developed microlearning programs that have multiple microlearning resources:

- As you create, implement, and evaluate the microlearning resources in steps 3, 4, and 5 of the MILE model, you can quickly change gears if a particular resource doesn't seem useful. Let's say you are having trouble designing or promoting a microlearning resource. Because each resource is shorter, it takes less time to create or curate, so it's easier to decide to throw out one resource and replace it with something else.
- I've also learned from designing large microlearning programs that step 3 can become extremely agile because you're developing so many small pieces to completion. Imagine creating a 45-minute e-learning module; when you review it, you have a new idea, but realize you just don't have the time or money to implement it. Now, imagine you're creating 10 five-minute modules, and after you finish one, you have that same idea. This presents the opportunity to implement that idea into the remaining nine modules, because you haven't created them yet. This was my biggest unexpected surprise of going micro—my quality went up because I'm able to be more agile than ever before! The end product gets better because of the smaller scale and incremental development inherent in a developing a program of microlearning resources.

In early versions of the MILE model, the steps weren't numbered. That was intentional because I thought you should be able to jump around between steps, and I didn't want it to feel so linear. But an editor convinced me that numbering the steps would make it clearer, and I have found the same, so the numbers have stayed. However, this does make it feel like you're going "back" a step when being agile.

Much like the speedometer in your car, when you go to an earlier step, **you have slowed down, but you are still moving forward.** This is true if you are developing a single microlearning resource or a full microlearning program. You may feel like you're going backward, but you are actually still moving forward; your progression simply slowed. This is key, and know that your product will be better in the end because you took the time to slow down.

RESOURCES

Thought leaders like Michael Allen (CEO of Allen Interactions) and Megan Torrance (CEO of TorranceLearning) have been talking for years about the importance of being agile in instructional design. Carla is lucky to have had both of them as mentors, and through conversations with them and years of project work, she can attest to the value of being agile. Requirements change, good ideas crop up, and feedback comes as we see our designs coming to life.

If you want to learn more about their approaches, consider these books:
- *Agile for Instructional Designers: Iterative Project Management to Achieve Results* by Megan Torrance
- *Michael Allen's Guide to E-Learning: Building Interactive, Fun, and Effective Learning Programs for Any Company* by Michael Allen
- *Leaving ADDIE for SAM: An Agile Model for Developing the Best Learning Experiences* by Michael Allen and Richard Sites

MILE Step 1: Identify Performance Objectives

In chapter 3 you determined if your microlearning resources would be used in preparation before a learning event, follow-up to reinforce a learning event, stand-alone training, or performance support. You also determined what you wanted that resource to be able to achieve within that category, based on addressing a performance need.

PRO TIP

When you break your content down to small discrete chunks that can stand on their own, you may have a lot of topics that feel very "knowledge" focused. As instructional designers, it's easy to focus on all the things people need to know to get to that ultimate goal of your terminal objective.

However, you should think about each objective, no matter how small, as a performance objective—what will people be able to do as a result of using this one resource? Because for most of your learners, it's not about what they know; it's what they do with that knowledge that sets them apart. And they won't engage with any piece of microlearning if they can't see how it will help them in a tangible way.

Now that you've got a vision for the performance gap you want to resolve, you should have a good handle on the objectives you want to achieve for the microlearning resource or program. In this step you'll think a little more formally about your objectives for this learning resource or program. You want to commit this to paper so you can refer back to it later as needed.

A typical learning objective is written in the form, "At the end of this training, the learner will be able to . . ." But you don't necessarily need to be that formal. Simply ask, "What will people be able to do differently because of this microlearning resource?"

If the objective is small enough that you could achieve that goal with a single microlearning resource, then you've finished this step of the MILE model. But if you are planning to create a series of related pieces, you have another important step. **Start with the terminal objective (what people will be able to do differently because of the program), and break it down into its enabling objectives—all the things they need to know or be able to do to get there.** Of course, if the microlearning resources are intended to come before or after a longer-form learning event, then you'll want to align your resources to the learning objectives of the longer program.

CASE STUDY: WRITING PERFORMANCE OBJECTIVES AND ENABLING OBJECTIVES FOR A STAND-ALONE MICROLEARNING PROGRAM

Len designs training for a large bank. He knows that dealing with unhappy customers is one of the hardest parts of a teller's job. He wants to design a stand-alone program of microlearning resources for tellers and identifies his terminal performance objective as, "Tellers will be able to handle calls from difficult customers."

Often, when we create classes that's enough. Len would create a class on handling difficult customers, including a de-escalation model and lots of role play to practice.

That's a fine terminal objective for the whole program, but for the individual microlearning resources, Len needs to dig deeper. He learns there are a few things that commonly cause customers to escalate. One of the more common situations is when a teller informs a customer about a hold on funds—that is, when the customer is depositing money into their account, but they won't be able to use that money (transfer or withdraw it) for several days. As a result, Len writes some of his enabling objectives like so:

- Tellers will be able to handle calls from difficult customers with a hold on funds.
- Tellers will be able to handle calls from difficult customers who have an overdraft on their account because of a hold on funds.

Len probably can't create an effective single piece of training that's just a few minutes long that teaches tellers how to handle calls from all types of difficult customers. But he can create a single piece of short-form content about how to handle calls from difficult customers with a hold on funds or any of the other top areas that tellers struggle with.

The enabling objectives are critical. They are what enable you to go micro (Torgerson 2016). When you design longer-form learning, like a half-day class (or even a 30-minute e-learning module), you usually focus on the high-level objectives and how the content will flow together to support it. You might not think about the enabling objectives, maybe because it's too in the weeds or it's obvious. But when you go micro, you need to think about how this content breaks down into its component parts. When designing a class, you focus on the flow of all the parts, but **when going micro, your focus shifts from having a good flow to having a series of performance-focused enabling objectives**.

PRO TIP

How do you actually decide how long the microlearning resource will be? The soundtrack in your head may sound something like this: "I could solve this in five minutes with short-form learning, but I could also see the possibilities of a 30-minute module. What should I do?"

The answer is twofold: The first question to ask yourself is, who is this for and how much do they need to know to be able to execute this task on the job? In the previous case study, where an enabling objective is, "Tellers will be able to handle calls from difficult customers with a hold on funds," your SMEs may remind you that there are a lot of reasons for that. You need to decide if tellers only need to know how to handle the two most common ones. Or if they need to know all the reasons, but that three of them are escalated to a bank manager. Or if the way to handle all of them is essentially the same, and you don't need to get into the details of the different reasons.

In all these cases, the content and skill could be addressed in a job aid or a short-format module. However, if the teller needs to know deeper details about the reasons for the different holds on funds, and how customers can avoid such a hold in the future, you may need more depth. Then a longer format may be needed. Or maybe you still create microlearning resources, designing one resource for each of the different types of holds.

Another question to consider is, how many different job roles need this content and to what depth? The topic of exceptions may be the same for both the tellers and the back-office employees who review the requests, but you may find that microlearning is the best option for the tellers, and longer-form learning is better for the back-office staff. You can provide different training for different groups! If you find yourself putting in extra content that is really only for a subset of your learner group, you should clearly flag it as optional for the others, or peel it off to be a separate learning resource for just those people for whom it is relevant.

And lastly for emphasis: Yes, you *always* need an objective. We speak across the nation about using microlearning, and we'll sometimes hear someone ask if you must have an objective for every piece of microlearning you create. The thinking is that if the piece of content is so small, you may not necessarily have a meaty performance objective that it addresses. While that may be true, you must have an objective, even if a very small one, for every piece of microlearning you create. If you can't articulate why a piece of content will be useful to the learner, then you shouldn't be creating it.

MILE Step 2: Determine Program Technology and Structure

When using microlearning, probably the most challenging question to ask yourself is, "How do I get this content to my learners?" With longer-form learning we usually create live or virtual classes or host e-learning materials on the LMS, but with microlearning we have many more options.

When you choose how to distribute your content you really need to go back to thinking about your use case, which we discussed in chapter 3. As you think about how these materials will be used (preparation before a learning event, follow-up to support a learning event, stand-alone training, or performance support), you should be able to identify the conditions under which the learner is most likely to consume your content. When will the learner use these materials, what will they be doing, and what will be the most natural way for them to reach for your materials?

Knowing this will make it clearer how to best distribute those materials. For example, let's say you want to provide follow-up materials to support a learning event. It may not be optimal to put those boosting materials on the LMS, because you'd prefer to push them to the learner in a different way—maybe as emails or push notifications on their phones. With microlearning, think beyond the LMS! Here's a list of several options for distributing microlearning content:

- LMS
- social collaborative system
- LXP
- email
- paper handouts (physical)
- PDFs (digital)
- posters
- software-help systems
- websites or portals
- a system to provide pop-up questions, text messages, or push notifications on the learner's computer or mobile device.

TOOLS

The "Ways You Can Distribute Microlearning Content" tool at the end of this chapter expands on the microlearning distribution options and provides examples of each, along with their pros and cons.

PRO TIP

There is a lot of excitement about learning experience platforms (LXPs), particularly as a platform for sharing microlearning resources. They are commonly referred to as the "Netflix of learning," because the idea is that the learner is in control of their learning, as opposed to being assigned learning content that they are required to complete, as is the case with an LMS.

The LXP focuses on informal learning, making it easy for learners to find and consume content they are interested in. The LXP makes it easy for people to search for and discover content. It can also recommend learning materials based on your login profile (your role, number of years with the company, academic background, and so on), and based on the other materials you have searched for or viewed. Further, you can follow other people in the organization, so you can find out what they are accessing or rating highly. The LXP can also recommend content that people with a profile similar to yours also consumed.

The learning team can also create pathways, so if I'm a junior associate and I want to become a senior associate, there could be a recommended pathway of courses and other learning materials to help me get there. And there could be several different paths that I can chose from, depending on my professional interests—what kind of specialized senior associate I want to be.

For more, see "Learning Experience Platform (LXP) Market Grows Up: Now Too Big To Ignore," by Josh Bersin. This article provides an excellent comparison of the functionality of LXPs and LMSs, where each has value, and how they are likely to evolve in the future.

Once you've identified the best tool for your use case, then you need to ask yourself what constraints that tool may have, what impact those constraints might have on the learner, and if those constraints would cause you to choose a different tool or change how you design your microlearning resources. Some of these are listed in the "cons" column of the "Ways You Can Distribute Microlearning Content" tool at the end of this chapter, and others will be based on the specific tool used by your organization or your organization's rules governing its use. For example, a system may have a limit on file size, may not allow certain file types, or other issues.

MILE Step 3: Create or Select Resources

Now that you've determined what you want to teach (step 1) and how you'll deliver it (step 2), it's time to actually curate, create, or crowdsource that content!

Designers often think about using an e-learning module when they have a micro-learning need. And there's the common myth that microlearning is always a video. But really, as we discussed in chapter 1, microlearning can come in a variety of formats (Figure 4-2):

- text-based resources
- e-learning
- video
- infographics
- podcasts.

Figure 4-2. Five Formats of Microlearning

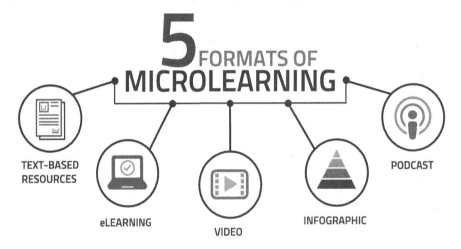

Do not limit yourself by thinking it's only one of these options! (See chapter 1 for more about each of these formats and how they can be used.)

Relative Effort to Develop Each Format

As you are choosing the format, you must also consider the relative cost to develop each. Regardless if you are considering the cost of your or your staff's time, or the actual dollars you spend with an external partner, this is an important consideration. You are always making trade-offs, and Table 4-1 helps you consider the relative effort to develop each format. It is important to keep this in mind as you consider the instructional value of each format for your topic and the performance need.

Table 4-1. The Cost to Develop Microlearning Resource Types

Resource Type	Cost to Develop	Notes
Text-based resource	$	Fast, easy, inexpensive—most have the software to develop these resources in-house
E-learning	$-$$$	Inexpensive if creating a simple page-turner, but can become more expensive with the level of complexity, interactivity, and graphics
Video	$-$$$$	Inexpensive when filmed using a smartphone, but can increase dramatically when using paid actors or a full production and editing crew
Infographic	$$	Relatively inexpensive to create; cost and quality goes up with increased sophistication
Podcast	$$	Relatively inexpensive; just need a good microphone and editing ability

The 3 Cs: Curate, Create, and Crowdsource

Once you know what you want to teach and have identified the format (or formats) you will use, then you need to get to work and generate those learning assets. In general, instructional designers create their own materials, and that's a good approach. But, as we just saw, it takes effort—sometimes a lot of effort—to create these different formats. So, before rushing to create something new, you should consider all the ways you may be able to obtain your learning assets.

We like to use Carla's 3Cs model, which tells you not only the three ways you can obtain content, but also the preferred order in which you should try to use these approaches: curate, create, crowdsource (Figure 4-3).

Figure 4-3. The 3 Cs: Curate, Create, and Crowdsource

CURATE ▶ CREATE ▶ CROWDSOURCE

Ultimately, you should curate first where possible. It has the biggest bang for your buck. If that doesn't work, then you can create your own materials. Finally, don't forget about using crowdsourcing when you can; but note that there are limited situations where it will be truly successful, so you should consider it third.

Curate

Curating happens when you collect the "best of the best" resources that already exist on the Internet or on your corporate intranet. With curation, your goal is to circumvent people searching the Internet or intranet for their learning content, which saves their time and ensures the resources align with the models or approaches in use by your organization. While Google is a quick way to find resources, learners are often overwhelmed by the volume of those resources. And even if the resources they're seeking are inside your organization, searching the intranet can be difficult.

Regardless of whether the content is external or internal to your organization, you can make the process of finding what your learners need more efficient than having them search for it themselves. But it takes time and careful evaluation to curate good content.

Pros

The biggest advantage of curation is that it is relatively quick. Certainly, you could spend a day or two finding the right resources, but that will be far less time than you would spend creating those resources yourself. Curation is also likely to produce high-quality content—oftentimes better than you can create on your own with the time and resources available.

Curated content can also be more rigorous because it's been developed by leading researchers, and it can have the advantage of credibility if it comes from known, trusted authors. For example, if you create leadership development curriculum, people are more likely to give greater credibility to materials from *Harvard Business Review* than the materials you create in-house.

Cons

Of course no approach is perfect, and there are lots of reasons instructional designers don't curate more often. The most common reason is copyright. In general, the rule on copyright issues is that you're breaking the law if you copy a microlearning resource (like a video) from somewhere else and put it onto your server; but you're fine if you link to it on the other person's site, because the owner of the content can still control it and is clearly the owner since the learner is accessing it on their site. However, your organization might not allow you to link outside your intranet. Or maybe the content you want to share is paid content—you have a membership to a site with that content, but it's unrealistic to get a membership for everyone in your organization.

The other big issue is that you can't customize this content to your unique needs. What if the article has a great model, but all the examples are from a different industry than the one you work in? Or maybe that video you've found is excellent, but it's 30 minutes long and you'd really like a five-minute summary—or just the five minutes at the end. Or maybe you like the content and the length, but it's dated and you'd like to use more contemporary graphics or terms. If you don't own the content, you can't make these kinds of revisions or alterations.

Finding Content: Consider Your Objectives

When curating content, you want to start by identifying your learning or performance objectives. Then, you'll search the Internet or your intranet for one or more resources to address each objective. As you review the resources you'll naturally know which ones are best for your purposes, and you'll ignore those that either don't meet your objective or don't teach it well.

The key is that you identify the objectives in general but don't get any more granular, because if you get too specific about what you want to be included in the resources you'll never find exactly what you're looking for. Not only will you spend too long trying to find that perfect resource, but you'll end up creating content when you probably could have curated it.

Create

The issues described for curation usually lead to creating your own materials. You can create something that's exactly what you need, integrated into your curriculum, and worded the way you want. It's great because it's customized.

Of course the advantages and disadvantages here are nearly the opposite of a curation approach.

Pros

The biggest advantage is that you can customize the content to your exact needs—just the content, tone, focus, length, and format you want. As a result you also own all copyright and thus can use the resource in any way you want and with as many people as you want. Frankly, it's this freedom and flexibility that drives organizations to create their own content.

Cons

The biggest challenge is that it takes time and resources to create this content. And you may not have the skills to create those materials the way you want. For example, your vision is to have a video like that one you saw online, but you don't have a day in a studio with a slate of actors to do that.

The big thing to note here is that while there are very valid reasons that drive you to create materials, when you go micro, sometimes curation is a more valid approach than you realize. There are so many good, short resources available on the Internet that you really should consider them as assets when you develop your microlearning programs.

Designing Content: Keep It Brief, Well Organized, and Engaging

The process you follow for designing microlearning resources will be similar to other learning materials you create, but perhaps with a few tweaks. Start by identifying your learning or performance objectives (see MILE step 1). Then, knowing you'll create one resource to address each objective, create an outline that identifies the few ideas, points, or concepts that will be included in each resource. As you outline it, ask yourself: What are the most critical thing(s) to being able to do this behavior?

Interview your SMEs for specific details or examples to use in teaching that content or supporting that behavior. Keep an eye on making things brief. If the SME starts offering too much information, remind them of the short, focused approach and the purpose of the specific resource. Ask, "Would the learner need to know that now?" to help you to stay focused on just what they would need in that short resource.

If you find you have more in your outline for a microlearning resource than you can realistically cover in about five to 10 minutes, start by asking if all that content is really needed. If it is, then you need to be agile and ask yourself if you should split the resource into multiple resources, each with a different learning or performance objective. Or you may realize that a micro approach just won't work, and a longer-form resource is needed to properly address the performance objective. Ultimately this will drive you back to step 1 of the MILE model, and is exactly the agile and iterative thinking we encourage!

After you outline the content, you'll design and develop each unique resource, just as you would any other learning material. Depending on the format, you need well-written text, quality images, good video footage, or crisp audio recordings to ensure the message and any interactions are clear and engaging. And it needs to be tested to make sure the content is accurate, you've achieved your desired level of quality, and any functionality is bug-free.

Crowdsource

Crowdsourcing happens when people throughout the organization share their favorite resources from the Internet (or the intranet, if there is a good internal library of content). Generally, this happens within a social collaborative platform (like Yammer, Jive, or even Facebook) or on your LXP. Crowdsourcing is another form of curation, but the curating is done by the employees, not the instructional designers.

Your employees may also create some content themselves, such as sharing their own best practices or opinions. Or they may augment existing content by adding comments to other people's posts, or giving posts or resources a star rating.

Crowdsourced content is best when the community and content generation are organic—that is, led by the employees. The training team can be a guide, but should not be a driver in the community.

Pros

There are a few big advantages to this approach. Most important, if the content is generated or shared by employees, their endorsement of the content means that it was helpful to them. There is no group better at knowing what resources help them than the people who do that job themselves!

You also get a great variety of opinions and approaches, which can generate new ideas. It's also great for sharing the tacit knowledge in your organization—that is, you can take the knowledge from the most experienced people in the organization that's not documented anywhere and share it with those who have less experience. This is especially important if you are expecting a large wave of retirement, as is the case in a number of fields. (Already there are industries that hire their retirees back as "consultants" to help fill this knowledge gap.)

Cons

There are a few issues that cause trouble for a crowdsourcing approach. First is credibility of the information—an employee could share something that is wrong. Some organizations, especially in highly regulated industries, will also have concerns about employees sharing their own best practices and things that work for them. For example, if a pharmaceutical sales rep writes in a discussion forum about an off-label use of their drug, the sales rep will be at risk of losing their job for appearing to suggest drug use for a nonapproved indication, the company could be at risk of receiving a warning letter from the FDA along with huge financial penalties, and the company could be sued if a healthcare professional used the drug in an off-label manner that then resulted in physical harm to a patient. This is the kind of risk any company wants to avoid! But in nonregulated areas there can be huge value in having employees share their best practices and approaches to the work they are doing.

The biggest barrier to crowdsourcing is *time*. Sure, the time required for the L&D team is generally lower; they need to create the structure for sharing, encourage its use, and monitor and moderate the community. But that means that the time required to find, create, and share those resources shifts to the employee.

As we said earlier, the employees' highest priority is *always* their operational duties. Their training comes next. And frankly, sharing their knowledge to train others comes after that. To get people to take time to share knowledge like this, you have to consciously create an environment where those behaviors are rewarded, such as public recognition or even rewards or bonuses based on team performance goals.

Overall, though, this is not a new problem, nor is it one seen only in corporate settings. In fact, in most online social communities, a pattern of behavior can be seen. This pattern is called the "90-9-1 rule," and it states that in any online social community, only 1 percent of the users will actively create new content; 9 percent will contribute a little, but mostly add to existing content (liking, sharing, starring); and the remaining 90 percent will lurk, that is, they will read but not contribute (Nielsen 2006).

Communities like Facebook, Twitter, and Instagram can thrive despite this because of the sheer number of people in the community. Even with just 1 percent of people creating new content, there is always new content for the lurkers to consume. **Ultimately, though, this means that in our organizations, where we have smaller social communities, crowdsourcing may not work unless we create very large groups or reward participation in some way.**

Sourcing Content: Engage Your Community

Like with the other approaches, when using a crowdsourcing strategy, you want to start by identifying your learning or performance objectives. Then, identify key topic areas that relate to each objective and post those in a portal where employees can share content. Often this is a discussion board on an LMS, a social collaborative system, or a social networking platform, but it could also be a wiki or shared web page where people can post links to their favorite resources.

Then find well-respected people in the organization and encourage them to contribute content—this could be responding to performance-based questions ("How do I do . . ." or "What's the best way to do . . ."), or simply sharing their favorite resources about a topic ("What's your favorite resource about . . ."). In a corporate environment, your L&D team may need to moderate the community to keep it active. Ideally, though, over time additional questions and topic areas will be posted by employees as you start to build a more robust community.

You will never overcome the 90-9-1 rule—participation inequality has occurred in every online community ever studied (Nielsen 2006). However, there are some things that you can do to encourage participation, so that fewer people will lurk and more people will participate to some degree:

- Host your content in a tool that makes it easier for people to contribute. For example, systems that allow people to click a "thumbs up" or click one of five stars enables the learner to add their opinion with a single click. Even systems that have easy-to-use forms for adding discussion posts and comments will make a difference.

- Host your content in a tool that generates automatic participation. This gets into data analytics, such as identifying the resources that the most people clicked on, or those resources that got the most five-star ratings by people in similar roles to the learner. A lot of learning experience platforms do this very well.

- The learning team can promote the best content, raising it to the top of the search results or the discussion page. Marking that content as "endorsed by the organization" can also highlight those resources that the organization feels are best for employees to consume. You can then let the poster know that you appreciated their post and give them positive feedback on it. Including their manager on such communication is valuable, because then the person who is responsible for their performance evaluation will know about their efforts too.

- Reward participation. This can take a number of forms in the corporate environment. A lot of corporate social tools give points for participation and then use badges and leaderboards to encourage participation. However, we've found this only works if learners see some sort of value in having the badges or being at the top of the leaderboard, which often comes from recognizing those with certain scores or badges. Better yet, have team goals that are best achieved by sharing expertise and knowledge with one another; if they can see how this helps them do their job better, they are more likely to participate. Note that when rewarding participation, you must ensure you are rewarding the quality of posts, not just those who post a lot. You want to be sure that when people are recognized for their posts or their position on the leaderboard, the feeling within the organization is that the person "must know their stuff" rather than the person "must have a lot of time on their hands."

PRO TIP

Regardless of your content development strategy—curate, create, or crowdsource— don't overthink things here. The value of microlearning is that you can try a microlearning resource, and if it doesn't work as well as you wanted, you can replace it with a new resource. If you are curating, it's often easy to find another relevant resource. If you are creating, it shouldn't take long to revise the current resource or just create a new one. And if you are crowdsourcing, you can add another discussion question for people to answer.

Focus on your performance objective and what the learner is most likely to need at that moment. Then just get started and iterate along the way until you are providing the resources that prove to have the greatest value to your learners.

MILE Step 4: Promote

In MILE step 2 you identified where you would host your content and how you would distribute it. Then, in MILE step 3, you curated resources, created your own resources, or identified your crowdsourcing topics or questions. Now, in MILE step 4, you need to implement those resources or crowdsourcing plan as you envisioned in MILE step 2.

If your program is required for people to complete, your primary job now is just to monitor the completion status of learners and contact them if they do not complete the microlearning resources on the prescribed schedule. This can be done manually or automated with your LMS.

However, if the program is not required, which oftentimes microlearning programs are not, then you have to think about how you are promoting the content. That is, how are you letting your learners know that the resources exist and enticing those learners to consume them or remember to use them at their moment of need?

The key here is:

- If they don't **know** it exists, they can't use it.

- If they don't **remember** it exists, they won't use it (Torgerson 2016).

So you need to find ways to continually alert your audience that the resources are available.

Strategies for Promoting Your Content

Really, your promotion strategies won't be any different from the ones you use with any other nonrequired training. Here are just a few ideas, many of which you've probably used before:

- List the program on your website, your LMS, your social collaborative system, or your LXP.
- Place banner ads on any of those sites.
- Send emails to all employees in the organization, or particular groups of employees (such as all people in a particular department, or all people who have been in a certain role for less than a year).
- Put posters, flyers, or QR codes in break rooms or other common areas.
- Put posters or flyers on bathroom doors.
- Ask managers to promote the materials with their teams at team meetings and in one-on-one meetings with their employees.
- Mention the materials in other related programming—during live classes and virtual instructor-led classes, and even at the end of other e-learning courses.
- Give prizes to people who complete the program (for example, to the first 10 people who complete all of the microlearning resources, or a random drawing from all the people who complete them by the end of the month).
- If your team has a newsletter or blog, make sure to mention your programs there. If possible, get other people to mention the program in their blogs and other social posts they make.
- Make sure you tag your content well so the search engine of the system where you post the content can find your content easily. Ask the administrator of your LMS, social collaborative system, LXP, or other systems if they have recommendations for how to tag your content for that system. You want your content to be as easy to search for as possible.

Making Your Content Sticky

The notion of "sticky" content comes from the field of marketing. Stickiness refers to content that is so engaging that people are likely to stay for a while or keep coming back to it. Because many microlearning resources are created as a library of content that serves as a reference or performance support, you want to consider how to make those resources sticky so people will keep coming back to them.

Research from the field of marketing has shown the strategies in Table 4-2 to be effective at creating stickiness.

Table 4-2. Marketing Strategies to Increase Content Stickiness

Marketing Strategy	Application to Microlearning
Ensure site navigation is immediately intuitive.	When coming to your site, people should be able to find desired resources easily.
Make text readable on any browser, including mobile browsers.	Know your audience well enough to know what browsers they are likely to use and if they'll access your materials on mobile devices.
Continually provide fresh content. It will prompt people to come back regularly to check what's new.	Develop and release your library of content over time. You don't have to wait for the entire program to be complete before sharing it with your learners.
Let people subscribe to your content. If they are subscribed you'll have an easier time prompting them to come back.	Send interested learners an email when you post new content. Let them sign up for your mailing list, or target people based on factors like job role, tenure, or consumption of past microlearning resources.
Include your personality wherever you can. It will make you seem more real and inviting.	All resources should be interesting and engaging, and written in an informal tone when possible.
Allow readers to engage by posting comments and responding to one another. This will encourage visitors to stick around and come back.	Allow social commenting on your resources when possible.
Provide a highlight reel of the most popular content.	Re-share your most popular resources. For example, have a banner ad for the "five most popular videos this month" and link that to a page listing those videos.
Create a competition or free offer. People respond very well to free things, and will, for example, subscribe to a blog in exchange for a gift.	Provide a prize to all people who use six or more resources, or to the top 10 users of the content library (in terms of amount of content consumed) in a month.
User testimonials and reviews establish credibility for new users. Similarly, list your awards and accomplishments.	Find ways to collect feedback on your microlearning resources and then share that. For example, beside each resource you could have an employee quote about why they found the resource helpful. If the content is curated from a site that has received awards for their content, make sure to tell your learners.
Provide a tease into similar content.	At the end of a resource, provide a link to other content on the same topic. This is one of the best ways to get users to dive deeper into your content.

Adapted from DeMers (2014).

Rollout and Promotion Plans

If you have a larger program, you'll want to have a plan for how to roll out the microlearning resources to learners—how will you distribute and promote the content, to whom, on what schedule, and how will you support it over time.

You probably have some ideas in mind for the rollout and implementation

TOOLS

At the end of the chapter is the "Rollout and Communication Considerations" job aid that provides questions to consider when building your rollout and communication plan.

plan from when you initiated the project. Now is the time to formalize your plans, get them on paper, and determine the time and resources needed for a successful implementation of your microlearning program. The good news is that you can take the same approach for the rollout and communication plan for your microlearning program as you would for any other learning program.

PRO TIP

Often, as you implement training, you are also creating a change for the organization. With that in mind, you should seek feedback as you develop and implement the plan—ask learners and leaders if they think this training will be useful. Getting their buy-in early and often will make a big difference in garnering support for your program. We discussed this in chapter 1, but that socializing should continue from when you have an initial vision for your microlearning program all the way through its launch.

The only caveat here in the context of microlearning is that you want to address anything about your approach that may seem "different" from typical learning programs you've created in the past. For example, if the learners will be accessing a new format or platform that they haven't before, you need to ensure they will be comfortable with that platform or format; you wouldn't want them to get frustrated by the mechanics of getting to and consuming the resource. And consider any logistics that may be different from what they are used to, like the program being optional, or if they will be expected to discuss the content in team meetings or in one-on-one meetings with their manager.

As trainers, we often implement the learning resources and then think we're done. But for your training to really have an impact, you need to consider how that new way of working will integrate into existing behaviors. In these situations you may also want to consider guidance from the field of change management.

RESOURCES

There are lots of great change management models. If you don't have one you follow, we like to use the ADKAR model from Prosci, which states that you must have five things in place for any change to stick (Hiatt 2006):

- Awareness of the need for change.
- Desire to support or participate in the change.
- Knowledge of how to change.
- Ability to demonstrate the needed skills and behaviors for the change.
- Reinforcement to make the change stick.

Most important, these build on one another, so you need to have the first in place before going on to the second, and so on.

MILE Step 5: Monitor, Modify, and Evaluate

As we've said before, microlearning allows you to be agile, so monitoring and modifying is important to a successful microlearning program. That gets us to evaluation, which is the focus of our next chapter.

What's Next?

Once you've implemented your curated or created microlearning resources, or started your crowdsourcing community, it's easy to think you're done. But now it's time to look at how successful the program was. Did it meet the objectives? Is there anything that needs to be modified or changed to make any single resource or the entire program more successful? This sort of evaluation is the focus of MILE step 5, and the next chapter.

Questions to Explore

- What are the performance objectives of your microlearning program?
- How is the performance objective reflected in each of your microlearning resources?

- Does *every* microlearning resource have a clear objective?
- What technology will you use to distribute your microlearning resources? If it's new technology, how will you support your learners and managers in using this new technology?
- What is the optimal format for each of your microlearning resources: text-based, e-learning, video, infographic, podcast, or some combination of these?
- How will you generate your learning materials? Will you curate, create, or crowdsource?
- How will you ensure that learners know your resources exist and that they remember to use them at their moment of need?
- Does your training relate to a change for the learner? If so, are the learners aware of the need to change and have a desire to change? If not, how will you use change management strategies to ensure that this is in place to enable your training to be successful?

Tools for Support

The MILE Model Job Aid

Use this worksheet to help you design a microlearning resource or program.

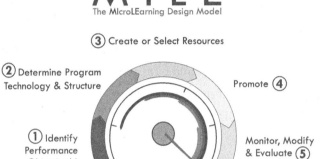

MILE Model Step	Things to Consider	My Notes

1. Identify Performance Objective(s)	• How will this microlearning content be used?
	  » Preparation before a learning event
	  » Follow-up to support a learning event
	  » Stand-alone training
	  » Performance support
	• Who will use this learning content? (Who is the intended audience?)
	• What will people be able to do differently because of this microlearning content?
	• If you have a large performance objective, what are the enabling objectives?
	• How will you keep the learning content for each enabling objective focused on performance?	

MILE Model Step	Things to Consider	My Notes

2. Determine Program Technology and Structure	• What microlearning formats are likely to work best to achieve your performance objective(s)?
	  » Text-based resources
	  » E-learning
	  » Video
	  » Infographics
	  » Podcasts
	• Given the formats you want to use and the audience who will use them, what is the best technology to distribute the microlearning resources?
	  » What constraints does that technology have, and would those constraints cause you to choose a different technology or a different approach?	

3. Create or Select Resources	• Identify one (or more) resource(s) for each enabling objective. • Use the 3 Cs: Curate, create, or crowdsource your content for those objectives. • If curating: Identify the resources you will link to. • If creating: Identify the format and key content points. Then build the microlearning resource(s), having only one objective per resource. • If curating: Create one or more discussion topics or questions per objective. • As you create or curate, ask yourself: What are the most critical thing(s) to being able to do this behavior?	

4. Promote	• Implement the resources as you planned in step 2.
	• Tell your audience about these resources, using as many communication channels as possible.
	• Remember:
	  » If they don't know it exists, they can't use it.
	  » If they don't remember it exists, they won't use it.	

5. Monitor, Modify, and Evaluate	• Regularly review your quantitative and qualitative data.
	  » Monitor usage, comments, likes, shares, and any other data you have.
	  » Use this data to revise the resource(s) as needed.
	• If curating: Validate links on a regular schedule.
	• If creating: Update, replace, or add to resources as needed to keep the content current and accurate.
	• If crowdsourcing: Participate in the community on a regular basis.
	• Consider both the ROI (return on investment) and ROE (return on expectations) of your resource(s).	

Ways You Can Distribute Microlearning Content

Use this tool to consider the variety of ways you can distribute microlearning content and the pros and cons of each.

Learning Management System (LMS)

Some you may have heard of: Moodle, SumTotal, Workday, Cornerstone, Desire2Learn, and Docebo.

An Example

Frank's organization uses an LMS to house all their learning content. Employees are assigned content; they log in to the LMS and are marked "complete" when they finish a course or resource.

Pros

Easy to track if and when people are accessing the content. Also easy to send automated emails to remind people to complete assigned courses.

Cons

It can be difficult for people to find content at their moment of need. If the person can self-assess and realize they need help, they probably won't seek that help from the LMS because most LMSs have weak interfaces and search capabilities. As Josh Bersin (2019) says, these systems "were never designed to be employee-centric. They were developed as 'Management' systems for learning."

Social Collaborative System

Some people call this "Facebook for work."

Some you may have heard of: Yammer and Jive; some also use SharePoint in this way.

An Example

Mary's organization uses a social collaborative system that enables employees to post questions and comments to each other, much like on Facebook and LinkedIn. Each corporate team also has a page where they can share content about themselves, much like a corporate Facebook page. The corporate university team uses their page to post information about upcoming programs, and to provide links to learning content.

Pros

It's easy for peers to share their favorite resources. Sharing resources among peers can be very effective because the people who are doing the job know what resources help them the most.

Corporate teams can make pages that function like websites or portals, enabling them to share a variety of content formats, organized in ways that are more user-friendly than an LMS.

Cons

It's hard to make your content stand out, and for users to find your content later. The life span of content on a social collaborative system is shorter, which can inhibit use of that content.

Learning Experience Platform (LXP)

Some people call this the "Netflix of learning."

Some you may have heard of: Degreed, Pathgather (acquired by Degreed), EdCast, and Valamis.

An Example
Michael's organization uses an LXP to share learning content. Employees can log in and search for the topics that they want to learn about. They start to create a personalized profile of content they have consumed, which then enables the system to recommend other content that they are likely to find useful. Employees can also follow other employees so they can consume the same content as others they respect. Michael finds that this system supports their microlearning efforts well because the content can be provided in very small pieces to support informal learning needs in the organization.

Pros
This is a good way to share content if you have the right logic and data to identify those people for whom each piece of content will be useful.

Cons
It can be challenging to get people to consume informal learning content because they focus on their operational duties as their first priority. Sometimes learning needs to be required for people to make time for it.

Email

An Example
After a one-hour VILT class is over, Jessica sends a series of follow-up emails to the participants. Every week for a month following the class, Jessica sends a short email focusing on a different topic from the class that she wants to reinforce.

Pros
Nearly every employee has access to email, and many of them have access on a variety of devices.

Cons
Messages sent by email can easily be lost in our crowded inboxes. The average office worker receives 121 emails per day (Campaign Monitor 2019)! And people that don't have desk jobs may only look at their email a few times per week. Employees' inboxes are noisy and crowded, and as a result, many emails are never even opened.

Paper Handouts (Physical)

An Example
Paul designs a half-day program on delivering exceptional customer service. In the class he teaches a four-step model for de-escalating an angry customer. Paul provides this four-step model on a small card that can be used during role plays in class, and then placed on the employee's desk to glance at any time an angry customer is encountered.

Pros
If you're using paper handouts, it's usually for content you expect the learner to refer back to later. These are generally performance support materials. If that support content is perceived as valuable reference material, the learner will hang it in their cube or keep it somewhere that they will be able to reference it easily. Seeing a job aid hanging on a cube wall is the holy grail for a piece of performance support, because then we know the learner is expecting to use it often!

Cons

Most paper resources get "filed" somewhere and never accessed again. Even if the learner remembers your resource exists, they will forget where they put it and still won't use that performance support at their moment of need.

This is the main reason people tend to go digital with such resources, sending a PDF handout instead of paper.

PDFs (Digital)

An Example

Kim's organization has accounting software for tracking customer invoices and payments. To help employees use this software well, Kim has electronic documents with screenshots that walk people through the most common or difficult tasks in the software.

Pros

PDF documents can be used for nearly any kind of content, from something you want the learner to read one time before a class, all the way to something they will refer to daily on the job.

The biggest benefit of providing resources digitally like this is that they can be hosted on a platform or filed on the user's computer and found more easily than paper resources.

Cons

Files are searchable, so the learner can find them more easily than paper handouts, but these files can still be hard to find in all the places we store our digital materials—especially now that many organizations have an LMS, an LXP, and a social collaborative system, not to mention all the shared network spaces where they store files too.

Also, digital resources can't be glanced at on the fly like a paper job aid hanging in someone's cube.

Posters

An Example

Daniel's organization is hyper-focused on cybersecurity. Daniel offers an e-learning module on the topic, but he knows that will do little to change ingrained behaviors.

So he creates posters that are hung in the hallways and break areas that remind employees of the top five cybersecurity threats and what employees can do to prevent them. These posters are planned to be up for an entire year. Daniel knows the posters will have more conscious recognition at the start of the campaign, and they will not be noticed as much over time, but those posters will continue to have a subtle impact, reminding employees every day as they walk down the hallway to their desks.

Pros

If you have something you want people to keep top of mind, then well-placed posters in the work environment are very valuable. This can fit with a boosting campaign or a longer-term change management effort.

Cons

Instructional designers tend to either not think of doing posters, or, when they do, they put too much content on them!

Our biggest advice is to partner with someone from your marketing department for help in doing this well. This can be as simple as a conversation over a cup of coffee, all the way to a complete partnership of work effort.

You also have to be very strategic with what content will be in your poster campaign. The posters may hang for months, so you must be promoting your most important content.

Notification Systems

Some you may have heard of: Axonify or Qstream (these provide pop-up questions on user login); Mobile Coach (sends regular text messages to the learner); or any app that can also send push notifications to a learner's phone.

An Example

Ashley works for a major retailer, and it has a lot of turnover in their sales associates, not to mention the additional part-time staff that are added during busy holiday seasons.

It's critical to ensure that those staff know what to do in safety situations that could put the staff or the public in harm, like what to do if the elevator stops working, if a parent reports a lost child, or if a customer becomes violent. No matter how new the employee is, the store wants certain behaviors and thinking to become automatic, particularly in response to safety situations.

Ashley's team is using a tool on their POS (point of sale) terminal so that a few times each week, when the employee first logs in at the start of their shift, they have to answer three quick questions. For each question, they get points for correct responses, along with very targeted feedback.

There are also leaderboards so store associates can see how they are doing compared with other associates. At the end of the quarter, the top 10 scoring employees get a gift card for the store.

One of the best ways to reinforce learning is through spaced repetition, and suppliers in this space have data showing impressive outcomes with their products. Many also have gamification elements like leaderboards that keep engagement high.

Pros

This will work extremely well for topics that the learner needs to keep top of mind, like compliance topics or sales product details. It's not as good for topics where you don't know if the topic will have relevance to the learner at that time, like having difficult conversations and other management topics.

Cons

There can be organizational issues here. Your learners will need to be comfortable with the idea that one or two times each week they will have questions to answer, either when they log in to their computer at the start of their day, or as a pop-up on their mobile device or via text message.

Of course, texting our employees has particular challenges because people generally see texting as something they do with friends and family, not their employer. And for hourly employees there's the added challenge of ensuring we are not texting them outside of their normal work hours (which can be especially challenging with part-time and shift workers).

Also, if you are sending pop-ups or text messages to an employee's cell phone, there are additional issues regarding whether the employee is using a company-issued phone. Generally, use of an employee's cell phone for these kinds of tasks works best if the employee opts in, so they can chose whether to participate with their personal phone.

If you have all those logistical issues addressed, then the idea of such a system can be tantalizing. But the questions you ask employees must be focused on the most important content, and generally questions should be about topics that are highly relevant to the learner. Large organizations who set these systems up well run the risk of having "everyone" wanting their content in the platform too. Then you can have trouble ensuring that only the most relevant and high-value content will be sent to the learner.

Software Help Systems

Some you may have heard of: WalkMe and Assima.

An Example

Steven's organization uses a sophisticated electronic medical records system in their healthcare clinics and hospitals. Anytime the learner is stuck, they can click a help menu in the software and get customized support based on where they are in the software. In addition, for all major tasks that are performed in the software, when the learner uses the help menu, they can chose to watch a brief video of the task being done, or they can read a page with step-by-step instructions and screenshots.

Pros

Software support is a classic example of an electronic performance support system (EPSS). While using the software, the learner can click the "help" menu and get specific help in the software. Depending on the platform, that help may already be targeted to their need, based on their most recent clicks in the software.

Certainly, the biggest advantage here is that while using software, the learner is easily able to self-assess (that is, they know immediately when things aren't working), and the system can provide help that is incredibly targeted to their need.

Cons

There really is no disadvantage to using this, except that it's limited to only being used with software systems.

Also, if the software system is mission critical or accesses a lot of confidential data, your organization may not allow you to install custom help materials in the system itself. For security purposes, the organization may insist that the training materials be hosted outside the live system.

Website or App

An Example

Dorothy's organization has a number of job aids, courses, and other support resources that are specific to the needs of each of their different departments. She sets up a separate webpage for each department, with those resources that are most relevant to the staff on that team.

Pros

Creating your own website or app is one of the most flexible ways to deliver your content.

Cons

You have to have programming skills and interface design skills to create such a portal. You may also need to program any tracking or search functionality yourself and find a server on which to host your site.

Ultimately, the effort involved to create a custom website or portal is often not worth it, which is why so many people will use an LMS, a social collaborative system, or an LXP to do this task.

Rollout and Communication Considerations

Consider the following questions when building your rollout and communication plan.

- Who is your target audience for these materials?
- How will they access the microlearning?
- Is the format new, or already familiar?
- Is the content related to a change for the learners?
- What new technology may need to be addressed—both from a communication and a logistics perspective?
- How will learners communicate any technical issues? Will they go to the IT help desk, directly to you, to their manager, or somewhere else?
- Who will help you troubleshoot any technical issues? Are they ready and available pre-rollout? During rollout?
- How will managers be informed of the microlearning program? Do they need any additional context or support ahead of the learners? Should they complete the training to be able to best support their employees?

References and Additional Resources

Allen, M. 2016. *Michael Allen's Guide to e-Learning: Building Interactive, Fun, and Effective Learning Programs for Any Company.* Hoboken, NJ: Wiley.

Allen, M., and R. Sites. 2012. *Leaving ADDIE for SAM: An Agile Model for Developing the Best Learning Experiences.* Alexandria, VA: ASTD Press.

Bersin, J. 2019. "Learning Experience Platform (LXP) Market Grows Up: Now Too Big to Ignore." Josh Bersin blog, March 8. joshbersin.com/2019/03/learning-experience -platform-lxp-market-grows-up-now-too-big-to-ignore.

Campaign Monitor. 2019. "The Shocking Truth About How Many Emails Are Sent." May 21. campaignmonitor.com/blog/email-marketing/2019/05/shocking-truth -about-how-many-emails-sent.

DeMers, J. 2014. "20 Sticky Features Your Website Needs to Convert Visitors." *Forbes*, July 29. forbes.com/sites/jaysondemers/2014/07/29/20-sticky-features-your-website -needs-to-convert-visitors.

Hiatt, J.M. 2006. *ADKAR: A Model for Change in Business, Government and Our Community.* Loveland, CO: Prosci Learning Center Publications.

Nielsen, J. 2006. "The 90-9-1 Rule for Participation Inequality in Social Media and Online Communities." Nielsen Norman Group, October 8. nngroup.com/articles /participation-inequality.

Torgerson, C. 2016. *The Microlearning Guide to Microlearning.* Torgerson Consulting.

Torrance, M. 2019. *Agile for Instructional Designers: Iterative Project Management to Achieve Results.* Alexandria, VA: ATD Press.

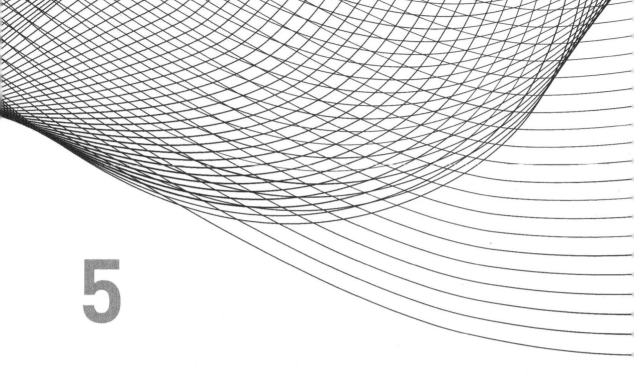

5

Transferring Learning and Evaluating Results: How Do You Demonstrate Success?

In This Chapter

- How to approach the measurement of your microlearning efforts
- Metrics that align best to measuring microlearning
- Examples of microlearning evaluation

The final step of the MILE model is to monitor, modify and evaluate. Monitor the learning resources and the overall program, use what you learn to modify the resources or program over time, and evaluate their effectiveness. One of the challenges every learning professional encounters when designing a learning solution is, "How do I measure success?" This question is an interesting one. Learning professionals are very aware of the importance of measurement, and you can probably rattle off all the reasons you should measure the effectiveness of a learning solution. At the same time, this may be the most difficult behavior for learning professionals to initiate.

Depending on the complexity of any given learning resource or program, it could be relatively easy to figure out its impact, or it could be quite challenging. There are a number of resources out there on measurement and evaluation, and many offer good guidance on the philosophy of measurement as well as some really cool formulas you can use to determine whether your solution hit the mark.

Learning professionals understand and appreciate the value of measuring a program's success. When done correctly, it demonstrates the effectiveness of the learning resources, reveals acquisition of knowledge or skills, and, in the best cases, shows business impact. But according to ATD's 2016 report *Evaluating Learning: Getting to Measurements That Matter*, only 35 percent of training and development professionals reported that their organizations evaluated the business results of learning programs to any extent.

Why is this? One of the biggest challenges is that it can take a lot of effort to determine what to measure and how to measure it, collect and analyze data, determine actionable next steps, and communicate the outcomes to stakeholders. For many in the training field, the fun part is building the learning solution, not necessarily figuring out how to measure it. Without examples that are relevant to specific job roles and industries, it can be difficult to take measurement techniques and apply them

RESOURCES

Want to read more on how our industry uses evaluation? Check out ATD's research reports *Evaluating Learning: Getting to Measurements That Matter* (2016) and *Effective Evaluation: Measuring Learning Programs for Success* (2019).

to a learning professional's own situation. To complicate measurement further, there are many factors beyond training that can both positively and negatively affect a learner's ability to perform on the job.

There is good news for learning professionals who find measurement and evaluation to be difficult or even daunting. Because the best microlearning resources are "singularly focused"—meaning they tackle one performance need at a time—it can make the evaluation of its effectiveness much simpler.

Where to Start

The best place to start is to think about why you are creating this piece of microlearning in the first place. What are you trying to achieve? Going back to the starting point and reflecting on what triggered the need for microlearning should reveal the answer. Are you trying to solve a performance gap, remind learners of a critical job task, or introduce something new? In earlier chapters we stressed the importance of understanding the goal for the program. Now you need to revisit that goal and ask if you were successful in achieving it.

As mentioned in chapter 1, the task of measuring and evaluating success should be considered, developed, and included in your initial plan for microlearning. If you did your homework when getting started, you should have a clear vision of what your learners need and what leadership is expecting. You don't need to overthink things at that early planning step, but you absolutely must know what you hope to achieve with the program—if you don't know your expectations for the program, you'll never know if you achieved them.

PRO TIP

Measurement can and should be kept simple. Don't assume that you have to track all the possible data and metrics for every learning solution you implement. Most learning professionals don't have the time or resources to do this, and it would be an ineffective use of time and resources even if they did. Instead, focus on the few learning solutions that you believe will have the greatest impact for the learners and the most impact on the business. Focus on the data and metrics needed to build an accurate picture of that microlearning resource or program's success—or failure.

A properly designed microlearning resource focuses on a single learning or performance objective. As a result, its evaluation can be kept simple. In fact, its evaluation should be kept simple. How? A good way to start thinking about how to measure the success of your microlearning is to reflect on the following questions:

- **What am I trying to achieve with this microlearning resource?** Think about the specific performance need you are trying to address. Is it a high-stakes performance gap, or a low-stakes one?

- **How important is it to measure the effectiveness of this specific microlearning resource?** Think about the intended impact of the resource. Will this address a critical performance need that can improve a business outcome? Measure it! Will it ensure learners are prepared for attending a live event? Maybe it's not necessary or worth the time and effort to measure this.

- **How critical is the job task or skill that the microlearning resource will support?** If it's extremely important for learners to get it right, you may want to consider a Level 4 evaluation or a return on investment (ROI) assessment. (We discuss the Kirkpatrick and the Phillips methodologies later in this chapter.) If the task is not so critical, then learner feedback may be all that's needed.

- **What kind of metrics will be useful, and why? Which metrics will stakeholders be interested in?** It's easy to get "metric madness" when thinking about all the possible metrics you could collect. Because microlearning focuses on a discrete performance need, it makes good sense to focus the metrics on only those that relate to the performance need—and nothing more. But before you decide, it's also wise to consider the type of metrics your stakeholders will want, if any. In later sections, we will explore the different types of metrics you can use to gather data in more detail.

- **Does the organization have the capability to capture those metrics? What tools or platforms are in place to capture metrics and data?** There are all kinds of tools and platforms to leverage the collection of data. These range from survey tools, social media–type elements such as likes and shares, and of course your LMS. We can also consider an EPSS and the experience application programming interface (xAPI), which expand the type and level of tracking we can do of a learner's digital footprint.

What Should Be Measured?

It is usually not necessary to measure every single learning resource you create, and the same holds true for microlearning. Microlearning can present a provocative question: Because a lot of it is informal learning—that is, not required—should microlearning be measured and evaluated? If it's not mandatory, why bother to measure it? Learning professionals are used to measuring formal learning. When compared with informal learning, formal learning is mandatory, requires more of an employee's time, and may require more budget, so measuring it ensures that the training is effective and meets the needs of the business. Even though formal learning suggests formal measurement, it's important to remember that good informal learning is also designed with performance objectives to help the learners improve in some way, and measurement can and should be considered.

The answer to "What microlearning should be measured?" needs to be addressed in two parts. First, we will review types of measurement metrics and techniques, and then we will address measurement in terms of the different ways that microlearning is used.

Types of Data

There are multiple types of data you can use to measure and evaluate learning. This section reviews several options and provides key considerations when implementing a microlearning resource or program. Many of these terms may already be familiar to you, but here we want to review the concepts that are already well-known in the industry and then relate them to measuring microlearning.

Both quantitative and qualitative metrics can be informative and useful when measuring the effectiveness of microlearning content. Quantitative metrics provide the "hard data": the numbers and information that can be summed up, averaged, or manipulated in other ways to provide a numerical view of effectiveness. Quantitative data are usually straightforward and generally objective. For example, metrics can be gathered on the number of times a new microlearning resource was accessed—a new microlearning job aid implemented to an audience of 100 learners and accessed 100 times could be viewed as successful. If this same microlearning resource was accessed 500 times by 100 unique learners, the rate of success is even higher.

On the other hand, qualitative data provides the rich "color commentary" about the learners' experience, where descriptions and details can be gathered. Qualitative data are often subjective in nature, because the individual learners are providing descriptions of their experience—or their managers are describing their performance.

Ideally, you should capture and analyze both types of data to build the clearest picture of the success of your microlearning efforts.

Quantitative Measurement

Quantitative metrics tend to be easier to collect and can provide enough data to form some conclusions about the success of your microlearning resource or program. Usage rates are one type of quantitative metric that can begin to reveal if the learners found a new microlearning resource valuable. Data on the number of downloads, number of times accessed, and number of page views are often quantitative measures. Each of these alone may not be enough, but when analyzed holistically they can start to tell an interesting story about the success of your microlearning content.

While considering usage rates is valid for several reasons and is recommended, it's still akin to marketing counting "eyeballs" compared with sales counting revenue. In other words, measuring usage tells you how helpful or interesting learners perceived a resource to be, but that usage may not correlate with the actual behavior change you are looking for, or what the business cares about.

Some additional examples of quantitative metrics that could be used with microlearning resources include:

- usage rates over time
- number of total views
- number of unique items viewed per person
- number of repeated views per person
- time spent viewing pages
- number of likes and shares
- badges earned
- scores.

When you capture metrics such as usage rates over time, the picture of how useful people found your resources becomes clearer and validated to a certain extent.

There is a potential "next level" of quantitative metrics—those that are related to your business outcomes. For example, the metrics noted previously show usage. They answer the questions, "Did learners complete the training?" and "Did they refer to it over time or when it was needed?" But the most valuable quantitative metrics can be the ones that show us the behavior change back on the job. These metrics may include:

- reduction in customer complaints
- change in speed of task execution
- increase in sales or market share
- increase in sales conversion or product adoption.

PRO TIP

Quantitative data are great for telling you if a program worked. But those data are more than just evaluative—they can help you course-correct too. For example, if you discover that one resource within a microlearning program wasn't used much you may want to find out why it wasn't used, or just remove it from the library of resources. Similarly, if a particular video resource was often replayed from 2:34 to 2:57 you will want to find out if that part was confusing—or extremely helpful.

As we've mentioned several times in this book, we believe that going micro will enable you to be more agile and responsive because the resources are short and it's easy to change or remove them. But those ideals are only attainable if you have the data to support your efforts. If you don't know how the resources are used, you have little ability to revise your resources or program in a thoughtful way.

Qualitative Measurement

While quantitative data provide numbers, facts, and figures, it's the qualitative data that usually bring the picture of success or failure to life. There are several types of qualitative data that could be captured, depending on the specific type of microlearning implemented, including:

- testimonials and anecdotes from learners or their managers
- testimonials and anecdotes from customers
- responses to surveys
- interviews
- case studies.

With microlearning, the best kinds of qualitative data are rich with descriptions of how the learners were successful after they completed the microlearning resource or program. When designing your microlearning, think about the descriptive data that would help to communicate the success of the microlearning to your learners and stakeholders.

PRO TIP

Qualitative data can be very time-consuming to collect and analyze. To lighten this burden, people sometimes use Likert scale surveys, which give them data that are easier to parse and report. While these surveys are quantitative, they feel more qualitative because they categorize subjective data while providing some level of quantitative understanding of the program.

For example, you could have a survey where you ask people if they feel more confident in their skills after completing the training. By having a five-point scale that people respond with, you can easily report numbers like "82 percent of people agree or strongly agree that they feel more confident in their skills after completing the training." These sorts of survey data can be a nice middle ground for those who want to collect qualitative data but don't have the time to invest in interviews and focus groups.

Data Collection Methods

Now that we've reviewed the different types of data you may want to collect about your microlearning resources or programs, let's consider the different ways you can capture them. The good news is that technology has come a long way, and there are a lot of digital ways to capture data versus doing a manual collection.

- **Surveys.** Who doesn't like a survey? Of course, we know a lot of people get annoyed when asked to complete a survey; the key to getting the learners to complete it is to keep it short. Given that a microlearning resource is focused on one performance objective, your survey should be limited to a few brief questions. For example, "On a scale of 1 to 5, how helpful was this training to you in completing this new job task?" A good general rule is that your survey should take less time to complete than your microlearning resource! The exception would be if you are surveying your learners after they complete an entire microlearning program—because it has more components, here it's OK to ask more questions.

- **Interviews.** These are a great way to capture qualitative data from a selection of learners (it's usually not practical or worth your time to interview all the learners who completed the microlearning). If you have the opportunity to do interviews, you can gather rich qualitative data that can be difficult to extract from a survey. Don't forget the manager when conducting interviews—they provide a unique perspective if they have been able to observe the employees back on the job for the objective for which you implemented microlearning. By the way, some of the best interviews Sue conducted while working in a corporate environment were informal—she would talk to learners during sales meetings or managers in the lunchroom to gather intel about training. When drafting your interview questions, consider open-ended ones like, "What did you think of the training?" "Tell me about how you accessed the content." "What was most helpful back on the job?" "Can you give me an example of why you thought it was helpful?"

- **EPSS, LMS, social collaborative systems, LXP, learning record store (LRS), and other content distribution and data collection platforms.** These tools are great for deploying your microlearning and are usually great for capturing the quantitative data discussed in the previous section. While many learning professionals are well versed in the functionality of implementing training with these platforms, it's not always clear what kind of back-end metrics are available. If you aren't sure, it's a good idea to talk to the supplier or your IT partners to find out exactly what kind of data and reports you can get.

- **Business reports.** Is your microlearning resource or program expected to have a critical impact on a specific business objective? If so, think about business reports generated by other functions such as sales, marketing, or customer service. For example, if your microlearning resource was designed as a stand-alone training to help field technicians fix a crucial equipment error, are there data tracked by customer service that showed a reduction in callbacks about this specific equipment malfunction where the technician had to come out a second (or more) time?

Using xAPI

No conversation about measuring microlearning would be complete without a discussion about xAPI (also known as the Experience API or Tin Can). xAPI is an e-learning specification that enables you to collect data about a wide range of experiences a person has during formal and informal training activities. It also enables you to correlate that with performance data. Many call xAPI the next version of SCORM. (SCORM is used to store learner data in an LMS.) While SCORM allows you to track which courses have been opened or completed and perhaps a score from a test at the end of the module, xAPI allows you to track so much more and stores the data in an LRS (learning record store).

PRO TIP

An EPSS can be used to implement microlearning in the flow of work. An EPSS helps the user complete a certain task in a guided way, providing just-in-time help as the user is working through the job task. A common example of an EPSS is the help embedded in those programs you can use to complete and file your taxes; on-screen support is readily available to help you at every step of the process.

An EPSS can include data that you can use to measure your microlearning, such as knowing which pieces of help were used, for how long, and even if the user's subsequent actions (such as use of the software) showed increased proficiency as a result. You can track what help the learners use and how they use it, whether it's an interactive text with steps and buttons, a simulation, or just a text-based support article. The closer learners are to the moment of need, the more they need this sort of just-in-time help. EPSS helps with this, brokering the right pieces of performance support for the exact need of the learner at that moment, and often collecting valuable data as well.

Some things you can track with xAPI include:

- usage data, including the number of views, likes, or shares
- learning experience data, like where they pause an e-learning program, scrub a video (slide the playback bar to advance quickly through the video), or stop out (where they exited the resource—for example, what page of the PDF or time of the video they reached when they stopped using it); you can even track things like what browser they are using, what time of day they're accessing your materials, for how long, and so on.

You can use these data to learn which of your resources people found most helpful, or if a lot of people stop out at the same spot, you can consider why. For example, we know of a training team that provided support for a piece of software used to do mission-critical work in a high-pressure environment. Under the help menu they offered three different lengths of each of their software tutorials (five minutes, eight minutes, and 12 minutes), each offering a different depth of explanation of the features. They found the following:

- 5-minute video tutorials: Nearly 100 percent of people who started the videos completed them.
- 8-minute video tutorials: Almost 80 percent of people who started the videos completed them.

- 12-minute video tutorials: Less than 20 percent of people who started the videos completed them.

With these data they could look at where in a 12-minute video people stopped to see if there were patterns in the stop-out point. However, in this case, the early stop-out was a consistent pattern found across multiple video topics, so they assumed that people preferred the shorter videos while trying to do such mission-critical tasks. Armed with this knowledge, they tried to make all future tutorials five minutes or less, and never longer than eight minutes.

RESOURCES

xAPI is still an emerging standard, but there is a lot of excitement for what's possible and how these kinds of data will influence the profession. If you are interested in learning more about xAPI, you should follow Megan Torrance's work. Visit her website at TorranceLearning.com/xapi.

Combining With HR Data

Where xAPI gets more exciting is when you combine these data with HR data, such as the person's role, geographic location, and number of years in role. Now you can segment your data so you can learn what resources one group finds helpful compared with another group.

For example, although hypothetical, the organization in the previous example might have found that the 20 percent of people who watched the 12-minute videos to the end were mostly technicians who needed that detail. The organization could then look at the overall data and see that the majority of technicians who used the tutorials consumed the 12-minute version, and that 90 percent of those technicians completed the 12-minute video. This tells a more nuanced story than knowing that less than 20 percent of people completed the 12 minute video; it tells you that the 12-minute version was helpful, but only to a specific subgroup. While the organization may continue to aim to provide videos that are no more than five minutes long for their general learner population, they may create longer videos just for technicians.

Combining With Performance Data

Things get most exciting when you combine these data with performance data. Now you can look at things like:

- Of my top-performing sellers, which microlearning resources did they access? Were there any that they stopped out of, and if so, where did stop-outs generally occur? Are there any of these resources that my lowest-performing sellers did not access? (This could tell you about any topics that less skilled people are not considering, but are perceived as valuable by those who have stronger performance.)

- Of the people with the lowest customer service skills, which microlearning resources did they consume (and to what level of completion), and was there a lift in their customer service skills after a few months?

Measurement and Evaluation Models

When thinking about measuring your microlearning resource or program, the good news is that you can use the models with which you are probably already familiar. The following models provide a range of options to consider based on what you need to evaluate.

The Kirkpatrick Model

The Kirkpatrick Model is an effective one to use when evaluating microlearning. Kirkpatrick's four levels of evaluation are widely used in the training and development arena, and they can be applied to microlearning resources and programs—both informal and formal. The levels provide an easy way to align the learning goals to learner outcomes relative to learning and performance expectations:

- Level 1: Reaction—how the learners react to the training (for example, satisfaction)
- Level 2: Learning—the learner's acquisition of knowledge and skill
- Level 3: Behavior—the learner's performance back on the job
- Level 4: Results—the degree to which business needs are met as a result of the training.

RESOURCES

Few authors in the learning field have the staying power of the Kirkpatrick family. Several books are available to learn more about the four levels of evaluating training and how to apply the levels back on the job. Here are two:
- *Implementing the Four Levels: A Practical Guide for Effective Evaluation of Training Programs* by Donald Kirkpatrick
- *Kirkpatrick's Four Levels of Training Evaluation* by James D. Kirkpatrick and Wendy Kayser Kirkpatrick.

All levels of the Kirkpatrick model can be used to measure the success of microlearning. The key is to choose the level and associated techniques that align with the specific objective of the microlearning resource or program. For example, it's most likely not necessary to use all four levels to measure a single microlearning resource. It would take too much time and too many resources. Our advice is to go to the highest level in the model that aligns to the objective of the microlearning resource. For example, if the microlearning is focused on the learner executing a very specific job task, and you are able to capture metrics on results, then measure to Level 4. If results would be too difficult to isolate or acquire, Level 3 might be more realistic.

CASE STUDY: MEASURE TO LEVEL 3 OR LEVEL 4?

A new fabrication machine is added to the shop floor of a textile manufacturer. While the machine operators have attended formal training on how to operate the machine, there is one task that requires multiple steps and is proving to be somewhat challenging, mainly because it is completed only once a week, and it's difficult to remember. To assist the machine operators with this specific task during the moment of need, you create a piece of microlearning—a three-minute video tutorial that can be accessed on a smartphone.

Level 3 metrics can be identified and tracked (for example, successful operation and completion of the task, more timely completion of the task, fewer errors in textile outputs related to the task, and number of times the microlearning was viewed now and over time). These are good metrics that demonstrate behavior change, but can you—and should you—measure Level 4 (the impact on the business)? If this microlearning resource addressed a critical new task that improved the operational effectiveness of the machine and led to shortened time to production, reduced work pauses to operate the machine, and increased profitability due to time saved, then yes! Level 4 results in this case could be demonstrated by all the metrics mentioned. But if the task doesn't have a clear connection to a specific business result, it's OK to measure only to Level 3.

Brinkerhoff's Success Case Method

Everyone loves to hear success stories! Brinkerhoff's Success Case Method (SCM) is designed to focus on identifying extreme examples of learning success—the most and least successful case studies or participants in a learning program.

SCM can be particularly helpful when defining success for microlearning, because it focuses on the learners who are achieving success after using the resource or program. The key is to be able to identify these learners as early as possible, capture their success, and identify how they used the training to achieve that success. This is particularly valuable when microlearning is used as informal learning, because successes can be shared and potentially drive more use and confidence with other learners. It can also give you invaluable qualitative data to share with leaders about the usefulness of the program.

While SCM usually focuses on specific cases, and may not be a representation of the entire pool of learners, best practices are often gleaned from successful use cases. Imagine you created a new stand-alone microlearning resource for sales representatives to address a very difficult customer objection. When you identify and interview even just one salesperson who achieved success, you will feel great hearing their story and their passion when they explain how well the resource helped them move their business forward with a very important customer. Not only will you feel great, but stakeholders will be glad to hear it too. On the flip side, a disastrous case study can highlight the need to make some additional changes if your solution did not hit the mark.

RESOURCES

The five steps of Brinkerhoff's Success Case Method include:
1. Focus and plan a success case study.
2. Create an "impact model" that defines what success should look like.
3. Design and implement a survey to search for best and worst cases.
4. Interview and document success cases.
5. Communicate findings, conclusions, and recommendations.

To learn more, browse articles and publications on the Brinkerhoff Evaluation Institute website: brinkerhoffevaluationinstitute.com/publications.html.

The Phillips ROI Methodology

Most learning professionals want to show that their efforts produce a return on investment (ROI). However, as discussed in the beginning of this chapter, very few actually conduct this level of measurement. The focus of the ROI Methodology is to measure whether the results of the microlearning program had a monetary value that exceeded the cost of building and implementing that program. The challenge in doing this can be the isolation of the effects of the program on performance and results.

RESOURCES

Jack and Patti Phillips provide this formula for calculating the return on investment of a learning program:

$$\text{ROI } (\%) = \frac{\text{Net Program Benefits}}{\text{Program Costs}} \times 100$$

For more information about the ROI Methodology, see the Phillips's books including *ROI Basics*, 2nd edition, and *Real World Training Evaluation*.

While calculating the ROI of something as broad as a leadership retreat can prove challenging, calculating ROI on a microlearning resource or program is easier because it focuses on a discrete performance need or gap. One of the simplest ways to isolate ROI for microlearning is to have a control group that does not receive the training to observe along with the microlearning learner group. If you can identify differences between these two groups after the launch of the microlearning resource or program, then you can credibly report the Level 4 Impact and an ROI for your microlearning program.

For example, let's say a microlearning resource is created for call center representatives to address a specific customer complaint and refund request. If the microlearning resource is launched to a pilot group of learners, you could track the success of the pilot group compared with the control group by looking at the pilot group's metrics. If the pilot group demonstrates a 10 percent reduction in customers choosing to discontinue use of the product and get a refund when compared with the control group, one could say that success was achieved. To get specific, the 10 percent reduction might translate to $20,000 in product refund avoidance. Let's further assume that it cost $5,000 in staff time to develop the program and minimal learner time to consume it. To calculate the ROI you would use the formula:

$$\text{ROI} = \frac{\$20{,}000 \text{ product refund avoidance} - \$5{,}000 \text{ program costs}}{\$5{,}000 \text{ program costs}} \times 100 = 300\% \text{ ROI}$$

CASE STUDY: DEFINING THE MEASUREMENT METRICS FOR LIFE-SAVING MICROLEARNING

Jeff is a learning professional in the human resources department for a large metropolitan medical center. Jeff's director has come to him asking for training to address an important safety issue that has arisen. In the past three months, there have been two electrocutions involving workers who were attempting to change an overhead ballast in a light fixture. One of the workers was treated and survived. The other worker fell six feet off a ladder to the floor, hit his head on the floor, and died from his injuries.

Subsequent investigations determined that the medical center was missing critical policies, procedures, and training that would have helped avoid these situations. As a result, the organization was fined for OSHA violations. As new procedures are being put in place to prevent exposure to electrical hazards, Jeff addresses several training needs for maintenance workers. They include ensuring awareness of electrical hazards in the medical center, providing steps to properly prevent exposure to electrical hazards, and knowing how to "lock out/tag out" circuits to electrical equipment to ensure that other workers are safe before repairing the equipment. Jeff creates two stand-alone microlearning resources: a short video on how to properly lock out/tag out a circuit and a job aid in the form of a poster with awareness precautions. (For example, "Grab your rubber insulating gloves before you go.") The poster is hung in every maintenance closet in the center, so it is seen on a daily basis.

As Jeff thinks about why he is building these microlearning resources, the answer is very clear: It's to protect the maintenance workers from injury or even death when changing a ballast. Several metrics are needed to determine the effectiveness of the microlearning resources—tracking and confirming that all maintenance workers completed the training (which is required in this case) and ongoing use of the microlearning program (which informs Jeff that the workers may be reviewing the training just prior to conducting the lock out/tag out skill). But the ultimate reason Jeff built the microlearning was to eliminate workplace accidents related to electrical exposure hazards when changing a ballast—and that is his most important metric.

Six months later, the medical center has not experienced similar safety issues. After isolating the impact of his microlearning plan, Jeff determines it has helped the medical center avoid repeated OSHA violations and thus offered a return on investment in avoiding costs (OSHA fines).

Think about why you are implementing microlearning, and it will point you to the business metrics. This can include quantitative data such as:

- number of complaints
- number of errors
- sales-growth percentage.

If your performance need is mission critical and you can't withhold microlearning from a control group, you can compare results with the baseline of how things were before the training was implemented. Of course, if there isn't an existing problem, but the organization is introducing a new model, skill, or technique, then the preprogram data may not be relevant. In either case, consider all the success metrics identified previously in this chapter and select the ones that are most relevant to your resource or program. To help you identify the metrics for the potential uses of microlearning, see the "Microlearning Measurement Job Aid" in the Tools section at the end of this chapter.

Now that we've covered types of data, methods to collect those data, and the models for measuring and evaluating learning, let's turn to applying all of it to microlearning.

Applying Measurement to Microlearning

In chapter 1, we discussed the four areas where microlearning can be used:

- preparation before a learning event
- follow-up to support a learning event
- stand-alone training
- performance support.

In the next sections, we take a closer look at the four areas and begin to address how you can measure each.

Preparation Before a Learning Event

Microlearning can be used to prepare learners for a formal training event, such as a live classroom program. In this case, a microlearning resource is deployed to a specific cohort of learners ahead of a longer-form learning program. This content is generally related to the classroom content, but should not be duplicative. The goal here is that by doing this learning in advance, the classroom instruction can move past that content

faster. Because the performance objective is preparation, the overall measure of success is to determine whether the learners came to the live event prepared with the knowledge delivered in the microlearning resource.

For example, if new employees were given a short video introducing the mission and vision of the company, you would expect that they would have some recall of this information, or at least could demonstrate awareness of the content. In another example, a sales team about to attend a sales training session could be given an interactive infographic that introduces a new customer type and buying characteristics. Again, you would expect that they have some recall of this information when they come to class.

Depending on the learning objective of the microlearning resource and the format type, there are several types of metrics that could be considered and gathered to build a picture of success, including the number of times a resource is accessed, total time spent with a resource, or the score on a short quiz. Table 5-1 outlines examples of some pre-event microlearning resources, associated metrics, and how success can be defined.

Follow-Up to Support a Learning Event

Microlearning can also be a valuable tool when used as follow-up to a learning event, such as a live classroom program. In this instance, microlearning is implemented to directly support, reinforce, or "boost" the most important performance objectives taught in the learning event. It can serve as reinforcement or extension for a key piece of knowledge, a specific task or skill, or an important concept that is critical for the learner to retain.

Because the objective is reinforcement, the overall measure of success is how well one or more of the discrete learning or performance objectives delivered in the live program were reinforced. In contrast to the previous section, the microlearning content is taken directly from the learning event. Examples of microlearning used to follow a learning event include:

- an email to capture two new skills they learned and commit to implement
- a handout or activity debrief used during the program with the "best answers" included
- an email campaign to remind participants of key concepts they learned in class
- pulse questions to encourage retention and application of key concepts.

PRO TIP

Sometimes, when evaluating microlearning that is used as preparation before a learning event or as follow-up after a learning event, you will evaluate it as part of the entire learning program. That is, you may choose not to isolate and evaluate the microlearning as separate from the longer-form learning event and will simply evaluate the ability of the entire program (both short- and long-form learning) to achieve its intended outcomes.

Table 5-1. Examples of Measuring and Evaluating Pre-Event Microlearning

Learners	Learning Event	Learning Objective	Microlearning Resource	Success Defined	Metrics to Inform Success
New employees	New hire orientation (live)	Recognize four corporate values	90-second video	New employees can identify the four corporate values	• Number of video views • Total time spent viewing • Trainer observations
Sales team	Quarterly sales training program (live)	Identify a new customer type and buying needs	Interactive infographic	Salespeople can describe new customer characteristics and differentiate them from existing customers	• Number of downloads • Number of views • Short quiz • Trainer observations
Equipment operator	New equipment training (live)	Prepare and initialize new packaging machine	Short gamified e-learning module	Equipment operators can identify the steps to set up the new machine in the correct order	• Number of times played • Length of time played • Number of badges earned • Scores
New virtual trainers	Virtual classroom facilitation training (virtual)	Set up microphone, speaker, and webcam for optimal AV experience	3-minute video tutorial about basic troubleshooting and AV setup for participants	Virtual classes are run smoothly from a participant AV perspective	Before facilitator training: • Number of video views • Length of time spent viewing During subsequent virtual classes: • Number of AV technical difficulties experienced • Number of unresolved audio issues • Number of unresolved video issues • Amount of time spent correcting or troubleshooting AV issues for participants

Measuring the success of a post-event microlearning resource requires you to go back to the program objectives and determine whether they have been achieved. This includes considering measures like the number of times a resource was used, the length of time it was used for, the number of likes and shares of the resource, interviews and surveys with learners a month after implementation, or even performance metrics like reduced customer complaints or improved customer satisfaction scores. Table 5-2 provides some examples.

Stand-Alone Training

A microlearning resource or program can also stand on its own—that is, there is no long-form training that it supports. The resource or program is simply one or more discrete, quickly consumed learning solution. In this situation, microlearning is implemented to address a specific performance need. In the case of a single microlearning resource, the objective is one specific performance need. For a microlearning program,

a set of related performance needs is being addressed. (Remember that when you create a series of microlearning resources, each one needs to stand on its own and address a separate objective.)

Because the objective is most likely application of new skills to the job, the overall measure of success is to identify whether the performance objective or objectives have been met and, ideally, are being applied on the job. Examples of stand-alone microlearning include:

- a mini-module to highlight a new customer objection and how to handle it effectively
- a short video series, in which each video answers a "how-to" question for managers about completing performance reviews
- a short screen-capture video series, in which each video shows viewers how to do a task in the new software
- a text-based PDF with clickable pop-ups that educates sales reps on how to describe a product feature.

You can measure these in lots of ways, including number of views, length of time played, scores on interactive practice activities, number of likes and shares, learner interviews or surveys, or even performance metrics like reduced customer complaints or improved customer satisfaction scores. Table 5-3 offers examples of some stand-alone training microlearning resources, associated metrics, and how success can be defined.

Table 5-2. Examples of Measuring and Evaluating Follow-Up Microlearning

Learners	Learning Event	Learning Objective	Follow-Up Microlearning Resource	Success Defined	Metrics to Inform Success
Home appliance customer service representatives	New hire training (virtual)	Guide a customer through troubleshooting a faulty cordless vacuum cleaner	Job aid with decision-tree algorithm to remind them of what they learned in the class	Representatives can solve 90 percent of calls or chat inquiries in one attempt	• Positive feedback, likes, and shares of the job aid • Reduced percentage or number of customer complaints • Survey to customers post-interaction • Survey to representatives one month post-training
Salespeople	New hire training (live)	Address a perceived problem with an established product that they sell	Scenario-based mini e-learning module	Salespeople can choose the correct steps to handle the discussion about the perceived product shortcoming	• Number of views per unique person • Number of total views • Length of time played • Scores • Survey at end of module
Senior marketing manager	Advanced marketing training (live)	Apply two new best practices for reducing the time needed to market a new brand	List of best practices identified in the class	Marketing managers adopt at least one new best practice for their brand	• Percentage or number of managers responding to email request with their chosen best practice • Interviews with managers two months post-program • Survey with managers two months post-program

Table 5-3. Examples of Measuring and Evaluating Stand-Alone Microlearning Resources or Programs

Learners	Learning Objective	Microlearning Resources	Success Defined	Metrics to Inform Success
Remote healthcare workers in developing countries	Multiple; includes how to keep accurate data records, how to repair a kerosene refrigerator, and how to ensure consistent temperatures in refrigeration units	Platform with 35 short videos, one on each of the various topics, accessible on any device	• Healthcare workers can apply the knowledge and skills to self-selected areas of need • Reduced incidence of issues • Increased access to medicine in local countries	• Number of views per unique person • Number of total views • Number of downloads • Number of times played • Number of likes and shares • Length of time played • Quiz scores • Survey results • Testimonials
Experienced salespeople	Introduce and apply elements of a new selling philosophy	Suite of self-directed interactive PDFs, short videos, and mini e-learning modules, accessible in any order	• Salespeople adopt and apply the new selling philosophy • Sales are expanded to new customers • Sales are accelerated for existing customers	• Number of downloads • Length of time played • Scores on interactive practice activities • Number of likes and shares • Learner surveys • Customer testimonials • Salespeople testimonials • Cases using Brinkerhoff's Success Case Method • Sales-data comparison of those who adopted and those who didn't • Increased customer conversions from awareness to adoption • Shortened buying cycle with existing customers

All employees of a financial services company	All employees are able to respond to specific customer concerns about company disclosure of cybersecurity breaches	Mini e-learning module with embedded activities and links to resources	• Employees effectively address customer cybersecurity concerns • Increased confidence level of employees when handling this concern • Increased employee confidence in how corporate handles cybersecurity concerns	• Number of views per unique person • Number of total views • Length of time played • Scores • Employee survey • Decreased number of calls to service desk over time specific to this inquiry

(Note: In this table, there is no column for "Learning Event" as in the previous tables, because the microlearning resource in this case is the event.)

TOOLS

Consult the two long-form case studies in the tools section at the end of this chapter for examples of how you might measure a single stand-alone microlearning resource and a formal program of stand-alone microlearning resources. Use the reflection questions at the end to see how you might have approached similar efforts.

Performance Support

Microlearning is a great option for providing performance support. When done correctly, a microlearning resource can provide that just-in-time answer when employees need a quick refresher while back on the job. They are highly motivated to seek an answer to their problem, and they want it short and fast! Many of the examples in the previous sections could also be used as performance support. Here are a few more microlearning examples:

- a mobile app with easy-to-access information
- a laminated job aid kept at an employee's desk or workspace
- an infographic
- short video tutorials
- a short slide deck with a voice-over.

How does one tackle measuring microlearning while the learner is back on the job? In chapter 3 we introduced Conrad Gottfredson and Bob Mosher's five moments of need, which focus on gaining and sustaining effective on-the-job performance from employees and work teams. When applied, a five moments of need solution allows employees to learn while performing their jobs. Gottfredson and Mosher modified and

TOOLS

Use the "Microlearning Measurement Table" tool at the end of this chapter to plan your own measurement and evaluation efforts for whichever of the four types of microlearning you pursue. Fill in the learners, the learning event (if applicable), the learning objectives, the microlearning resource, how you'll define success, and the metrics you'll use.

validated 18 business-impact outcomes proposed by Gloria Gery in her work and aligned them to the five moments of need (Figure 5-1).

Figure 5-1. The Five Moments of Need Impact

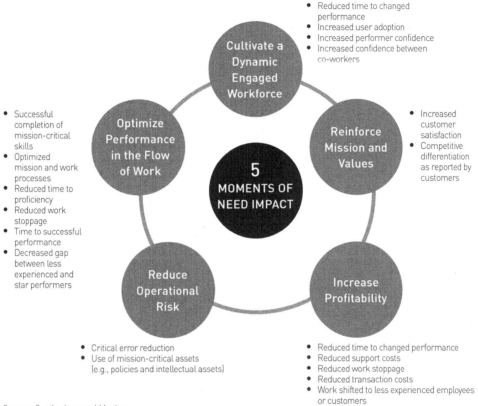

Source: Gottfredson and Mosher.

These 18 business-impact metrics are great examples of business outcomes that could be tracked and measured to see if microlearning achieved the desired effect. To do this, Gottfredson and Mosher advise using a performance support infrastructure with a fully functioning EPSS. One of the benefits is its ability to track and provide these metrics. Specifically, when imple-

RESOURCES

To learn more about measuring performance in the flow of work using business-impact metrics, read Conrad Gottfredson's article "Beyond Kirkpatrick: Measuring Performance in the Flow of Work."

menting a piece of microlearning as performance support, wouldn't you want to know if it was used more than once? This can be an indicator of success, because a resource that is accessed repeatedly implies that it is helpful to the user. Table 5-4 provides examples of microlearning used as performance support and the associated metrics to identify.

Table 5-4. Examples of Measuring and Evaluating Performance Support Microlearning

Learners	Learning Objective	Microlearning Resources	Success Defined	Metrics to Inform Success
People managers at a large software company	Address critical conversations aligned to company culture and performance management expectations	Mini e-learning modules with embedded video and branching (one per situation)	Managers quickly and effectively handle the most common critical conversations	• Number of views per unique person • Number of total views • Frequency of individual scenarios played • Length of time played • Scores • Number of likes and shares • Learner testimonials • Manager survey • Employee satisfaction survey
Employees who infrequently incur work-related expenses	Complete an entertainment-related expense report	Job aid tutorial	Employees will complete an expense report with no errors after conducting a business meal	• Number of errors in business-meal-related expense reporting • Reduction in errors for business-meal-related expense reporting • Number of expense reports flagged to revise and resubmit
New instructional designers	Apply the key characteristics of the modern learner to new projects	Interactive infographic	New instructional designers apply modern-learner concepts to new learning resources	• Number of views • Number of downloads • Learner testimonials • Audit of learning resources produced by new designers

Return on Expectations

Return on expectations (ROE) can seem so simple, yet it's often overlooked by learning professionals. Reflect on these questions when considering measuring your microlearning:

- **Did the learners proactively ask for support, resources, or training?** Sometimes we're lucky enough that the learners come to us and ask for a training resource or assistance. When learners ask for training, it implies they have a high level of motivation to complete whatever microlearning you build and implement. The learner proactively answers the WIIFM question.

- **Did leaders or stakeholders ask for it?** Here, the business has identified a need and is asking for a solution. Once you validate the need, you can build your microlearning resource. When you are thinking about the types of metrics that demonstrate the effectiveness of your microlearning, keep in mind that leaders may not be interested in every metric you can measure—they usually just want to know that it worked, and that it had a positive impact on the business.

In both cases, ask yourself what their expectations were for the program and if you met them, leaving the stakeholders satisfied with your work. ROE is about identifying learner or stakeholder expectations and then determining how well you responded to them. For example, if learners were asking for a quick fix to a performance problem, did you meet their needs quickly, even if the solution was relatively simple?

PRO TIP

ROE is really important—if people believe you are meeting their needs, then you don't need as much data to back up your measurement and evaluation. That is, you don't have to prove that the solution is helpful, because your constituents already know it themselves.

But there is an important caution here. If the focus is entirely on meeting learner expectations and those learners don't communicate their satisfaction to their leaders, then leaders won't know the program was helpful. This is especially critical with informal learning, where the focus is on providing resources the learner finds helpful at their moment of need—without knowing that learners find the resources to be helpful, leaders might cut your program.

In these cases, holding focus groups (or even just informal conversations) with learners to collect these sentiments and then sharing feedback with leaders will go a very long way. Informal learning is tricky because everyone takes it at different times, and many learners don't talk about it with their managers—it was just the resource that helped them get the job done. So it's critical to look out for and collect feedback from learners that you can share with leadership.

> ### The Data Suggest It Failed. Why?
>
> What if you analyze the data and the evidence suggests that your microlearning resource or program failed? While it's important to take a humble approach and consider that it could have been a number of things within your control, there are many other factors that can contribute to a learner's lack of performance or use of the microlearning resource you delivered.
>
> Thomas Gilbert's Behavioral Engineering Model shows that there are other factors outside training that can blunt employee performance (Chevalier 2003; Gilbert 2013). The six-box model covers the individual and environmental reasons for poor performance, along with the information, instrumentation, and motivation factors. These factors range from individual variables (such as lack of motivation due to personal issues or being placed in the wrong job) to corporate level variables (such as a misaligned performance management process or a toxic culture). Armed with this knowledge, learning professionals can determine why a microlearning resource may succeed or fail.
>
> If your microlearning fails, try to determine the root cause—it could be your approach, or it could be something larger. For example, if there is an environmental barrier such as an incentive plan that does not reward the right performance, learners may skip the microlearning resource because they believe that they will not be rewarded for adopting the new behavior.

Measuring a Microlearning Program

We have focused most of the attention in this chapter on the details of measuring a single microlearning resource. In many ways, it is theoretically easier to measure a microlearning resource compared with any other course, class, or program, simply because of the nature of a microlearning resource—it is very short and focuses on a discrete learning or performance need.

How does a learning professional measure a microlearning program—that is, a larger program comprising many microlearning resources? Of course you want to evaluate each of the individual resources (which was most viewed, which did people find most and least helpful, and so on). In addition, because the length of the overall program is longer, you can also consider some of the more traditional evaluation methods you would use for longer-form learning. For example, once someone completes a particular number of resources, you can send them a survey or interview them to get a richer understanding of their use of the whole program.

There isn't a straightforward answer to measuring a microlearning program because it depends on what you need to measure and why. But, generally speaking, it's good practice to focus on the overall effectiveness of your program as well as the effectiveness of the individual microlearning resources that comprise it. The challenge is that if the program is informal (not required), you may get some variation on completion. But, if the performance of the learners who completed the program improved when compared with those who did not, then you have a good story to tell.

Here are some of the ways to measure a larger microlearning program when it's informal:

- **Metrics by user group.** If you have one homogenous learner group, you can track which resources were the most used or measure the overall performance improvement of the learner group. If you have multiple groups, you can also identify those resources that were most used by one group (such as sales professionals) compared with those that were most used by another group (such as marketers).

- **Metrics by resource.** Track and measure the associated performance improvement expected with each resource.

- **Overall program metrics.** While microlearning resources should be able to stand on their own or be completed in any order, you can measure the total number of resources completed. For example, if you have 10 microlearning resources in your program and 80 percent of the learners completed all 10, that sounds pretty good. However if only 20 percent of the learners completed all 10 resources, then you may want to take a step back to figure out why (maybe they were unaware of the program, they didn't think they needed it, they didn't have the time, and so on). You might even find that although only 20 percent of people completed all 10 resources, 80 percent completed eight resources, and there are two that people consistently didn't use. And while total completions don't tell you anything about behavior change, it's a good place to start. From there, you can take a look at behavior change back on the job.

What's Next?

Measurement and evaluation of microlearning, and of all learning solutions you create, should be an integral part of the design process. It's not always easy, and for those who may not feel data-savvy or business minded, there are lots of tools and resources to help you get the job done. Regardless of your comfort and skill level in this area, it's important to focus on the most important data and metrics that tell the story about the success of your microlearning, and more important, the success of your learners in adopting and implementing behavior change and performance improvement. In the next chapter, we'll consider planning the next steps for your microlearning efforts.

Questions to Explore

- What do you really need to measure for a specific microlearing resource?
- What are the expectations for this microlearning resource or program from your learners or leaders? What ROE can you express?
- Do you have the right tools or platform in place to capture the data needed? If not, how hard would it be to get a tool in place (such as a free online survey tool if your LMS doesn't have one)?
- Is manual data collection possible? Would it be worth your time and effort?
- Who in your organization may be knowledgable about metrics, measurement, and evaluation that could assist you (think market research, marketing, and so on)?
- Who in your network has experience with measuring microlearning? What would you ask them about their approach?
- What do your stakeholders expect regarding measurement and evaluation— a simple summary approach or data they can dig in to? What do they really want to know? For example, was the microlearning great or did performance improve?
- What measurement techniques do you currently use or have you used in the past that may apply?

Tools for Support

Microlearning Measurement Table

This table can be used to identify and plan the measurement and success of your microlearning resource or program. For each microlearning resource, fill in the learners, the learning event (if applicable), the learning objective, how you'll define success, and the metrics you'll use.

Microlearning Resource	Learners	Learning Event (if micro is used to support)	Learning Objective	Success Defined	Metrics to Inform Success

Microlearning Measurement Job Aid

Use this job aid to guide you in aligning your microlearning evaluation to your use case. Think about the way you intend to use microlearning and choose the appropriate column. Then read each row for tips on how to measure your microlearning.

	How Will You Use Microlearning?			
	Preparation Before a Learning Event	**Follow-Up to Support a Learning Event**	**Stand-Alone Training**	**Performance Support**
What Is the Performance Need?	Prepare for the learning event.	Close an existing performance gap.	Introduce a new skill.	Support a critical job task.
How Is Success Defined?	Learners arrive to the learning event having acquired the critical information needed.	Performance gap is closed or reduced.	New skill is adopted and sustained.	Increase in efficiency. Decrease in errors.
Should I Measure Impact to Performance?	Probably not—even if the impact on the live event is high, it doesn't relate to business outcomes. Instead, make it required to ensure completion.	If the impact is high when the job task is done correctly, then yes.	If the impact is high when the job task is done correctly, then yes.	If the impact is high when the job task is done correctly, then yes.

What Can Be Measured?	• Completion rates prior to attending the event
	• Knowledge acquisition (Kirkpatrick's Level 2)
		• The number or percent of employees with the gap closed
		• Increased business impact (metrics depend on the situation):
		  » increased sales
		  » sales lost to competitors
			Depends on the skill—take cues from the performance need, such as:
			• The number or percent of employees who adopted the new skill
			• Increased business impact (metrics depend on the situation):
			  » increased sales
			  » sales lost to competitors
				• The number or percent of employees with the gap closed
				• Decreased errors
				• Increased business impact (metrics depend on the situation):
				  » increased sales
				  » sales lost to competitors

How to Measure?	• Tracked completions via LMS • Pop quiz • In-event observations	• Number of downloads, views, likes, or shares (anything that reflects usage) • Sales data • Any reports that quantify data related to the specific job task (e.g., employee response time, customer satisfaction data, or error reports)	• LMS, LRS, LXP, or EPSS data • Short survey to learners and managers • Manager observations • Sales or other operational data (e.g., if the increase in sales or operational impact can be isolated and attributed to the training)	• EPSS or LRS data • Sales data • Number of downloads, views, likes, and shares (anything that reflects usage) • Any reports that quantify data related to the specific job task (e.g., employee response time, customer satisfaction data, and error reports)

Case Study: Simple Evaluation for a Stand-Alone Microlearning Resource

Meet Jim

Jim works in the compliance department of a global medical device company. The company sells sophisticated medical equipment used in hospitals and specialty clinics. These devices enable physicians and specialists to deliver the highest-quality care to their patients. As a result, these high-tech devices are connected to computer networks so their data can be transmitted electronically to other computer systems and the patient's electronic medical record.

That connection to the network makes those devices susceptible to cyberattack. The large, specialized medical centers that buy these kinds of products have entire teams of people dedicated to cybersecurity and will make purchasing decisions based in part on the technical security of the product.

Jim's company thoroughly tests the functionality and security of its equipment before it is released, and it has built-in antivirus software and software security features. However, there are always bug fixes and improvements to the software that are released post-sale, many of which are automatically installed for customers. This is a natural part of having a high-tech product and is expected by the IT and procurement staff at hospitals and clinics.

However, as is required by law in most countries, when these software releases correct a cyber-security vulnerability, the specific vulnerability must be communicated to the consumer through a vulnerability disclosure statement. These communications are managed by the compliance department of the medical device company in which Jim works.

As a trainer in the compliance department, Jim knows that when a vulnerability disclosure statement is released to a client, that client is likely to talk to their sales rep about it. Sometimes the customer calls with concerns, and sometimes they just have questions the next time the rep comes in for a visit.

The Training Need

The compliance team has found that sales reps are very well trained on their products and how to sell them, but they have very little understanding of the post-sale security work that is done. Reps know that security is of utmost importance to their customers and they know the company does post-sale software updates to keep their products secure. But many reps don't know that vulnerability disclosure statements are sent to clients, and then they feel blindsided when their customers ask about them.

The Solution

Jim creates a small piece of microlearning specifically about vulnerability disclosures: What they are, what they communicate, and how a rep should respond to customer concerns. Because of the focused topic, it's short—only about five minutes.

Ideally, Jim would like to have this training content released to sales reps when a vulnerability disclosure is released for a product that rep sells. That is, he would like to have just-in-time training for each rep when the vulnerability disclosure statement is relevant to them. However, due to the large number of products that are sold, the variability in timing of security updates, and the large number of reps to train, Jim is forced to send the training to all reps at one time. He knows, though, that every rep is likely to have a vulnerability disclosure statement released for a product they sell within the next few months, so he's satisfied that this is an acceptable compromise.

Because it's a compliance-related topic, the training content is put on the LMS and made mandatory. All reps and their managers receive an email that it must be completed within the next 30 days.

The Evaluation

Jim evaluates the success of this microlearning resource in a few key ways. The simplest is that because the microlearning resource is on the LMS, he can track if people actually took the training by the deadline. The training is required so they have about a 95 percent completion rate among sales reps and sales managers.

Of course that tells Jim that the training was completed, but not if it made a difference. So then Jim looks at the number of calls and emails to the customer service team from reps. The customer service team has a call center where they track the number of calls received on a variety of topics. Jim is able to look at these data to see if the number of calls from reps about vulnerability disclosure statements went down. He even asks the manager of that team to ask his staff if, when they get such calls, the reps seem to have a better understanding of vulnerability disclosures.

Jim also goes to the managers of the 10 largest sales teams and asks them to follow up with their reps after the training period is over. Do they better understand vulnerability disclosures and how to handle them with their accounts? Jim even provides the manager with some talking points that could be used if the rep confesses that they still don't understand vulnerability disclosures.

Jim could send emails to these sales managers asking for their support, but he knows he'll get better buy-in by just talking with them. He knows business gets done through relationships, so he arranges a 30-minute call with each of them instead. He talks briefly about the training need, why it's important, and even educates the managers a little on the coordinated vulnerability disclosure process. He gets their buy-in to supporting the training initiative with their reps. He also schedules another call a few weeks later to check in with each one after the training period to get their honest feedback about how well the training seemed to work for their reps.

The Results

- 95 percent completion rate of the training by the 30-day deadline
- No change in total number of calls and emails to the customer service team from reps in the past three months
- 30 percent reduction in number of calls from reps regarding vulnerability disclosures
- Six of the 10 managers interviewed one month post-release of the training agreed that the training had helped their sales reps
- Eight of the 10 managers interviewed two months post-release of the training agreed that the training had helped their sales reps

Questions for Reflection

- If faced with the same situation as Jim, would you have taken the same approach to evaluation?
- Do you consider Jim's microlearning program successful? Why or why not?

- If interviewing the managers was not an option, how else could Jim have collected manager feedback?
- Given the dynamic nature of cybersecurity vulnerability, what techniques can Jim employ to sustain what the reps learned?

Overview

As you can see from this example, a single piece of stand-alone microlearning is targeted to a single organizational need. So evaluating it can be relatively straightforward—did you successfully affect the one thing you were trying to address? In this case, that's the sales rep's awareness of and confidence in discussing cybersecurity vulnerability disclosures.

Doing this evaluation just required Jim to be thoughtful at the start of the project in recognizing the one thing he was trying to influence. Based on that objective, he needed to be willing to talk to people to ask if the training helped. He could have used email, but relying on a more personal approach worked better for him. He was also fortunate that this call topic was measured at his call center, so he had one piece of hard data to pull.

Could Jim have gone data crazy and looked for more metrics to analyze? Yes, but in this case, it probably wouldn't have been necessary. Given the additional time and effort it would have taken to identify baseline customer service center data on this issue, gather post-microlearning metrics, and then analyze all of it, along with the fact that the business wasn't pressuring him about it, Jim spent his time wisely with his evaluation choices.

Case Study: Robust Evaluation for a Formal Learning Program of Stand-Alone Microlearning Resources

Meet Mary

Mary is a training manager supporting all the marketing teams in a large software development company. The company has 10 different products and each product is supported by several marketing teams, such as email marketing, social marketing, and print marketing. In total, there are 30 different marketing teams worldwide, with more than 500 marketers.

The marketers on these teams are at various levels in their career, and so are at different levels of capability in terms of marketing their products. The company would like for all marketing staff to get better at basic and advanced marketing skills. Much of that could probably be learned through experience on the job, but the organization wants to accelerate that growth and development. Employee surveys have shown that employees would also appreciate such resources aimed at helping them in their career development.

In addition, an even more important gap is that few marketers on any team are able to recognize when a customer is engaged with a single product in a way that suggests they would be ripe for cross-product marketing—that is, marketing a different product within their suite of products. This is seen as a critical way to delight customers while growing the business. The goal here is that marketing efforts do not feel like the company is trying to sell you on more products, but that they are helpfully reaching out to tell you about another product in their suite that is likely to improve your productivity. Yes, this turns into increased revenue, but more important, it results in more loyal and committed customers—those "raving fans" that every business wants to have.

Using cross-product marketing to create these fans is something that employees are hearing about a lot from company leadership, and it's an industry trend common in the software industry, but Mary knows this is an area where her marketers could improve.

The Solution

Mary's team creates a program of microlearning modules. She identifies all the key content areas important to marketing, such as market segmentation, identifying how to reach people in those target segments, and how to message appropriately to them. She keeps a focus on one learning objective per resource to keep the topics focused and bite-sized.

Then Mary tags the topics by the teams for whom they are most appropriate. She and her SMEs are able to identify which teams are most likely to need which topics, based on the kind of product they support and the kind of marketing they do. She also ranks all the topics as beginner, intermediate, or advanced, to identify a likely progression through the assets.

This creates a matrix of mini-modules that each can stand alone. In the end she has about 100 resources identified, across a variety of topics, and at a variety of levels of advancing difficulty. To the outsider, 100 resources may seem like a lot, but she knows each topic will take three to 10 minutes to teach, so she estimates having about 10 to 12 hours of content that needs to be developed. They plan to create most of this content, but about 20 percent will be curated from the Internet. Certainly, it's a large program, but she figures it can be designed and developed by her small team in three to six months.

With this content matrix in place, Mary knows all the topics that need to be taught. She is able to not only develop the resources, but also create recommended pathways through the content. An entry-level employee supporting a given product will be recommended to consume certain assets, but the same entry-level employee supporting a different product will be recommended to consume other assets. And those associates with more experience will start with more advanced assets, assuming they have the basic skills already in place.

Despite having recommended pathways, the learner has ultimate freedom and flexibility to consume any content in any order they wish. When the employee logs into the system, recommendations are offered, but the learner can consume any of the content they want in any order they want.

By having discrete learning modules that can stand alone, Mary can recommend different pieces of content to different learners based on their relevance to each person. She recognizes that not every employee needs to know about every facet of segmentation—and that by forcing someone to consume content about an area that is less relevant, that person will disengage from the entire program, including those parts that are useful to them in their role.

Making Learning Required

Mary knows that in her fast-paced software company, just providing a great informal learning program won't be enough. Sure, associates say they want a program like this, but if they are not given time during the workweek to do it and are not held accountable, they simply won't do it. The pressure to do their operational duties will be too great, and her program will be seen as a great resource that no one has time to use, even if each resource is just five minutes long.

So Mary finds ways to make this informal learning program formal. She wants to get the managers of all the marketing teams on board for supporting this training, but she realizes that getting their buy-in will not be simple. These teams are busy and managers are first responsible for their operational goals and metrics. So she starts just with the managers of the marketing teams for two of their 10 products. That's seven managers, enabling her to reach seven of the 30 marketing teams in her first wave of this program launch.

Because Mary's company is global, it's impossible for her to meet with these seven managers face-to-face, but she has a video-based conference call with all of them together. She tells them about the program and how it will enable each of their marketing employees to perform better and, more important, achieve cross-product marketing, an initiative that all managers are hearing about regularly from the CEO, and in the industry.

She gets their commitment that this would be a good initiative to support with their employees' time. But then she takes it one step further. She gets each manager to make it tangible: Each team will have one hour a week blocked on their calendars for engaging with the program. The agreement is this will be time that's blocked on calendars and is treated like a team meeting, but everyone will be learning independently. It's at the start of the day so people aren't distracted by other tasks. It's hard at first, but managers check in with their team members to hold them accountable to making learning the priority for that time, and eventually it becomes part of the team culture to use this time for learning.

In addition, each manager has a one-on-one meeting with each of their staff once every two weeks. In that meeting, they agree to take 10 minutes to discuss the most valuable thing the employee learned from the program in the past two weeks and how that influenced their work. This helps to hold employees accountable for doing their learning, makes the learning actionable, and enables them to ask questions and get coaching from their manager.

Each team also has a monthly team meeting, and they take 10 minutes in that meeting to have staff share the best takeaways from what they've learned in the past month and how that is causing them to think or work differently. The goal here is for the team to cross-pollinate their ideas, with a discussion led by the manager who is familiar with what all staff members are learning and working on.

Mary checks in with these seven managers regularly to hold them accountable. Are they ensuring that their employees take dedicated time for learning, are they checking in during one-on-ones, and are they taking time for it during team meetings? She knows that just as much as employees need to be held accountable to doing their learning, managers need to be held accountable to supporting the program too.

After a few months, Mary starts a similar process with the managers for the marketing teams of three more products, and continues in this way until all managers are supporting this initiative.

Evaluating the Program

Step 1: Evaluating Manager Support

As Mary works through the process of getting managers bought in and supportive of the program, one of the things she evaluates is the manager buy-in and support. She's doing biweekly 30-minute calls with each of the seven managers so she can assess how the training is being supported and ensure managers continue to support the program. In this way, she's really evaluating her change management efforts with the managers.

Before each call with a manager, she takes a quick look at her data to review the usage of the microlearning resources by that manager's team. With this information, she can tell if the team members are using the one hour per week they are expected to dedicate to learning from these resources. As she's checking in with managers to see how things are going with the program, she listens for barriers that could be preventing their team's use of the program and how she can help. This is an area where her relationship-building skills are key. She knows that change management is not about telling managers to tell their people to take training, rather it's about making it something managers are actively supporting and learners are getting real value from.

Step 2: Evaluating Resource Usefulness

After the program has been in place for a few weeks, Mary looks weekly at the data to see how useful the resources are. The data she looks at include:

- Which resources are accessed the most?
- Of those resources that are accessed, which are the least likely to be completed? Of those, are there trends in the point in a resource where people stop consuming the content?
- Do people tend to follow the learning pathways as she anticipated? Or are there other pieces of content that they are finding more helpful than those she flagged?

With this, Mary is finding out which resources are most useful, if any resources need to be revised, and if the recommended pathways should be revised.

Step 3: Evaluating Employee Performance Improvement

Then, to measure the actual success of the program, she takes both a quantitative and qualitative approach. As the program progresses, when she checks in with managers, she's also asking if their staff seem to be not only aware of more advanced marketing principles, but also achieving more. Managers should have a sense of whether their employees are performing better.

The marketing teams also track all kinds of metrics to tell them about the success of their marketing efforts, such as conversion rates and customer usage of their products. These metrics show them the success of their marketing campaigns and if the training efforts are causing their marketers to work differently or achieve more with their efforts.

Results

- Weekly data show that each marketing team is accessing 50 percent of the program resources flagged as relevant to them, and this is increasing week over week.
- Of all 100 resources in the program:
  - » 10 resources have been accessed by all marketers
  - » 20 resources have not been accessed by any marketer.
- Anecdotal feedback from calls with marketing managers:
  - » overall positive; the resources are welcomed
  - » carving out an hour a week for learning works for some teams but not others
  - » looking at marketing and customer metrics (conversion rates and customer usage) is premature at this time.

Questions for Reflection

- Do you consider Mary's microlearning program successful? Why or why not?
- If faced with the same situation as Mary, would you have taken the same approach to evaluation?
- What other evaluation options could Mary have considered?
- If Mary couldn't conduct calls with each manager, how else could she have collected data?
- How could Mary evaluate the resource effectiveness by user type (for example, junior associate versus experienced marketer)?
- What metrics could help Mary determine if there was business impact? How often should Mary check in with the marketing teams to collect these metrics?
- How will Mary sustain her microlearning program to stay relevant?

Overview

As you can see from this example, Mary used a number of microlearning resources and essentially created a curriculum of microlearning resources for these marketers to take. The value of using microlearning is that she was able to break concepts down into small pieces, allowing marketers to consume those pieces that were most relevant to them, and create a more customized and individualized curriculum for each person.

Mary used her strong relationship-building skills to ensure manager buy-in and manage this change for the organization. Without this focus, Mary likely would have created a program that few people used and had little value to the organization.

Because there are multiple microlearning resources, and because Mary worked so much with the managers, her evaluation was far more robust than in the previous case study. She evaluated the learners' use of the microlearning resources and used that to continually improve those resources. This also gave her a good sense of the overall program usage, which led directly into her conversations with managers. These conversations provided another way for her to evaluate the success of her program and enabled her to intervene with change management support as needed.

Of course, Mary was also lucky that the marketing teams track so many metrics that tell them the success of their marketing campaigns. While she doesn't yet have enough data to make conclusions, she knows this will be increasingly useful in the future to give her a sense of how well the program is working at actually changing behavior.

Mary has been pretty thorough in her evaluation efforts, but given the size of the program, it makes sense for her to invest this level of effort in monitoring its success and iteratively revising resources as needed to ensure it is most successful.

References and Additional Resources

ATD (Association for Talent Development). 2016. *Evaluating Learning: Getting to Measurements That Matter.* Alexandria, VA: ATD Press.

ATD (Association for Talent Development). 2018. "ATD Microlearning: 5 Techniques to Improve Job Proficiency and Prove ROI on Training Investments." October 4. td.org/videos/microlearning-5-techniques-to-improve-job-proficiency-and-prove -roi-on-training-investments.

ATD (Association for Talent Development). 2019. *Effective Evaluation: Measuring Learning Programs for Success.* Alexandria, VA: ATD Press.

Brinkerhoff, R.O. 2003. *The Success Case Method.* San Francisco: Berrett-Koehler.

Chevalier, R. 2003. "Updating the Behavior Engineering Model." *Performance Improvement* 42: 8-14.

EdApp Microlearning. 2019. "Measuring the Success of Your Microlearning." youtu.be/k9DKbEz0V-0.

Gal, G., and R. Nachmias. 2011. "Implementing On-Line Learning and Performance Support Using an EPSS." *Interdisciplinary Journal of E-Learning and Learning Objects* 7:213–124.

Gilbert, T. 2013. *Human Competence: Engineering Worthy Performance,* Tribute Edition. San Francisco: Pfeiffer.

Gottfredson, C. 2019. "Beyond Kirkpatrick: Measuring Performance in the Flow of Work." The 5 Moments of Need, June 26. 5momentsofneed.com/module/news .htm?newsId=7997.

Hogle, P. 2018. "Integrate Learning Into the Workflow With These 3 Tools." *Learning Solutions,* December 13. learningsolutionsmag.com/articles/integrate-learning-into -the-workflow-with-these-3-tools.

Israel, M. 2017. "Microlearning: The Assessment Factor." InSync Training blog, December 26. blog.insynctraining.com/microlearning-the-assessment-factor.

Kirkpatrick, D., and J.D. Kirkpatrick. 2007. *Implementing the Four Levels: A Practical Guide for Effective Evaluation of Training Programs.* San Francisco: Berrett-Koehler Publishers.

Kirkpatrick, J.D., and W.K. Kirkpatrick. 2016. *Kirkpatrick's Four Levels of Training Evaluation.* Alexandria, VA: ATD Press.

Performitiv. 2018. "Measuring Microlearning." Whitepaper. performitiv.com/wp-content /uploads/2018/06/Performitiv_MicroLearning_Measurement.pdf.

Phillips, P.P., and J.J. Phillips. 2015. *Real-World Training Evaluation.* Alexandria, VA: ATD Press.

Phillips, P.P., and J.J. Phillips. 2019. *Return on Investment Basics,* 2nd edition. Alexandria, VA: ATD Press.

Putman, S., J.L. Effron, and M. Bowe. 2017. *Investigating Performance: Design and Outcomes With xAPI.* Narberth, PA: MakingBetter.

TorranceLearning. n.d. "Helping You With xAPI." www.torrancelearning.com/xapi.

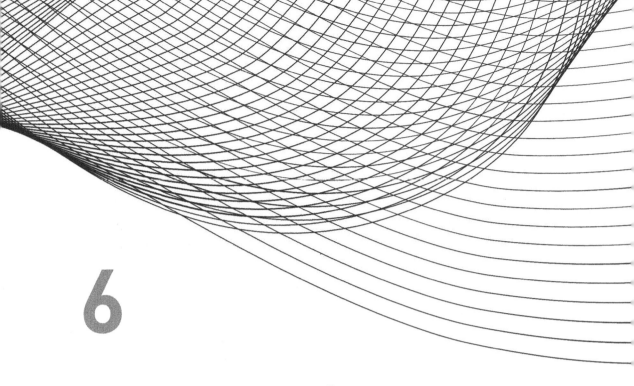

6

Planning Next Steps:
Where Do You Go From Here?

In This Chapter:

- Reflecting on the current state of microlearning in your organization
- What to do next if you are successful (or not)
- Gaining momentum to embed microlearning in your design approach
- Accountability for the learners, the stakeholders, and the learning team

Now that you have read the first five chapters of this book, you should have a solid understanding of microlearning, the value it can bring to addressing learning and performance needs for your learners, the foundational knowledge needed to design and build microlearning to meet these needs, and even how to evaluate your efforts. You should also begin to see important connections to the business when microlearning is used to solve specific performance gaps or needs. As with anything new, it can feel exciting and overwhelming as you get started. With all this new information, tools, and resources, where do you go from here? In this chapter, we explore how to take the next steps that make sense for you.

To figure out where to go from here, you need to first determine where you are today in your microlearning adoption journey. It's really difficult to build a solid plan without first reflecting on your current situation. In fact, without taking a moment to determine where you are today, you may feel even more overwhelmed and unorganized. You need to consider your current state to be able to determine if the efforts you are putting forth seem to be achieving the things you want. Skipping this reflection step can hinder your efforts, and, at worst, lead to an unsuccessful introduction of microlearning.

Think of it this way—imagine you are hosting a party and one of your guests is having trouble finding your house. They call to let you know they are lost and need your help to get back on the right route. The first question you probably will ask them is, "Where are you now?" They could be circling the streets in your neighborhood, or they could be many miles away. In either case, you can't give clear directions without first knowing where they are. Likewise, you can't give your team or stakeholders a good sense of where you intend to go if you can't express where it is you are currently at, or where you're coming from. Visionary learning leaders are able to describe the current state, paint a picture of the future state and its possibilities, and express it extremely well.

Reflecting on Where You Are With Microlearning

To reflect on where you and your organization are at currently, it's helpful to think about your use of microlearning right now. Is it new to you? Or maybe it's familiar but you haven't introduced any microlearning resources for your learners. Maybe you have designed and developed a few microlearning resources, but haven't yet embedded microlearning in the range of solutions you offered. Some of you may consider yourselves microlearning "regulars" and may feel quite comfortable and confident in designing microlearning at the right time, place, and need for your learners. The next few sections will provide self-reflection questions to help you to identify and determine if you have explored the possibilities for your current situation before moving to the next level.

New to Microlearning

Earlier in this book we recommended that if you have never built or introduced microlearning and you are learning the fundamentals, you should start small. By small, we mean it's best to start with one microlearning resource versus tackling a large microlearning program. By building a single microlearning resource and getting it out there, you will learn so much about your learners and how the organization responds to microlearning. Small successes with one microlearning resource will build your confidence, gently introduce microlearning to your organization, and provide valuable lessons in a low-risk way.

Consider doing a "microlearning pilot." Is there a performance need that has surfaced with a small user group? An easy job aid you can create to help learners in the moment they need it? Go for it! You can learn and course-correct easily with a small project, and because you are being agile, that project is likely to be successful. And with that success will come other projects because business teams elsewhere in the organization will see what you are able to achieve.

Pilot Everything!—A Note From Sue

I learned long ago that when introducing a new learning initiative—whether it was a new format, a new piece of technology, or a new curriculum—calling it a pilot immediately reduced the perceived risk by my stakeholders. When implementing my first e-learning module 20 years ago for a new product launch, stakeholders were very concerned that the learners would not be able to effectively learn the new product details if they weren't in a three-ring binder with lots of pages and lots of text on every page. I ended up calling the e-learning module a pilot and made the printed version available as a backup resource only if the learners wanted it.

Needless to say, most of the learners appreciated the fun and engaging new way to learn, and most skipped downloading the paper version. Key lessons learned from the pilot were incorporated into future e-learning modules, and most everyone was pleased. If I had positioned these efforts as a "new program" and the e-learning module wasn't engaging and effective, there would have been a lot of complaining from the learners and stakeholders. But, under the guise of a pilot, you can circle back and couch any major missteps as lessons learned.

A long time has passed since then and I still pilot everything I can. I always consider the possibility of a pilot when introducing something new because it has been so helpful to me in pressure-testing new initiatives and building trust with my stakeholders.

Dabbled in Microlearning

If you have already initiated some microlearning in your organization, congratulations! If you read the book to this point, perhaps you could relate to some of the examples and have tried some of the techniques and formats discussed. For you, it's important to think about how well or not so well your microlearning journey has gone. These questions would be relevant to you:

- How would I rate the effectiveness of each microlearning resource or program I have implemented?
- Did each microlearning resource meet the criteria for the definition of microlearning (refer to chapter 1)? If not, does it matter? (If you met the performance need, you're probably fine!)
- Which formats did I use? If multiple formats were used, was one preferred over others?
- Have I leveraged most, if not all, of the steps outlined in the MILE model (refer to chapter 4)? If not, why not?
- What was the reaction and feedback from learners? Did performance improve? Were gaps closed? Did it help in the moment of need?
- What was the reaction and feedback from the stakeholders?
- Was there perceived value from the stakeholders? From the learners?

TOOLS

Use the "Microlearning Pilot Template" tool at the end of this chapter to draft a plan for any microlearning pilot effort.

Microlearning Is a Mainstay

If you regularly implement microlearning, congratulations for being ahead of the curve! Hopefully you picked up some new ideas and pearls of wisdom from earlier chapters about how to really make your microlearning effective and engaging. Before expanding your use of microlearning, consider the following questions:

- How would I evaluate the overall effectiveness of microlearning in my organization? Is there a noticeable and measurable impact?
- Is microlearning a go-to approach for everything, and is this appropriate given the performance needs of my learners?
- Have I explored all the possibilities of formats and topics best suited to microlearning in my organization?

- Have I leveraged most, if not all, of the steps outlined in the MILE model? If not, why?
- Is microlearning reserved for a specific user type or job role? If so, could it be effectively expanded to other groups?

No matter where you land on the spectrum of microlearning implementation, the most frequent piece of advice we give is to **remember that microlearning is not a panacea!** The biggest curse of a successful implementation is that everyone in the business comes to you, wanting you to build microlearning programs for them, even if microlearning is not their best solution. Those business partners see the great results you are achieving elsewhere in the organization, and they want you to replicate those results for their unit. But it's up to you to recognize where microlearning will have the greatest value and where it will not.

As you probably know, microlearning is a great tool to have, but it's not the tool for everything. Imagine having only a flathead screwdriver in your toolbox at home. Its main purpose is for tightening screws, such as a screw holding a knob on a kitchen drawer, or when putting together a piece of furniture. Sure, it can be multipurpose—you can use a flathead screwdriver to open a can of paint, pry open a jar, and even chip ice off the inside of your freezer. But, while a screwdriver is great for a lot of tasks, it isn't great for all tasks. In some cases, it can even be dangerous. Imagine using the blunt end of a screwdriver to drive a nail into a wall. It might ultimately get the job done, but considering the handle doesn't have enough weight to create the force needed to drive the nail and it usually doesn't have a flat edge, it's more likely that you will hurt yourself. A hammer would be the best choice in this case. The point here is to use microlearning for the right learning needs, but not all needs.

To ensure you are using microlearning for the right reasons at the right time and the right place, go back and review chapter 3. You need to understand the performance need, and have the right format for the right audience to achieve success with microlearning.

What to Do Next If You Are Successful

If you implemented microlearning as a single resource or as a larger microlearning program and it was deemed a success, shout it from the rooftop! It's so important to celebrate successes as learning professionals, and as human beings. Take the time to capture your success and share it with the individuals or groups in your organization for which the news will resonate.

At first it might feel a bit self-serving to share your successes. However, it really isn't about you—it's about the learners you helped to do something better at work. You enabled them to improve their performance. When framed in this manner, it makes it easier to share your success with others. And it's more than just communicating the success of the microlearning; it's about marketing the success. Why? Marketing your microlearning success promotes awareness, increases use of the resource or program, and sustains this and similar resources and programs.

How can a learning professional share their microlearning success? There are many ways to do this. Sue's favorite way to share success is usually in the form of a short PowerPoint presentation with visuals of the learning resource evaluation metrics as well as comments from the learners. However, this was determined by how she was able to get time with her stakeholders, and it was usually in a conference room with limited time. Think about how your stakeholders like to receive information and communicate your successes accordingly. Some options include:

- a presentation in a live meeting
- a short video with learner or manager testimonials
- a short email
- infographics
- employee recognition (create or provide an award for the learner or team who achieves the highest score, completes the most courses, or demonstrates the most performance improvement).

Again, choose the communication method and channel that makes the most sense for your organization and your stakeholders.

Knowing What Message to Share

How will you know which data and outcomes from your microlearning matter most? The answer lies in having a dialogue with each of the different stakeholder groups. Keep in mind that in the context of microlearning, the outcomes are usually just like your microlearning: very specific and focused on improving one performance or learning need. Focus on identifying success stories that include the desired outcomes and will resonate with the different stakeholder groups. Let's look at some desired outcomes that resonate with different groups, pulled from our experience working with businesses leaders and their learners over many years.

Senior Leadership

These people are most interested in positive impact or acceleration of revenue, growth, market share, or other financial measures of your business that are relevant in your industry. Note that a positive impact could be expressed in a number of ways. For example, "reduced employee errors" could also be expressed as "accelerated sales processes," and while many senior leaders do care about how positive impact was achieved, as long as it was accomplished in a compliant manner, the details behind it may be less important. They just want to know that you as the learning professional are doing your job well and helping the business succeed; as a result, you are focused on the details, not them. Refer to chapter 1 for more on how to approach senior leadership.

Operational Leaders

These people are most interested in increased employee self-sufficiency to solve a problem instead of going to a manager for assistance, reduced errors, and shortened time to do an operational duty (for example, operate a piece of equipment, answer a customer call, or handle an objection). They could also focus on acceleration of new hire onboarding (resulting in greater speed to proficiency and with less manager assistance).

Leaders of Support Units (Such As IT, Marketing, or Safety)

These people are most interested in increased use of a specific tool, process, or system by employees, customers, or clients. They may also be interested in increased productivity in a specific area, efficiencies gained or time reduced to solving a specific operational or business problem, and reduced incidence of organizational issues like safety or compliance violations.

Learners and Employees

These people are most interested in increased confidence or ability to complete a task, apply a new skill, solve a problem effectively, help a customer, or to simply perform better at a specific aspect of their job. They may also be interested in improving the skills needed for them to achieve their next role.

* * *

Keep in mind that these ideas are a starting point and can certainly overlap across the different groups. In any case, it is always a good idea to avoid assumptions and simply ask those people what data, metrics, and outcomes would mean the most to them. Armed with that knowledge, you can do your best to incorporate those things up front when building your plan and then share your successes in the language that will resonate most with them. The point here is that while the actual outcome of your microlearning may be hyper-specific, consider communicating the success story with phrases and language that really mean something to the groups noted. How you express your success is critical because different stakeholder groups care about different things.

CASE STUDY: COMMUNICATING SUCCESS

At a recent training conference, Sue taught a workshop for life science learning professionals focused on strategies and tactics for planning and executing an effective plan of action (POA) meeting. A POA is a live meeting used in the life sciences to inform sales reps about new marketing strategies and tactics, giving the sales teams an opportunity to practice using new tools and resources. Planning for POA meetings at most organizations can be complex and time-consuming, and require lots of cross-functional collaboration with several departments such as sales, marketing, market access, operations, and meeting planning. The life sciences learning professional has a lot to do: Identify and design the learning solutions for multiple audiences, incorporate training on marketing tools that are in various states of development, train facilitators, and measure results—all while running their day-to-day training duties.

One of the tools Sue mentioned during her workshop was a POA planning checklist. It wasn't handed out during the workshop, but Sue made it available upon request after the program. The checklist could be considered boost learning or performance support, because it was a brief, one-page document that outlined the POA planning steps referred to during the workshop.

After the workshop, many of the participants reached out via email to request the checklist. Sue sent it out and asked them to share any success stories they had in using it. Given it was a training conference with attendees from all different organizations, feedback and follow-up can be limited and variable. However, in reflecting on the overall workshop, Sue compiled some interesting data:

- workshop room was full to capacity—suggests the topic was of interest to potential learners
- about half of the workshop participants requested the checklist—suggests people found the content useful and thought the tool might be useful back on the job
- six weeks post workshop, 10 percent of the participants had emailed Sue with positive feedback on how they used the checklist, and some had shared the checklist with other departments—demonstrates that the tool was effective back on the job, enough so that they felt compelled to share that with her.

How has Sue communicated this initial success to others? She incorporated these metrics into slides that discuss the overall POA thought-leadership strategy and tactics, and shared comments received from workshop participants during virtual and live meetings with clients. She will continue to monitor and collect feedback on the checklist to continue to tell the success story.

What to Do Next If You Aren't Successful

While we hope this doesn't happen, let's face it—not every program will be a smashing success, and having programs that are less successful than we expect happens to all of us from time to time. One of Sue's favorite anecdotes to share with staff, training managers, and students over the years is about the importance and role of failure in the journey to achieve success:

Michael Jordan is a professional basketball player who played 15 seasons in the NBA for the Chicago Bulls and the Washington Wizards. He won the NBA playoffs six times and scored a total of 32,292 points in his NBA career, making him the third-highest-scoring player of all time. Michael Jordan is not associated with failure. But this quote from him puts everything in perspective: "I've missed more than 9,000 shots in my career. I've lost almost 300 games. Twenty-six times, I've been trusted to take the game-winning shot and missed. I've failed over and over and over again in my life. And that is why I succeed."

The point here is that no one thinks of Michael Jordan as a failure, and that's in part because he learned from each and every time things didn't go the way he wanted. If you introduced microlearning and it did not go as planned, it's time to take a step back and evaluate the situation. We have worked with so many colleagues who immediately want to pick apart what went wrong. Stop. No matter how bad it was, try to find at least one thing that went well. These are the things you will want to remember and continue. Then, analyze what went wrong. Review any data and metrics you can get (chapter 5 discusses this in detail). Some questions to ask include:

- Why did the microlearning program not achieve its goal?
- What is the feedback from the learners? The supervisors?
- Was the objective aligned to the need?
- Was the right format chosen for the situation? For example, did you build an instructional video when they really needed a single page with talking points for handling a customer objection?
- Was the timing of implementation off?
- Was it socialized and promoted properly among stakeholder groups?
- Was the microlearning program easily accessible at the time it was needed?

If you implemented microlearning and it did not go as planned, try to view the failure as a step in the journey toward success. Oftentimes, when we've seen microlearning miss the mark, it's usually because the original performance or learning need was not clearly identified and the resulting microlearning was not aligned to meet that need. Alternatively, in the case of informal learning (when learning is not mandatory), it's because key learner or leadership groups were not fully aware of the program, so they didn't promote or use the program as much as expected.

As we mentioned earlier in this chapter, at times like these it can also be helpful to call the program a pilot—even if you haven't called it that before. Calling it a pilot gives you permission to reflect on areas for improvement and try it again another time. For example, rather than going to your stakeholders to report that a program didn't go well (and you know they already know it too!), you could say, "I'm considering this a pilot. Sure, it didn't go as well as we'd hoped, but we learned a lot, which will enable us to be more successful next time." Then list the top three things you learned and how you will change them moving forward.

Gaining Momentum to Embed Microlearning in Your Design Approach

Adopting a new habit or behavior is hard. Not only is it hard for the learners, but it is hard for us as learning professionals too. Think about it—in adopting and embedding microlearning as a regular tool in your toolbox, you are a learner too, learning new ways to think about performance challenges and how to support them. You must change how you think about your work and change the way you do your work so microlearning can be used on a regular basis when it will bring the most value and impact for your learners. To help with this, look for ways to gain momentum for your microlearning efforts:

- **Look for a quick win.** Pick a topic that lends itself easily to a microlearning format, such as compliance training. Or, think about that request for training you get hounded about but never have time to create—could the need be solved using a microlearning resource? The point is, a quick win is easy; it's something that would be high impact with low effort. If you can implement a microlearning resource in two weeks to three months (depending on your organizational culture) with few resources and it squarely meets an important need, it's a quick win.
- **Do a pilot.** Calling something a pilot provides an environment where failure is more acceptable (it is a pilot after all) so you can try some new things, like microlearning. If you have successfully implemented individual microlearning resources, consider whether a robust microlearning program would be of value to a particular set of performance needs.

- **Incorporate microlearning in your design planning.** To really gain momentum, embed microlearning in your instructional design processes and practices. It shouldn't be an afterthought; it should be a key element of your design considerations and a great tool to use given the right situation.
- **Incorporate microlearning in your annual planning.** If you are the one who puts together the learning plan and budget for your learners, department, or organization, consider identifying and putting in resources for microlearning opportunities. In our experience, it's much easier to get funding at the beginning of a fiscal year than in the middle. Think about not only any costs to design the microlearning content but also the funding requirements of the format type. If you are producing high-end video or are considering a microlearning delivery platform, you will likely need to build a business case and determine approximate costs. Whether it's low or high in spend, it's still a good idea to have an explanation of how microlearning will be used and which performance problem or need it will solve.
- **Communicate the activity and the results.** Whenever you implement microlearning, communicate to the learners, managers, and stakeholders about what is happening, when it will happen, and why it is important. Communication helps not only with the learners participating in the program, but also drives buy-in from others and ultimately creates champions for the resource or program. After you communicate that the resources are being launched, also communicate the results. Let people know about the specific and measurable positive impact the microlearning had on the user group or the organization. And if the results are less than ideal, tell them what you think the issues are and how you are course-correcting.
- **Become a microlearning expert.** Read as much as you can, keep this book handy as a desk reference, and talk to other learning professionals who are experimenting with or using microlearning on a regular basis. These activities build your expertise and help you to stay energized about embedding

TOOLS

Use the "Microlearning Communication Plan" tool at the end of this chapter and the two templates included to track and manage how you're communicating about your microlearning resource or program with learners, managers, and stakeholders.

microlearning in your work. And while you may consider yourself more of a novice than an expert, your microlearning expertise is likely much ahead of the business you serve. Go forth with confidence!

Developing Accountability for All

To ensure that microlearning—or any organizational learning for that matter—sticks, you need to build accountability around it in the workplace. This means establishing expectations that everyone does their part to contribute to promoting and participating in learning, and supporting one another in using their new skills. Because organizations are investing so much in employee development (spending overall on employee learning has steadily increased in the past six years), it's imperative that everyone holds themselves accountable—otherwise it's a huge waste of resources for all involved (ATD 2018).

Ideally, the organization provides the opportunity to learn and sets the expectation that learning is important for the business and for the individual. The managers support the organization's stance by ensuring employees are aware of learning opportunities, allowing learners time to attend, supporting pull-through with coaching back on the job, and "walking the talk" by participating as learners themselves. The learners recognize that while the organization and the managers provide the opportunity, they can't do the training for them. Learners have to do the work to acquire, learn, and apply the training on the job—in other words, be accountable to themselves. Finally, learning professionals need to be accountable to delivering high-quality, relevant, and engaging learning programs that meet business and performance needs.

Based on our personal experiences, accountability in the workplace can vary widely from one organization to another. Ideally you would love to have a corporate culture that encourages and supports learning at all levels—employees, managers, and executives—but that is rare; people get focused on their operational duties and it takes special leaders to create a corporate culture that focuses on more than just the operational metrics. The corporate culture can often influence the learning culture and associated accountability, or lack thereof. How can you develop accountability around the context of learning, and specifically microlearning, in the organization you serve? Let's consider it from three angles: the learners, the stakeholders, and the learning team.

The Learners

When considering holding learners accountable, it is helpful to first understand a little bit about the current workforce and their expectations for learning in the workplace.

According to Gallup (n.d.), only four in 10 employees strongly agree they have opportunities at work to learn and grow. Yet Millennials rank the opportunity to learn and grow in a job as number 1, above all other considerations, and 69 percent of non-Millennials also say it is important to them. Whether it is real or perceived, these data suggest that the majority of employees believe they don't have enough opportunities to participate in or receive learning at work.

Now, consider the needs of the modern learner. Research tells us that the modern learner is often overwhelmed, distracted, and impatient in the workplace. They use more devices and systems than ever before, rapidly switch from one device to another, are overloaded with information, distribute attention thinly across many things, and can be found across many age brackets (Bull City Learning 2012). In fact, when seeking help to solve a work problem, most modern learners won't watch a video longer than four minutes (Bersin by Deloitte 2014). So congratulations on reading this book to the end! As a modern learner, you bucked the trend.

How can the modern learner be held accountable when they have all these influences working against them? Good microlearning is a great solution to meet the needs of the modern learner. It is quick, can be delivered in a variety of formats, and is focused on a single performance or learning need—which is all the modern learner has time for! Learners can be held accountable in part by appealing to and engaging them effectively. You can also hold learners accountable by getting their managers involved. For informal learning, creating awareness with the manager can be especially helpful— if the manager sees value in the resource, they will likely recommend and reiterate that their team members participate. To help the manager, consider the support tools they might need to coach and assist their employees to be successful. A coaching guide is always a good idea!

One easy way to hold learners accountable is to make microlearning mandatory. This works well for some topics and may be expected, such as with compliance training. However, while forcing your learners to complete a training resource holds them accountable, it doesn't exactly feel warm and fuzzy, nor does it drive engagement. Expressing to the learners how the micro-

TOOLS

Check out the "Creating a Coaching Guide for a Microlearning Resource or Program" tool at the end of this chapter for tips on creating detailed but concise coaching guides—those that managers in the organization will use.

learning content will help them be better at their job can contribute to addressing the

WIIFM, which can drive engagement and accountability. And, even if the training is required, make sure they know the reason for the training and what's in it for them!

RESOURCES

For more details about engaging the modern learner, Bull City Learning has a recorded webinar that covers this topic in detail. In the webinar, Nathan Pienkowski and Garry O'Grady (2015) outline six strategies for engaging the modern learner:
- **Be useful.** Learners must be able to apply what they've learned to their jobs.
- **Be brief.** The content must be able to be consumed quickly.
- **Be visual.** Avoid a lot of text-heavy information in your materials. A visually appealing design will draw the learner in to the content.
- **Make it active.** Involve the learners, making them active participants rather than passive consumers.
- **Be everywhere.** Modern learners should be able to access their learning materials in a variety of ways.
- **Sell it.** Learners need to know why a training program is needed. Tell them what's in it for them, and how it will help them do their job better.

If you prefer to read about this content, check out Sue's blog post "Six Tips for Reaching the Life Sciences Modern Learner."

The Stakeholders

Stakeholders—senior leadership, operational leaders, support unit leaders, and managers—are critical to the success of any new learning initiative, including microlearning. Why would they be critical when the learner is the one who should be participating in and completing the microlearning? The stakeholder could be the first-line or second-line manager to the learner. If this is the case, they have a vested interest in their direct report's performance, and will likely be held accountable for any positive or negative outcomes.

Managers can use your help in supporting their employees' participation in the microlearning program. Think about the typical things that managers would need in this scenario, because it's no different from supporting them for other types of training. Let the manager know what's included in the microlearning program, and the performance need addressed. Give examples of the behavior change they should expect to see in their employees. Provide a coaching guide, which can include key questions they may receive and how to effectively answer them. To gain manager accountability and buy-in, proactively ask for feedback on the value of the microlearning from their perspective, as well as any feedback they glean from employees who complete the training. When managers feel confident and prepared, they tend to lead with confidence and will encourage their employees to use the microlearning because they can also be a confident mentor and coach on the content.

Managers can get involved by looking at data and reports from the LMS, LXP, or other systems to view employee access and use of microlearning content (assuming it is deployed from a system for which there is tracking and they have access). Again, if you are successful in identifying the right performance or learning need and you implement some really great microlearning, the supervisor will be eager for success too—and they should be able to provide firsthand observations of results. Letting the supervisor know that you are looking for feedback is a great way to get them more involved and accountable. And certainly involve the stakeholders afterward when you have results—they like to celebrate too when their team does a good job! And if it didn't go as well as planned, they probably have great insights as to what could be improved or ideas for how to course-correct.

If the stakeholder is not in a direct supervisory role to the learner but holds another role, such as in marketing, IT, HR, or sales, they may still have a vested interest in the program or the learner's success, albeit indirectly. Why? Improved performance of the learner as a result of good microlearning can lead to positive business outcomes. To help drive accountability with these stakeholders, communicate the value of the microlearning before it is launched—let them know what it is and why it is being implemented. This is especially important for groups like IT because they may play an active and integral role in the effective launch and implementation of your microlearning program. Communicate during development and implementation to let them know it is happening—this program helps create awareness and garner their support before and during the time the learners are going through the training.

The Learning Team

We've always found it fascinating that when something new arrives on the learning scene, the group you would expect to be the most excited should be the learning team. Yet, this isn't always the case. Even though microlearning makes a lot of sense and should be a consistent tool in the learning team's toolbox, we can clearly recall times when we were faced with resistance to change. What's also interesting is that the resistance to change had little to do with the training itself, but usually had to do with the concern of adding another task to their already too long to-do lists, a concern about being able to execute successfully enough, and so forth.

Like other innovations in training and development, microlearning can be faced with resistance too. The best way to address any resistance is to consider a change management approach. (As we mentioned in chapter 4, we like to use the ADKAR change management model, and it fits here too!) First explain what microlearning is and why it is important as learning professionals to adopt microlearning content. Then identify the opportunities where microlearning could have an impact and get your team members excited to try something new. Involve the team every step of the way, set clear expectations, and educate them on how to create effective microlearning. Then, as any good manager would do, "inspect what you expect" and follow up to ensure you hold your employees accountable, recognize their efforts, and reward them for a job well done.

As a side note, don't forget to help the learning team prioritize their work if it does seem like there is too much on their plate! It's hard to say no when stakeholders ask us to create more training. In some ways, it's a sign that you and your team are doing great work. To continue to have enough time to do all that great work, it's helpful to conduct prioritization exercises routinely to ensure your resources are focused on the right things at the right time, and to ensure they shift accordingly when the business needs change.

Sometimes the learning team or the subject matter experts may believe that something short is not enough for the learner. They are used to building longer-form learning content and think that "there must be more that they need to know." Learning professionals may also worry that their job could be at risk if they are not building longer-form content for their learners. These objections can easily be debunked by educating the team on the value of microlearning for the modern learner, having a targeted approach to deciding when to implement microlearning resources, and using microlearning when it makes the most sense (and not all the time). Support the learning team through these conversations and their own behavior change—maybe even create a microlearning infographic to help the learning team! The result will be a group of savvy learning professionals who have another awesome tool in their toolbox.

Your Quick Microlearning Guide

Here is the advice we often share with clients, participants in our workshops, and other colleagues interested in building microlearning.

1. **Conduct a microlearning pilot!** See earlier in the chapter and the "Microlearning Pilot Template" tool for details.

2. **Be specific.** We probably sound like a broken record at this point in the book, but being specific is so important for designing good microlearning. However, we often hear clients asking to add "just one more thing" to a microlearning resource in the design phase. If it's relevant and aligned to the specific performance or learning need, then great. But if it's a "nice to know" nugget, it's unlikely to be remembered by the learner anyway. Just. Leave. It. Out.

3. **Focus on performance.** When you focus on the performance gap or need of the learner, you help them improve back on the job. Not only does this address the WIIFM, it's really satisfying for the learner too.

4. **Be brief.** Do everything in your power to ensure your microlearning gives the learner only what they need, and nothing more. Design with short attention spans in mind and anticipate that your modern learners are being distracted even during the micro time span. Resist the urge to add more in and encourage your clients and stakeholders to do the same. Why? Go back to the second tip.

5. **Be engaging.** This is especially important if your microlearning will be informal learning (not required). If you build it and it's not engaging, your learners just won't do it. And nobody likes boring training, no matter how short! Engaging learning doesn't have to be fancy or expensive; it just has to capture the learner's attention and draw them in. A good WIIFM may be all you need, if you use it well.

6. **Focus on the learners.** This sounds like stating the obvious, but if we had a dollar for every time a client or stakeholder wanted to build microlearning or include content for some reason that wasn't exactly focused on the learner. . . . You really want to focus on the user and the use case. One of our clients has a selling approach for sales reps; the microlearning program is set up so these busy sales reps have the option of taking any of the pieces of microlearning they want and skipping over any they do not find relevant or helpful. This hyper-focus on the need of the busy sales reps kept us very focused on staying practical, having a strong WIIFM, and really keeping each resource short and to the point: What would they find

helpful? What would turn them off? The result was a great microlearning program that was truly focused on the learners.

7. **Capture metrics.** This one always generates a look of anguish. But you don't have to capture every single metric, just a few important ones. It takes a little work up front, but the payoff is huge. In the end, you'll be so glad you did it! Refer to chapter 5 for details on metrics and measurement.

PRO TIP

For a great example of a microlearning program (and platform) that is specific to the learner's needs, visit the Immunization Academy website.

This site provides microlearning resources on a wide range of very specific immunization topics. While the microlearning video library is huge, it is unlikely anyone would need to view all of them. It is designed so that healthcare workers in community clinics in Africa can search and navigate for the specific need they have and watch a short instructional video to learn how to complete that task.

For example, the video "How to Maintain Kerosene Refrigerators" is so specific that if you don't have a kerosene refrigerator, you wouldn't watch it. But if you do have one, you can watch a three-minute video that explains the importance of maintaining the refrigerator; what tasks to conduct on a daily, weekly, and periodic schedule; and how to conduct basic maintenance.

What's Next?

What's next is really up to you! As technology improves and learning professionals get more savvy about microlearning, consider the possibilities about how you can use it to drive very specific performance outcomes in the workplace. And continue to focus on enabling learners to access and consume learning quickly, efficiently, and even right at the moment they need it, during the flow of work.

Along with the movement toward shorter-form learning is a renewed interest in personalized and adaptive learning—that is, providing different pieces of microlearning for different learners to better meet their unique needs. For example, we are working on a project right now where the target audience is 600 people globally. They all have the same role at the organization, but some have a few years of experience while others have more than 15 years. When we user-tested one prototype, the feedback was mixed; some loved it, and others said it was too simple. They asked if we could instead create a series of different modules aimed at these different groups? With microlearning and adaptive delivery to different employees (based on years of experience), we sure could!

Part of the excitement about this kind of personalization and customization comes from finally having the right technology to deliver content in these ways. The technology to track and manage all of this is really exciting not only for what it can do, but also because it shifts from a "big brother is watching you" mentality about training to, "How can we analyze the workflow to help employees excel in the workplace?" Learning experience platforms, discussed in chapter 4, are a great example of an emerging technology to consider, as are the boost learning programs we described in chapter 3.

Another exciting trend with microlearning is workflow learning, or the idea of giving people support resources so they can learn how to do their tasks while actually doing those tasks, rather than stopping their work to learn (even if only for a few minutes). The idea is that you could give much better support to your employees, have less training, and see better performance outcomes by offering support right in the flow of their work. In the past, this was an ideal that was hard to execute, but with emerging technologies you can better provide just-in-time resources for your learners when, where, and how they need. See more about workflow learning in chapter 3.

We encourage you to embrace microlearning and add it as a key tool in your learning resource toolbox. When microlearning is focused on a single performance objective and is implemented at the right time through the right channel for your learners, it can be a very powerful business accelerator.

Questions to Explore

- How would you describe the current state of microlearning in your organization?
- What do you envision the role of microlearning to be in your organization in the future? What value can it bring?
- How would you describe the current learning culture in your organization? How would the introduction of a new microlearning resource or program be received?
- What would a microlearning pilot entail? Who could help you implement a pilot?

- How much communication is needed to support and drive microlearning? How could you plan for this?
- Have you marketed your training to stakeholders before? What worked, and what didn't?
- What communication channels would be most effective in your organization for communicating about microlearning resources?
- How comfortable are you with communicating the success of learning?
- Which microlearning resources have you implemented that would make a great success case for marketing to stakeholders?
- How can you engage and support the managers of the learners? Would coaching guides be helpful?

Tools for Support

Microlearning Pilot Template

A pilot is a great way to try microlearning in a low-risk way to determine potential value and impact without necessarily using a lot of resources. A pilot, by definition, is not the full-blown plan. Use the template below to draft a plan for a microlearning pilot.

Microlearning Pilot Title: _____

Background and Business Need What is the current situation?	
The Opportunity How will the organization benefit if the pilot is successful?	
The Objective What performance gap will be addressed? What would success look like?	
The Solution What would a complete and comprehensive microlearning solution look like?	
The Pilot What elements of the comprehensive solution will be implemented for the pilot? Who is the audience?	*(Consider how you can scale back the audience, length, timeline, or other element of the training for the pilot.)*
Resources What amount of time, people, and budget will be needed to conduct the pilot?	
Risks What are the potential risks of conducting the pilot, and how would the risks be mitigated (if necessary)?	*(Examples could include the performance gap being closed partially or not at all, leading to no positive change or a negative impact on a process.)*
Timing When will the pilot be conducted (once, over a period of days, weeks, or months)?	
Lessons Learned What worked well? What did not? What could have gone better? (Think about everything from planning all the way through implementation.)	Lesson 1: Lesson 2: Lesson 3:
Recommendations What would be adjusted if the full microlearning solution were to be implemented? What would you stop, start, or continue?	Recommendation 1: Recommendation 2: Recommendation 3:

Microlearning Communication Plan

When implementing microlearning, be sure to communicate to the learners, managers, and stakeholders about what is happening, when it will happen, and why it is important. The first table provides tips and considerations for the communications. The second and third tables can be used as templates to track and manage the communications. Keep in mind that this tool is comprehensive and may be more than you need for communicating a specific microlearning resource, so select the elements that apply to your situation. However, for a microlearning program that has multiple resources, or when a new release is available, the communication plan may be larger or ongoing over time.

	Audience		
	Learners	Managers	Stakeholders
Objective	☐ Create awareness of the training and why it is important (WIIFM) ☐ Notify about microlearning availability and how to access	☐ Create awareness of the training and why it is important (WIIFM) ☐ Notify of microlearning availability and how to share with their team	☐ Create awareness of the training and why it is important (WIIFM) ☐ Notify of microlearning availability and how to share with others
What to Communicate • before long-form training • after long-form training • for stand-alone training • for performance support	☐ Notify of microlearning availability, how to access, due date (if mandatory), or how they can get credit for their efforts (if informal) ☐ Periodic reminders to create ongoing awareness	☐ Notify of microlearning availability, how to access, and due date (if mandatory) ☐ Set expectation to check in with learners to ensure completion or use as appropriate ☐ Provide coaching tips ☐ Set up periodic reminders to create ongoing awareness ☐ Inform of results (consider periodic updates if learners complete over a period of time)	☐ Notify of microlearning availability and inform of expectations set with learners and managers ☐ Inform of results (consider periodic updates if learners complete over a period of time)

Continued on the next page.

	Audience		
	Learners	**Managers**	**Stakeholders**
Timing • before long-form training	☐ Ensure learners have enough time to complete prior to the long-form training (the microlearning may not take long, but the learner may need to carve out time to do it)	☐ Notify in advance of learners being notified ☐ Ensure managers are aware and have ample time to connect with the employee (if necessary)	☐ Notify in advance of learners and managers being notified
Timing • after long-form training	☐ Determine frequency of communications that support retention (e.g., every two days, once a week, once every three weeks)	☐ Notify in advance of learners (e.g., consider sending details of your approach prior to the long-form training date)	☐ Notify in advance of learners and managers
Timing • stand-alone training • performance support	☐ Determine ideal timeframe (e.g., one week prior to launch)	☐ Notify in advance of learners	☐ Notify in advance of learners and managers

Customize the following table to help you track and manage communications. Adjust the headers as needed to align with your microlearning resource or program.

	Timing *(change weekly headers as needed; for example, add more weeks or change to monthly or quarterly for ongoing microlearning programs)*					
	Week 1	**Week 2**	**Week 3**	**Week 4**	**Week 5**	**Week 6**
Communication 1						
Communication 2						
Communication 3						
Communication 4						

Customize the following table to help you track and manage the logistics of your communications. Adjust the headers as needed to align with your microlearning resource or program, then fill in the related details for that communication.

	Communication #1	Communication #2	Communication #3
Launch Date			
Audience (learner, manager, stakeholder, all)			
Communication Objective (awareness, action needed, sharing results)			
Delivery Method (email, LMS, in-app notification, manager cascade)			
Responsible (Who will create and send the communication?)			
Accountable (Who will make sure it happens?)			
Consulted (Who needs to be consulted on the communication?)			
Informed (Who needs to be informed?)			
Designed (Insert due date or check when complete)			
Developed (Insert due date or check when complete)			
Reviewed (insert due date or check when complete)			
Delivered (insert due date or check when complete)			

Creating a Coaching Guide for a Microlearning Resource or Program

A coaching guide is an excellent way to let managers know what their employees are learning, and to help them engage with their staff members on those topics. It also enables them to act as a mentor and coach on the topics their employees are learning about.

Of course it's great for managers to take the training themselves, but sometimes that's not possible—they have their own operational duties and training to attend! That said, it can be helpful to let managers know what's being covered in the microlearning resource or program so they can properly support their employees back on the job.

Coaching guides can have varying levels of detail, but shorter is better; if a leader doesn't have time to consume the microlearning themselves, they certainly won't read your five-page coaching guide!

With that in mind, consider including these topics in your coaching guide:

- **Performance objective.** What on-the-job performance is this intended to support or improve? What things should the manager look for to know the performance is improving (or not improving)?
- **Key content.** What core messages are being shared in this training? Provide a short summary of the microlearning content.
- **Challenges.** What areas of that content are likely to be the most difficult for employees? Are there any suggestions for how the manager can support the learner in these situations? Also consider if there are other barriers outside learning that may get in the way of the employees' performance.
- **Key questions to ask.** What are some questions the manager can ask in a one-on-one meeting with the employee to start a conversation about this topic?

Another option is to give the manager access to the microlearning resource or program. It's always short, the manager can probably make time to consume it, and they get exposed to exactly what their learners see. Text-based job aids can also serve as the coaching guide for the manager, along with a few guiding questions.

For a microlearning program, it may not be feasible to create a coaching guide for every element of the program, especially if there are numerous resources from which the learners can choose. In this case, consider the overarching program goals and align the coaching guide accordingly. If the microlearning program is informal, provide guiding questions for the manager to ask the employee, such as:

- Which topics in the program do you think are most relevant to you? Does that align with your performance goals or personal development goals?
- How will this help you?
- What is your plan to complete in terms of timing?
- When do you expect to apply what you learned, or in which situations?

References and Additional Resources

Association for Talent Development (ATD). 2018. *2018 State of the Industry.* Alexandria, VA: ATD Press.

Bersin by Deloitte. 2014. "Meet the Modern Learner." Infographic.

Bull City Learning. 2012. "Demystifying Microlearning for the Learning Leader." Bull City Learning blog. blog.bullcitylearning.com/webinar-recording-demystifying -microlearning-for-learning-leaders.

Gallup. n.d. "Workplace Learning & Development Programs." Gallup. www.gallup.com /learning/248381/workplace-programs.aspx.

Gutierrez, K. 2018. "Numbers Don't lie: Why Microlearning Is Better for Your Learners (and You Too)." Shift Learning blog, September 27. shiftelearning.com/blog /numbers-dont-lie-why-bite-sized-learning-is-better-for-your-learners-and-you-too.

Hessing, T. 2014. "Pilot and Implementation Planning." Six Sigma Study Guide, June 8. sixsigmastudyguide.com/pilot-implementation-planning.

Iannone, S. 2019. "Six Tips for Reaching the Life Sciences Modern Learner." Bull City Blue blog. bullcityblue.com/blog/six-tips-reaching-modern-learner.

Kapp, K., and R. Defelice. 2019. *Microlearning: Short and Sweet.* Alexandria, VA: ATD Press.

Pienkowski, N., and G. O'Grady. 2015. "Six Strategies for Engaging the Modern Learner." Bull City Learning webinar. vimeo.com/140815130.

"Pilot Project Plan Template." studylib.net/doc/8501760/project-pilot-plan-template.

Acknowledgments

Carla

This book would not have been possible without my husband and biggest supporter, Thomas Wortman. Tom, you have always been there to kick ideas around, give honest feedback, and help me find time for all my professional dreams while juggling work and being a mom. I still remember when I told you that ATD asked me to write this book and you said "Why not?" You are the best thing that's ever happened to me and I don't know what I'd do without you. I love you more than you know.

To my son John, who enables me to see the world through fresh eyes every day. Your curiosity and wonder amaze me, and help me see the world for all its beauty and joy. We'll have even more time to play now that Mom's finished this project, and I can't wait to build LEGOs with you. I'll race you to the toy box!

To the rest of my family . . . my mom and dad, Len and Jennette Torgerson, and my brother and his family, Trevor, Haylee, Mackenzie, and Griffin Torgerson. Although we're miles apart, I still carry with me the lessons you've all taught me over the years. I feel lucky knowing that whatever life throws at me—both good and bad—you'll always be there to support me.

Sue Iannone, I'm so glad you agreed to do this book with me. You bring such a wealth of experience and understanding of the training and development field. I learned so much from working with you on this book! You challenged and stretched my thinking in tangible ways, and this book is far better because of that. You always help me think about what makes for good training and how to be the best consultant for our clients. Thank you!

Jennifer Hoeke, an enormous thank you for continuing to partner with me on all my graphics. You understand the intersection of graphic design and instruction better than anyone I know and my work is always better for it. I can't tell you how much I appreciate the opportunity to collaborate with you on all this. I am a better instructional designer when you're in the room.

There are tons of other people who have shaped my professional career. I know I'll miss somebody, but here's a stab. Megan Torrance and Michael Allen—I'm so lucky to be able to call you mentors. Thank you for sharing your wisdom and, most of all, your time with me. In addition, a huge thank you to Ethan Edwards, Julie Dirksen, Bill Mills, Kassie LaBorie, Bob Mosher, Lisa Toenniges, Nathan Pienkowski, and the late John Sadowski; you all shaped my thinking about what makes good instruction and had a tremendous impact on me. And thank you also to current and past ATD staff, including Courtney Vital, Vanessa Fludd, Jason Sturges, Nikki O'Keeffe, and Justin Brusino, who gave me countless opportunities and feedback that helped me get where I am today. Thank you also to Craig Montgomerie and George Buck, the professors who first introduced me to the world of computer-based instruction and provided a solid foundation for all my work decades later.

And finally, to the thousands of instructional designers across the nation that I've had the pleasure of meeting in classes or presentations, or working with as clients over the past 15 or more years. I have learned from each and every one of you.

Sue

Writing a book is harder than I ever imagined. Accomplishing this bucket-list item would not have been remotely possible without all the people who touched my life and helped me in some way.

To my kids, Kyle and Sophia. While I tried to work on the book when you weren't around, there were times when I had to hide in my office to meet a deadline. The next time you peek in my office and ask if I'm working on the book, I'm excited to say that my new answer will be "no." I hope that watching Mom go through this process has inspired you to read more often. The big cozy chair is always waiting to snuggle you while you read in Mommy's office. I will read Dog Man or Junie B. Jones books anytime with you!

To my mother, Carole Bernhard, for your unwavering support. During one of the most difficult and challenging times in my life, you thought I was crazy for taking on another large project, yet you were there for me in so many ways—cooking dinners, feeding the koi when I traveled, spending time with Kyle and Sophia when I needed time to work on the book, and listening to me when I needed to be heard. Thanks Mama, you are the best.

To my father, Dr. Ron Iannone. Your logical, practical, "matter-of-fact" approach to solving any problem has rubbed off on me in so many ways. This helped me achieve success in the business world and equipped me to tackle the never-ending list of challenges that come with parenting a special needs child. Thanks Dad.

To all my siblings and my large, loud blended extended family. You are always excited when I share my career news and happenings; your support means the world to me.

To the awesome bosses I've worked for, and the ones who were downright terrible. I learned so much from each one of you. Jeff Wilson—thank you for taking a chance on a 21-year-old kid from Long Island with a biology degree and teaching me how to sell, be a great manager, and enjoy a burger on a toasted English muffin. Gary Grewal— thank you for teaching me the basics of all things training, grooming me to become an awesome classroom trainer, and for your ridiculous sense of humor. Trish Wetzel— thank you for teaching me to navigate the most excruciating and difficult workplace situations as I emerged as a senior learning leader. Your guidance, advice, and caring nature were priceless.

To Carla Torgerson, when you asked me to co-author this book, I was flattered that you wanted me to join you in this venture. I also thought you were nuts. I'm so glad I said yes! I have learned so much from you in this process. I appreciate so many things about you, but most of all I appreciate that you challenged me to do my best. Together we made a powerful team and produced a book we can both be proud of.

To Garry O'Grady, who reached out to me several years ago with this crazy idea to start a life sciences learning agency. You helped me transition from the corporate training world and realize my career aspiration of "going over to the dark side." It's definitely not dark and it is so much fun being a partner with you in this business. Your ability to sort through ambiguity and identify a path forward with clients is impressive.

There are so many people who deserve recognition, so forgive me for anyone I've missed! Thanks to Vicki Colman for your enthusiasm and love of training; Kevin Kruse for pushing me to find my voice and share my opinion even when it was controversial; Dawn Brehm for your transparency and always thinking of me; George Schmidt for setting the example of what exceptional performance consulting looks like and nudging me to join the LTEN board of directors; and Gary Evans for your refreshing leadership style.

My 25-year career in the pharmaceutical and biotech industries was an incredible journey. To the thousands of people I trained over the years, I learned so much from you. Watching the light bulb go off in your head when you learned how to do the job was enough to keep me going. It was humbling to play a role helping you to ultimately help patients suffering from all kinds of chronic conditions and diseases.

Carla and Sue

We are deeply indebted to Garry O'Grady, Nathan Pienkowski, and Michael Woodward, the partners at Bull City Learning and Bull City Blue. You have given us the flexibility to pursue this project, despite how crazy the idea was at times. Thank you for providing us the space to write this book as we simultaneously helped clients solve performance problems and delivered learning solutions.

We also thank all the staff at Bull City Learning and Bull City Blue. You've been there to share ideas, be understanding about our crazy schedules, and give words of encouragement and support. We are so lucky to work with each and every one of you: Alice Bumgarner, Allison Warren, Andrew Creter, Callie Carter, Elisabeth Ulrich, Feng Zheng, Gordon Pruitt, Hannah O'Grady, James O'Grady, Jenn Sabo, Jennifer Hogge, Jillian Bowlin, Jim Wright, Joy Brewster, Kristen Collosso, Laura Mazurak, Sara Talladira, Shantel Smith, Vivian Voight, and Zoe Voigt.

An immense thank you to Conrad Gottfredson and Bob Mosher for allowing us to share some of your work in this book. Thank you, Bob and Con, for sharing your thinking and expertise with us. Our work with microlearning as performance support is heavily influenced by the foundational work you have done, and this book is better because we've stood on your shoulders.

A huge thank you to Jack Harlow, Caroline Coppel, Eliza Blanchard, Melissa Jones, and all the other ATD Press staff for partnering with us to see this to completion. You all provided invaluable insights and support that enabled this book to become a reality.

We must admit that as we've been writing this book, we've had many times when we wanted to pause the publication schedule—not just for a few days or weeks because we were busy, but for months or years so we could "finish" our thinking. The truth is we will probably never finish thinking about the best ways to teach people and improve performance. We're sure the day this hits bookstores we'll have another good idea. But we share these ideas as a snapshot in time—where our work has brought us at this point—and hope that we will all continue to evolve and grow our thinking over time. Our learners will be better for it!

Writing this book has been a little like the journey of pregnancy and childbirth—the excitement, the anxiety, the exhaustion. But, as with many difficult things a great gift comes at the end. We hope you find useful ideas and suggestions within these pages. Modify them and refine them to work best for you with your learners. And let us know how it goes! We always love to hear from others who, like us, are trying to figure out the best ways to improve training and workplace performance.

— Carla and Sue
December 2019

About the Authors

Carla Torgerson, MEd, MBA, has more than 15 years of experience as an instructional designer and instructional strategist both on internal teams and in several consulting firms. She has worked with numerous Fortune 500 clients including Intuit, McDonald's, Netflix, Facebook, Fidelity, Cargill, Medtronic, Merck, and Best Western. She has designed solutions ranging from $15,000 to more than $2 million.

Carla has presented her thought leadership in the areas of e-learning, mobile learning, and microlearning across the nation at conferences, events, and workshops of leading learning organizations, including ATD and The eLearning Guild. Additionally, Carla developed MILE, the MIcroLEarning Design Model and is the author of *The Microlearning Guide to Microlearning*.

Carla is a consummate consultant who specializes in designing learning solutions to meet the needs of her clients, their businesses, and their learners. She is able to see training needs from both the perspective of the business and the learner, enabling her to create solutions that balance the needs of both groups and delight her clients. Carla has deep expertise in designing interactive and engaging learning materials, particularly in electronic environments, and using Agile and iterative approaches to achieve quality solutions that improve performance.

Carla is currently a director of instructional design at Bull City Learning, a specialized e-learning agency that provides digital learning solutions for companies in a wide range of industries, as well as nonprofit organizations. Bull City Learning offers a full suite of solutions including learning needs assessments, curriculum design, content development, and training deployment support.

Carla has a master of education (MEd) focused on technology-based education, and a master of business administration (MBA), which helps her see training through a business lens.

Carla grew up in western Canada where she developed a love for downhill skiing, biking, and camping. She currently lives in North Carolina with her awesome husband, Tom, and their very curious seven-year-old son, John. She loves to travel with her family, and they have explored the United States from coast to coast.

Connect with Carla on LinkedIn for insights and announcements at linkedin.com /in/carlatorgerson.

Sue Iannone, CPLP, has 25 years of learning-leadership experience in the commercial pharmaceutical and biotech space. Since 2016 she has been the vice president and a partner of Bull City Blue, an end-to-end learning agency created to address the needs of training and talent development organizations within the life science industry.

Under Sue's leadership, Bull City Blue has served a multitude of organizations to solve their complex learning and performance problems of local and global scale. Sue has helped learning leaders build strategic business plans for training teams, develop product launch learning processes and tools, create learning solutions for sales meetings, overhaul new hire learning pathways, and create training to meet countless other business needs. Sue has worked with several Fortune 500 organizations in the life sciences including AbbVie, Biogen, Philips, Sanofi, Merck, and Celgene.

Prior to joining Bull City Blue, Sue served as the director of Inflammation & Immunology Commercial Training at Celgene and as vice president for the board of directors of the Life Sciences Trainers and Educators Network (LTEN). Having worked for small, medium, and large biotech companies in her career, Sue has led the design and development of numerous learning initiatives—including more than 20 product launches. She has also led multiple performance-consulting initiatives designed to increase the effectiveness of the learning organizations in which she served.

Sue's deep understanding of the life sciences training space informs the articles and workshops she's crafted for both national entities such as ATD and the eLearning Guild, as well as industry-specific organizations like LTEN. Always interested in helping others succeed, Sue mentors life science learning leaders who are tackling challenging workplace problems and coaches aspiring learning leaders to identify knowledge, skills, and experiences to strengthen their career path. She also coaches CPLP candidates as they prepare for their certification.

Sue holds a bachelor of science in biology and is a Certified Professional in Learning and Performance (CPLP) since 2007—this unique combination makes her well suited to serve the learning needs of her life science clients.

Sue lives in New Jersey with her two children, Kyle and Sophia. You can find her leading Sophia's Girl Scout troop activities and advocating for Kyle's autism-related needs. Her penchant for baking delicious cookies and cakes combined with her love of fixing things around the house has earned her the nickname "Martha MacGyver" from her friends.

Connect with Sue on LinkedIn for insights and announcements at linkedin.com /in/sueiannone.

Index